Mikhail Bakhtin

Rhetoric, Poetics, Dialogics, Rhetoricality

Mikhail Bakhtin

Rhetoric, Poetics, Dialogics, Rhetoricality

Don Bialostosky

Parlor Press
Anderson, South Carolina
www.parlorpress.com

Parlor Press LLC, Anderson, South Carolina, USA

© 2016 by Parlor Press.
All rights reserved.
Printed in the United States of America

SAN: 254-8879

Library of Congress Cataloging-in-Publication Data

Names: Bialostosky, Don H. author.
Title: Mikhail Bakhtin : rhetoric, poetics, dialogics, rhetoricality / Don
  Bialostosky.
Description: Anderson, South Carolina : Parlor Press, 2016. | Includes
  bibliographical references and index.
Identifiers: LCCN 2015043978| ISBN 9781602357259 (pbk. : acid-free paper) |
  ISBN 9781602357266 (hardcover : acid-free paper)
Subjects: LCSH: Bakhtin, M. M. (Mikhail Mikhaæilovich), 1895-1975--Criticism
  and interpretation.
Classification: LCC PG2947.B3 B53 2016 | DDC 801/.95092--dc23
LC record available at http://lccn.loc.gov/2015043978

Cover design by David Blakesley
Printed on acid-free paper.

1 2 3 4 5
First Edition

Parlor Press, LLC is an independent publisher of scholarly and trade titles in print and multimedia formats. This book is available in paper, hardcover, and digital formats from Parlor Press on the World Wide Web at http://www.parlorpress.com or through online and brick-and-mortar bookstores. For submission information or to find out about Parlor Press publications, write to Parlor Press, 3015 Brackenberry Drive, Anderson, SC 29621, or e-mail editor@parlorpress.com.

Contents

Abbreviations Used in Text and Notes   *vi*
Preface   *ix*
1. Introduction   *3*

Part I. Dialogics, Rhetoric, Criticism

2. Dialogics as an Art of Discourse   *19*
3. Booth, Bakhtin, and the Culture of Criticism   *40*
4. Rhetoric, Literary Criticism, Theory, and Bakhtin   *53*
5. Bakhtin and Rhetorical Criticism   *67*
6. Antilogics, Dialogics, and Sophistic Social Psychology   *75*

Part II. Architectonics, Poetics, Rhetoricality, Liberal Education

7. Bakhtin's "Rough Draft"   *85*
8. Architectonics, Rhetoric, and Poetics in the Bakhtin School's Early Phenomenological and Sociological Texts   *102*
9. Aristotle's *Rhetoric* and Bakhtin's Discourse Theory   *121*
10. Rereading the Place of Rhetoric in Aristotle's *Poetics* in Light of Bakhtin's Discourse Theory: Rhetoric as *Dianoia*, Poetics as an Imitation of Rhetoric   *137*
11. Liberal Education, Writing, and the Dialogic Self   *148*

Notes   *161*
Works Cited   *169*
About the Author   *179*
Index   *181*

Abbreviations Used in Text and Notes

AA	Bakhtin, M. M. *Art and Answerability: Early Philosophical Essays of M. M. Bakhtin*. Ed. Michael Holquist and Vadim Liapunov. Trans. Vadim Liapunov. Austin: U of Texas P, 1990.
DI	Bakhtin, M. M. *The Dialogic Imagination: Four Essays by M. M. Bakhtin*. Ed. Michael Holquist. Trans. Caryl Emerson and Michael Holquist. Austin: U of Texas P, 1981.
DLDA	Voloshinov, V. N. "Discourse in Life and Discourse in Art." *Freudianism: A Critical Sketch*. Ed. Neil H. Bruss. Trans. I. R. Titunik. Bloomington: Indiana UP, 1987.
MPL	Voloshinov, V. N. *Marxism and the Philosophy of Language*. Trans. L. Matejka and I. R. Titunik. New York: Seminar, 1973.
PDP	Bakhtin, M. M. *Problems of Dostoevsky's Poetics*. Ed. and trans. Caryl Emerson. Minneapolis: U of Minnesota P, 1984.
PMN	Rorty, Richard. *Philosophy and the Mirror of Nature*. Princeton: Princeton UP, 1979.
SG	Bakhtin, M. M. "The Problem of Speech Genres." *Speech Genres and Other Late Essays*. Ed. Michael Holquist and Caryl Emerson. Trans. Vern W. McGee. Austin: U of Texas P, 1986.
TM	Gadamer, Hans-Georg. *Truth and Method*. New York: Seabury, 1975.
TPA	Bakhtin, M. M. *Toward a Philosophy of the Act*. Ed. Vadim Liapunov and Michael Holquist. Trans. Vadim Liapunov. Austin: U of Texas P. 1993.

In Memory of
Wayne Booth

Preface

In 1983, my then new colleague at State University of New York at Stony Brook, Peter Elbow, kindly invited me, a then new Romanticist in the English department, to present a paper at the 1984 Conference on College Composition and Communication (CCCC) convention on Mikhail Bakhtin's implications for authentic voice in composition. It would be my first CCCC convention, conveniently in New York City. The last chapter in this volume grew out of the paper I wrote for Peter, enhanced and recontextualized first at a conference on Interpretive Communities and the Undergraduate Writer in Chicago and again at the invitation of Patty Harkin and John Schilb, who included it in their Modern Language Association (MLA) volume *Contending With Words* and thereby included me in the community of rhetoric and composition scholars that has, over the past thirty years, become my primary scholarly community.

Rhetoric had been with me from my undergraduate days at the University of Chicago, where I first met it through Wayne Booth—later my thesis director—to whose memory I dedicate this volume, and Charles Wegener, my undergraduate mentor and first teacher of a formal course on rhetoric my sophomore year. Composition has grown to accompany rhetoric for me through those early invitations, through the great opportunity I had to organize a rhetorical theory colloquium at the University of Toledo in the late eighties and early nineties, through my time in the rhetoric and composition program at Penn State in the nineties and into the beginning of the new century, and most recently in the composition, literacy, pedagogy, and rhetoric group that I joined at the University of Pittsburgh in 2003. Colleagues in all these institutions too numerous to name here have enriched my investment in the field and prompted much of the thinking this volume represents, as have colleagues I have met at the CCCCs, the Rhetoric Society of America conferences, and conferences of the International Society for the History of Rhetoric.

The community of theorists and scholars that quickly gathered around the emerging translations of the Bakhtin School also sustained and provoked the work that is gathered here. The late Michael Sprinker, then at Oregon State University and later a colleague at Stony Brook, generously hosted my visit from the University of Washington to meet and hear Michael Holquist before *The Dialogic Imagination* came out in 1981. Clive Thomson welcomed me to a gathering on Bakhtin that he organized at the University of Toronto again early in the eighties—a conference that was the starting point for a series of biennial international Bakhtin conferences, the most recent of which I attended in Stockholm in 2014. He also involved me in the early years of reviewing articles for the *Bakhtin Newsletter* that chronicled annual publications on the Bakhtin School until the numbers became too numerous to keep up with.

I make these acknowledgments partly to situate the thirty years of work finally gathered in this volume, even more to call attention, in good Bakhtinian form, to the many interlocutors whose voices prompted and shaped my own and to the academic institutions that constitute the sphere of communication in which they were produced and previously published. Editors of collections and journals and publishers, too, are part of that sphere, and I am grateful to all of the following for permission to include my previously published work here:

- The Modern Language Association for "Dialogics as an Art of Discourse in Literary Criticism," *PMLA* (1986), and "Liberal Education, Writing, and the Dialogic Self," in *Contending with Words*, edited by Patricia Harkin and John Schilb (1991).
- *Critical Studies* for "Dialogic, Pragmatic, and Hermeneutic Conversation: Bakhtin, Gadamer, Rorty" (1989).
- Fred J. Antczak for "Booth, Bakhtin, and the Culture of Criticism" in *Rhetoric and Pluralism: Legacies of Wayne Booth* (1975).
- Rhetoric Society of America for "Architectonics, Rhetoric, and Poetics in the Bakhtin School's Early Phenomenological and Sociological Texts" (2006), and for "Bakhtin and the Future of Rhetorical Criticism: A Response to Halasek and Bernard-Donals" I am also grateful to Kay Halasek and Michael Bernard-Donals, two scholars in the field who have since published books on Bakhtin, for inviting me to respond to

their session on Bakhtin and Rhetorical Criticism at the 1990 MLA Convention.
- Sage Publications for "Rhetoric in Literary Criticism and Theory" in *The Sage Handbook of Rhetorical Studies,* edited by Andrea A. Lunsford, Kirt H. Wilson, and Rosa Eberly (2009).
- *Rhetoric Review* for "Bakhtin's 'Rough Draft': Toward a Philosophy of the Act, Ethics, and Composition Studies" (1999); its reviewers John Schilb and James Zebroski made the piece better.
- Cambridge University Press for "Antilogics, Dialogics, and Sophistic Social Psychology: Michael Billig's Reinvention of Bakhtin from Protagorean Rhetoric" in *Rhetoric, Pragmatism, Sophistry,* edited by Steven Mailloux (1995).
- Wiley for "Aristotle's *Rhetoric* and Bakhtin's Discourse Theory" in *A Companion to Rhetoric and Rhetorical Criticism* edited by Walter Jost and Wendy Olmsted (2004).

I have combined and modified some of these pieces as seemed warranted. Chapter 10 has not previously been published, though an earlier version has been circulating on my Academia.edu website.

I am grateful to David Blakesley at Parlor Press for venturing to publish a collection composed of widely dispersed previously published work that few presses these days would be willing to take a chance on. I hope that his faith in this project will be justified.

It has been a long time since my work has appeared in a monograph and so a long time since I have been able to acknowledge my wife Sue at the start of a book. The more than quarter century we had cared for each other when I wrote my last preface approaches half a century, the children she has been primary care-person for are grown, and two of them have their own children, on whom she lavishes the thoughtful love that our own children enjoyed. She has looked closely over the text of this book, which has risked many errors in its assemblage from previous versions, as she has closely read my previous ones. Though so many years accumulate so many things to say thank you for that saying it feels inadequate, I will say it again with love.

Mikhail Bakhtin

1. Introduction

Rhetoric appears to be a marginal topic for the Bakhtin School and for most Bakhtin scholars, but many rhetorical critics, theorists, and teachers have nonetheless found the school's work compelling and challenging. Explicit remarks about rhetoric, garnered from the translated work of Mikhail Bakhtin and his two colleagues and collaborators Pavel Medvedev and V. N. Voloshinov, could be gathered in a few pages, though more pages than the indexes to those translations would indicate. Most of Bakhtin's remarks appear hostile and reductive, the work of a commentator unsympathetic to rhetoric and interested in it as little more than a foil for his own speculations on the novel and dialogic discourse. Numerous critical books have placed the school's work in relation to other schools of criticism, theory, and philosophy, but again their arguments and their indices are nearly barren of reference to rhetoric.

And yet, since Wayne Booth engaged Bakhtin as a rhetorical critic in his second edition of *The Rhetoric of Fiction* (1982) and I delivered a talk on Bakhtin and composition at the Conference on College Composition and Communication in 1984 and Charles Schuster opened the topic of "Bakhtin as Rhetorical Theorist" (1985) in *College English,* a substantial body of rhetorical scholarship has engaged with and appropriated Bakhtin's and his colleagues' writing for rhetorical and composition studies. Numerous syllabi in communication, rhetoric, and composition programs include Bakhtin's work, as does Bizzell and Hertzberg's anthology *The Rhetorical Tradition.* Two important books elaborate a Bakhtinian composition theory, Kay Halasek's *A Pedagogy of Possibility* and Frank Farmer's *Saying and Silence,* and a Landmark Essays volume edited by Farmer, *Bakhtin, Rhetoric, and Writing*, gathers some of the numerous articles and book chapters in communication and composition that find Bakhtin School work salient for rhetorical criticism, theory, and pedagogy. No book-length study of the Bakhtin School's implications for rhetoric has emerged to date.

In all this work, students of rhetoric have not just jumped thoughtlessly on the now slowing Bakhtin bandwagon—a crowded and noisy vehicle once overflowing with scholars from numerous disciplines and national scholarly traditions, jostling each other, snatching at various bits of Bakhtiniana for various purposes, forming nonce friendships while sometimes calling on the driver (if there were one) to throw each other off—but they have found themselves there willy-nilly. Students of rhetoric were not in on the appropriations that followed the first publication of English translations from the School in *Readings in Russian Poetics* (1962) or of Bakhtin's book *Rabelais and His World* in 1968 or of the translations in the 1970s from Voloshinov's and Medvedev's writings or the early and largely neglected translation of Bakhtin's *Problems of Dostoevsky's Poetics* (1973), but with the translation of Bakhtin's essays in *The Dialogic Imagination* (1981), they quickly saw challenges and relevancies in Bakhtin's work that made them climb onto the back of the wagon just as it was getting crowded.

My own first encounter in 1980 came just before *The Dialogic Imagination*, prompted by an authority that rhetoricians honor, a footnote in one of Walter Ong's books pointing to the selections in *Readings in Russian Poetics*. I was not looking for insights into rhetoric at the time, however, but for a twentieth-century theorist of narrative who could help me develop what I then called a narrative poetics of speech, an account of narration that sees it as speech responding to prior speech as it reports it (see my "Bakhtin versus Chatman on Narrative" and "Dialogics, Narratology, and the Virtual Space of Discourse"). The selections in the *Russian Poetics* volume, the chapter on discourse from Bakhtin's *Problems of Dostoevsky's Poetics* and the chapter on reported speech from Voloshinov's *Marxism and the Philosophy of Language* were exactly what I was looking for to help me elaborate in a modern idiom the insight I had first worked out by contrasting Plato's account of poetic diction in his *Republic* with Aristotle's account of manner and diction in the *Poetics* (see my *Making Tales* and "Narrative Diction and the Poetics of Speech").

Poetics, not rhetoric, was my focus, but narrative poetics, as I had learned it from my thesis advisor, Wayne Booth, was a point of intersection of those two classical disciplines; so rhetoric was already potentially entailed as well. This connection has been borne out in my subsequent inquiries and in the following chapters that discover intimate connections between rhetoric and poetics in the Bakhtin School and recover those same connections from a reading of Aristotle's *Poetics* and *Rhetoric* against the grain, what P. Christopher Smith might call in his Heideggerian idiom a "destructive" reading.

It will help readers to make sense of the following chapters to know that my work with Booth was part of an education at the University of Chicago that involved me in a twentieth-century revival of an ancient array of disciplines among which rhetoric had a well-established place. The program in the Analysis of Ideas and the Study of Methods, in which I was one of the first undergraduate majors in the late 1960s, required its students to take a sequence of courses in methods—Poetics, Rhetoric, and Logic—a revival of the trivium (with poetics taking, as it sometimes did, the place of grammar) that engaged us with classical instantiations of these verbal disciplines, especially the authoritative Aristotelian texts, and with modern reformulations of them. Richard McKeon was a founder of this program, still teaching in it when I was an undergraduate though I did not sit at his feet. One of his students, Charles Wegener, taught the poetics and the rhetoric courses I took. Booth, scion of the Chicago School of Aristotelian literary criticism and already author of *The Rhetoric of Fiction,* was a member of the program's faculty and one of my undergraduate and graduate teachers as well as my thesis advisor.

I provide this autobiographical background not because I think my own history is of great importance in itself but because, as the story of the intellectual formation of a late twentieth- and early twenty-first century student of rhetoric, it identifies my affiliations and orientation and, as a reader of Bakhtin, it marks my peculiarity—perhaps, since Bakhtin says all our utterances are unique, my uniqueness. I have a number of colleagues in rhetorical studies shaped by work in Ideas and Methods at Chicago, most of them as graduate students or as post-doctoral faculty in the program rather than undergraduates—among them Eugene Garver, Walter Jost, James Kastely, Fred Antczak, and Wendy Olmsted. It is my Chicago School teachers and colleagues, however, not my Ideas and Methods colleagues, who also have engaged with the Bakhtin School. Bakhtin had, after all, written much about the novel, the poetic/rhetorical genre central to Boothian and post-Boothian Chicago critics. Booth himself took the measure of Bakhtin, a writer who had anticipated some of the arguments of *The Rhetoric of Fiction* forty years *avant la lettre,* and found a place for him in his pluralism. I discuss his engagement with Bakhtin in Chapter 4. David Richter and James Phelan, like me students of Booth, both drew Bakhtin into their Aristotelian orbits. They figure briefly in Chapter 5. I do not think they would dispute that I am the only one of us to become exorbitant from that orbit, revolutionized around a new center of intellectual gravity or a new constellation of ideas. Pulled away from Aristotle, however, I was never beyond his pull, and my turn away from him to the Bakhtin School has been articulated, in almost every essay in this volume, with and against the background of Aristotelian terms, premises, preferences, yes, even prejudices.

In this orientation to Aristotle, I have much in common with many of the other rhetoricians who have engaged with Bakhtin's work but very little in common with all the other contemporary critics and theorists who have engaged with him. Most of those in the West involved in the translation, appropriation, and elaboration of Bakhtin's work have brought to it investments in the schools of late twentieth-century literary theory—structuralism, deconstruction, Marxism, feminism, humanism—or in the early twentieth-century intellectual figures, disciplines, and movements that shaped Bakhtin's own work—neo-Kantianism, "life philosophy," sociology, formalism. Aristotle and neo-Aristotelians do not figure on their interpretive horizons any more than rhetoric does. And even my interest in rhetoric in its "trivial" affiliations with poetics and dialectic—a continuation of interests first developed in the Ideas and Methods curriculum—sets me apart from many other rhetoricians who have entered the disciplinary domains of composition or communication in flight from literature or at any rate with preferences for a civic rhetoric over the epideictic rhetoric more easily affiliated with poetics and "literary" interests; Jeffrey Walker's revisionist history of rhetoric is an important exception here. Dialectic, in the guise of "philosophy," has been more frequently on their minds as a prestigious challenger to rhetoric's intellectual legitimacy.

But if I am peculiar among Bakhtinians in my persistent orientation to Aristotle and among rhetoricians in my interest in poetics and the trivium, I find that my peculiarities position me to see both my contemporaries and the Bakhtin School in a distinctive light. No contemporary intellectual disciplines are closer to their classical roots in Aristotle than rhetoric and poetics. His texts that name and essentially invent the science of poetics and the art of rhetoric continue to be required reading for contemporary students of both. His definitions of their objects and ends, his distinctions of their principal parts, his hierarchies among those parts, and his accounts of the points of intersection and difference between the two disciplines still shape the expectations and questions that guide inquiry in these fields and the curricula that guide instruction.

In rhetoric Aristotle's authority is widely acknowledged. George Kennedy, the most recent translator into English of Aristotle's *Rhetoric*, writes, "It has been more studied in modern times than it ever was in antiquity and the Middle Ages. Most teachers of composition, communication, and speech regard it as a seminal work that organizes its subject into essential parts, provides insight into the bases of speech acts, creates categories and terminology for discussing discourse, and illustrates and applies its teachings so that they can be used in society" (ix). Though some theorists and historians of rhetoric have recently been reinterpreting Isocrates as an alternative classical predecessor or seeking other authorities for an alternative rhetorical theory and practice, Aristotle sets the authoritative background against which those reinterpretations, like Janet Atwill's or Ekaterina Haskins's, must pose themselves.

In poetics, conducted most often these days under the heading of criticism and theory, there is less direct acknowledgment of Aristotle's contemporary authority, but it remains considerable. Stephen Halliwell, a recent translator and expositor of the *Poetics,* notes a "fragmentation of Aristotle's conception of poetry, by selective quotation of particular dicta. . . . The removal of ideas and pronouncements from their context allows the characteristically eclectic modern theorist or critic to gesture towards Aristotle's significance as a pioneer in the field, but without incurring any suspicion or taint of real Aristotelianism" (*Aristotle's Poetics* 317–18). Halliwell, however, discerns a more pervasive contemporary afterlife of the *Poetics,*

> for apart from producing lines of enquiry and thought which are still with us, it has also helped to shape the formation of fundamental concepts and issues in the modern tradition of literary, and especially dramatic, theory and criticism. These concepts are apt to seem inescapable, so deeply embedded are they in common attitudes to poetry and drama. Though we no longer live in an age of neo-classicism, it would take a more radical and drastic break with the past of European culture than even the more brutal forms of modernism have effected to efface altogether the traces of the *Poetics*' continuing presence and insidious influence. . . . [T]he interpreter of the treatise is, therefore, whether he likes it or not, partially constrained from the start by interests and presuppositions which the work itself has been instrumental in creating. (*Aristotle's Poetics* 286)

With or without explicit acknowledgment, then, Aristotelian presuppositions have underwritten structuralist narratology and classically inflected theories of tragic drama. Though my forebears, the Chicago Aristotelians, no longer hold forth from Chicago, their mid-century dispute with the Coleridgean premises of the New Critics revealed (to someone like me, at least) that the conflict was really between two schools of thought in the Aristotelian tradition, one of which held to the priority of plot, while the other made his view of poetic diction primary. Taking language as the material out of which poems are made, the New Critics, like their formalist counterparts in Russia earlier in the twentieth century, followed Aristotle's account of poetic language, even if they were heretical in giving the matter more importance than the object of imitation. It would not be stretching the point too far to say that post-structuralist critics shared this premise with their New Critical, formalist, and structuralist predecessors but took the materiality of language more seriously than they did. In this sense the celebrated rigor of Paul de Man might be seen as his pushing Aristotle's account of poetic diction to its logical conclusion without any under-the-table recourse to objects of poetic imitation.

Be that as it may, some of what Halliwell calls our most "deeply embedded" common understandings of rhetoric and poetics do indeed originate in Aristotle's account of them. That narratives narrate story or plot, for example, feels like the way things are, but it is an Aristotelian premise that makes it difficult even to imagine alternatives. That rhetoric is a kind of reasoning, albeit a diminished kind, is another such premise, which it may seem genuinely heretical to question. That poetry should be universal, more philosophical than history, is a parallel belief that we owe to the *Poetics*. That the most important trope for both rhetoric and poetics is metaphor is hard to deny, and our teaching of style in both arts bears out our belief in its centrality. That poetic style should be distinguished from everyday language and that rhetorical style should above all be clear derive from Aristotle. We have shared Aristotle's view that delivery is a degraded and unfortunate necessity in rhetoric and that it has nothing to do with poetics. Many writers and critics have shared his view that narrative is the weak sister of drama and that that narrative is best that narrates least.

So in bringing expectations formed by Aristotle's *Rhetoric* and *Poetics* and the arts of the trivium to the Bakhtin School, I bring terms of contemporary relevance even if they are not, especially on the poetic side, terms widely recognized as Aristotelian, but the question remains as to whether the Bakhtin School is productively responsive to these terms. Much of the following volume is my affirmative answer to this question, but it is important to say at the outset that Bakhtin himself seems in his work on Dostoevsky and the novel to orient his argument against the backdrop of the arts of the trivium and their Aristotelian formulations. His dialogic accounts of language and of the novel position themselves, on the one hand, against poetics and grammar, and on the other, against dialectic. We could almost say that his "dialogics," if you will, tries to take the place of rhetoric, as a third discursive art positioned vis à vis the other two arts of the trivium; it tries, that is, to displace rhetoric as he understands it from that place. He and his colleagues powerfully critique the grammatical orientations to language of Saussure and the formalists, and he also sets novelistic discourse against poetic discourse (at least in what he repeatedly calls the strict and narrow sense). He also differentiates language as he finds it in Dostoevsky and the novel from dialectic, sometimes identified as Hegelian, sometimes not. But he does not turn to rhetoric as the needed alternative to the other arts. Instead he emphasizes its monologism and its formal constraints in contrast to the polyphonic and dialogic language he celebrates and analyzes. He turns against the Soviet avatar of the rhetoric of fiction, Victor Vinogradov, in his effort to formulate discourse in the novel, against classical rhetoric as a way of talking about pre-novelistic discourse in the Menippean tradition. In his "poetics" of Dostoevsky's fiction, he turns the hierarchy of classical Aristotelian poetics on its head. His hostile remarks on rhetoric may reflect its status as the art of discourse already established in the position he wants his own dialogics to occupy, closer to home, as it were, than either grammar and its affiliated poetics or dialectic. I will argue in Chapters 8 and 9 for an expanded rhetorical understanding of his theory of discourse that would let that theory occupy not only the position but also reclaim the name "rhetoric" in a rich pre-disciplinary sense.

The relevance of an approach to Bakhtin informed by an interest in the arts of the trivium may also be inferred from the critical reception of the Bakhtin School's work, which has come from contemporary advocates of dialectic and grammar as well as of rhetoric. Fredric Jameson's re-disciplining of dialogic to dialectical oppositions and Seymour Chatman's subordination of dialogic terms to structuralist narratological grammatical categories are but two of numerous indications that the reception of Bakhtin's work has revealed the "trivial" investments of recent theorists as well as the "triviality" of his own work (see my "Dialogics, Narratology, and the Virtual Space of Discourse"). The attempts of rhetoricians like Kay Halasek to frame a "dialogic rhetoric" appear to be part of the larger story of the contemporary trivium's attempt to assimilate Bakhtin's account of language and verbal practice to its established categories or adjust those categories to include his account. It would be possible to retell a considerable part of the story of the appropriation of Bakhtin School work in the seventies and eighties in terms of the contemporary practitioners of dialectic, grammar, and rhetoric instead of in terms of the names of contemporary schools of criticism and theory. For my present purposes, however, simply to recognize the possibility of telling such a story is already to see the relevance of these arts to the reception of the Bakhtin School without my actually needing to tell it more than piecemeal (see my "Dialogics, Literary Theory, and the Liberal Arts" for a fuller development of this story).

That so many theorists and critics tried to come to terms with Bakhtin School work on language and literature bespeaks that work's originality and power, but it also bespeaks the moment that the work emerged into Western critical discussions and the peculiar order and manner in which it was translated and brought forward. Bakhtin did not enjoy a long public career in which his work came out as it was produced in the contexts that provoked it, or in which it was translated and disseminated as it came out, and it might well have had nothing like the impact it did in the West had it appeared more "normally." He published in Russian an earlier version of the Dostoevsky book in 1929, the year he was "arrested on suspicion of having participated in an organization described as anti-Soviet" and exiled to Kazakhstan (Hirschkop 168–69). His other work of the previous decade—one of post-revolution intellectual ferment, extraordinary productivity, collaboration with Voloshinov, Medvedev and others in several circles of intellectuals—and his work of the next thirty years—a period of exile, isolation from colleagues, teaching in provincial obscurity and again extraordinary productivity—remained unpublished, except for a brief 1919 manifesto, until his very existence was rediscovered by admirers of the Dostoevsky book in the early 1960s in the Soviet Union during a period of post-Stalinist liberalization. Voloshinov and Medvedev published in the 1920s but perished in the 1930s, the first taken by cancer, the other executed by the authorities; they were translated into English in the 1970s.

Subsequent publication and translation of the School's work have been shaped by the interests and investments of editors and translators and the audiences they anticipated, not by the author or his anticipated audiences. The editors' and translators' selection and arrangement of texts, their publication of a series of major English translations representing Bakhtin's work from the end of the 1920s through the 1950s in little more than a decade (1981 to 1993), and their translation and publication of work from the 1930s through the 1950s before the work of the 1920s has profoundly affected its uptake. So has the effort by some of his translators and editors to identify him as the author of works published under Voloshinov's and Medvedev's names and the efforts of others, now in the ascendancy, to attribute the works to the authors under whose names they were published, while still acknowledging close intellectual exchange between them and Bakhtin and important relations between their work and his.

I cannot think of another thinker of such consequence rescued from near oblivion at the end of his life and re-presented to the world by so many advocates with such divergent interests to so many purposes at a moment of such intellectual excitement. *Rabelais and His World,* with its celebration of lower class language and culture, hit the bookstores in 1968, the year of international student unrest. The moment of "theory" in the West was reaching its apex as Bakhtin School work on language and literature was brought out in the 1970s and 1980s, and representatives of the major theoretical schools—

deconstruction's De Man, Marxism's Jameson and Williams, structuralism's Todorov, psychoanalysis's Kristeva and many, many others—took them seriously. Patricia Bizzell describes the choice to include Bakhtin in *The Rhetorical Tradition* as an investment in an "extremely hot" figure, "a real growth stock," because "the 'dialogic' coordinates fit well with current interest in the social construction of knowledge and with current issues in composition pedagogy" (112). Though the temperature has cooled and stock in Bakhtin has gone down since she wrote this, the School's work has been widely assimilated and continues to be assigned, read, and cited in current work in the field.

"The dialogic" was the rubric under which Bakhtin's most influential work for rhetoric and composition was presented by Holquist and Emerson in *The Dialogic Imagination* (1981), a compilation of work from the 1930s with a title Bakhtin himself never used. Revolving around this central collection, *Problems of Dostoevsky's Poetics,* the 1929 book substantially revised in the early 1960s and retranslated and published in 1984, and *Speech Genres and Other Late Essays,* including the titular essay from the early 1950s and work coming down to the 1970s, along with Voloshinov's 1926 essay "Discourse in Life and Discourse in Art" and his 1929 *Marxism and the Philosophy of Language,* both of which had been translated and published in English in the 1970s, were the principal Bakhtin School canon for scholars of rhetoric and composition. These are the texts where language and society and dialogic genres and gestures are codified and the texts where rhetoric makes its brief appearances, usually wearing a black hat. Readers of Bakhtin in Russian told us in the 1980s that there were early philosophical manuscripts with religious overtones, phenomenological and neo-Kantian terms, and with no focus on language or the novel, that could diminish the importance of the texts that were important to us. We waited, however, until 1990 for the first translation of some of these early manuscripts under the title *Art and Answerability*—another title invented by editors rather than by Bakhtin—and until 1993 for translation of what may be the earliest manuscript, entitled, again by editors, *Toward a Philosophy of the Act.* Awaiting these late translations of early work, we published books that touched on Bakhtin's phenomenology without access to his earliest phenomenological manuscript (Bernard-Donals) and criticized our discipline's preoccupation with the linguistic and sociological texts we had in translation on the strength of second-hand accounts from Slavicists of the more ethically serious philosophical texts we still did not have (Ewald; see Chapter 7). Those of us dependent on translators have been alerted that the translations we have come to depend on (and in some cases the Russian texts they were based upon) have been re-edited in a Russian edition of his complete works. At the same time the scholarly project of recovering the context of the School's work, the authors to whom it responded, the way its members responded to one another, and the degree of their originality in their original context has been the most recent project of a group of Bakhtin scholars who have gained access since the fall of the Soviet Union to archival materials previously unavailable. They have brought us interesting discoveries of sources and influence and necessary corrections to earlier myths and mistakes. Their frequent deprecations of the uninformed interpretations of scholars dependent on earlier translations put us all on notice that a philological regime has begun to assert its authority over authors deeply suspicious of philology and to restrict interpretations of the texts it claims to the period of their production and the language of their origin, even to declare a moratorium on further appropriations of Bakhtin School texts until they have completed the work of interpreting and situating them in their original contexts.

It is too late, however, to try to put this genie back in its bottle. The translations, whatever local difficulties they may have, are too consistent and too pertinent to too many questions that have concerned too many of their readers to hold the presses on further appropriation and elaboration of them until the final scholarly editions and unlikely-to-appear new translations have been made. Too many of us have already been persuaded by the translations and thought our ways too far down the lines they have opened and brought the ideas they have given rise to in us to bear on too many matters of concern to rescind what we have said or suspend our further thinking, even if we must correct occasional errors and be especially cautious in discussing matters of biography and originality. At least one of the scholars involved in both the editing and the historical situating of Bakhtin's work assured participants in a session at the 2014 International Bakhtin Conference that we could for the most part rely on the translations we have. We can take Bakhtin's celebration of the productivity and diversity of responsive understanding as sufficient warrant to continue our elaborations of Bakhtin School work in translation in the domains of thought that engage us in our own moment and our own fields of interest. The work was and is fresh and provocative to many of us (though from the beginning there were those like Richard Poirier who found it old hat), and it has become a fruitful starting point for thinking we cannot now unthink. But being a contemporary Bakhtinian is now more like being a contemporary Aristotelian than it was when the Bakhtin School texts first came out in translation. Then it felt as if those texts were speaking directly to us and what interested us; now, even when our project is to think *with* the terms and claims they give us about what interests us here and now, we must recall the scholarship that mediates them to us and remember that they had a life and place in their own place and time.

What, then, we might ask, makes a writer who has nothing much good to say about rhetoric so compelling and fruitful for students of rhetoric now? Our interest in him is not a matter of academic fashion, which in any event has now passed. Some of it may come from rhetoricians' disposition to defend themselves when attacked, especially when the attack is widely read and the position of rhetoric in the academy is vulnerable. But I think the attraction is principally that of likeness in difference—of a thinker engaged with language and human interactions in ways that resonate with disciplined rhetorical ways of thinking but don't quite fit them and prompt us to think again about them. His work alerts us to limitations in our rhetorical models and at the same time suggests ways to transcend them, even at the risk of losing rhetoric, or at least rhetoric as we know it. The priority of audience in the rhetorical transaction, the institutional delimitation of rhetorical situations and genres, the impersonality of topoi, the abjection of delivery, the distinction of rhetoric from poetics, the very disciplinary distinctiveness of rhetoric itself all come into question in an intellectual world where nonetheless terms and topics of rhetorical interest seem always to be before us. His work has pushed its rhetorical readers both to transform rhetoric into something new and strange and to reassert its distinctiveness more sharply in opposition to him.

My own work gathered here from the past thirty years linking Bakhtin, rhetoric, and the arts of the trivium has moved in both these directions, roughly represented by the two parts of this book. In the first part, in response to the early translated work on Dostoevsky and the novel, I have posited a Bakhtinian "dialogics" as an alternative and counterpart to rhetoric and the other arts of the trivium, pushing rhetoric, as Bakhtin did in those works, toward a sharpened definition as a contentious and competitive art focused on winning over others. In a domain of once-established verbal arts still shaping the expectations of philosophers and critics, even when they are no longer the explicit and dominant form of the curriculum, I have introduced dialogics as a fourth art that calls attention to its distinctiveness from the others even as it calls out their persisting, if varied, manifestations in the work of significant contemporaries. In Chapter 2, "Dialogics as an Art of Discourse," I inaugurate this project by setting dialogics off against rhetoric and dialectic as Aristotle distinguishes them at the outset of the *Rhetoric* and by situating the art of dialogics I propose in relation to several recent accounts of self-conscious discursive practice—Tzvetan Todorov's Bakhtin-inspired "dialogic criticism," Merle Brown's account of "communal creativity" in F. R. Leavis's late work, Richard Rorty's pragmatist "conversation" and Hans-Georg Gadamer's hermeneutic "conversation." Chapter 3, "Booth, Bakhtin, and the Culture of Criticism," examines the rhetorical criticism and pluralism of Wayne Booth from the perspective of dialogics and reviews Booth's attempt to come to terms with Bakhtin's work. Chapter 4, "Rhetoric, Literary Criticism, Theory, and Bakhtin," presents an account of rhetorical criticism in literary studies, which elaborates a Bakhtinian re-description of the classical figures of thought growing out of Jeanne Fahnestock's characterization of those figures as "interactional devices." Chapter 5, "Bakhtin and Rhetorical Criticism," includes an early response to the early work of two major Bakhtinians in rhetoric and composition, Kay Halasek and Michael Bernard-Donals, and points to a wider set of potentially productive sites to develop a Bakhtinian rhetorical criticism. Chapter 6, "Antilogics, Dialogics, and Sophistic Social Psychology," articulates dialogics with the revival of the sophists in recent rhetorical theory (the other hot "growth stock" in rhetorical theory that Bizzell identifies) by examining sociologist Michael Billig's account of a Protagorean rhetoric. In this chapter, the polemically sharpened definition of rhetoric that characterized the earlier chapters begins to dissolve into an un-institutionalized discursive process, a "rhetoricality" that the second part of the book examines.

In that second part, influenced by the late translation of Bakhtin's earliest work on architectonics, or first philosophy, I have recognized, preceding all the institutionalized arts and disciplines, a "rhetorical" discursive world that justifies Bender and Wellbery's prescient characterization of Bakhtin's works as "virtual treatises on the nature and functioning of rhetoricality" (p. 37), a "generalized rhetoric that penetrates to the deepest levels of human experience, . . . bound to no specific set of institutions, . . . no longer the title of a doctrine and a practice . . . [but] something like the condition of our existence" (p. 25). From this perspective, a disciplined art of dialogics looks restrictive, an attempt to fix and regulate the flux and interplay of an inescapably dynamic and risky pre-disciplinary existential situation. The first chapter of this part, Chapter 7, "Bakhtin's 'Rough Draft,'" refutes a reading of *Toward a Philosophy of the Act* by Slavicists Morson and Emerson that elevated the importance of ethics and diminished the accounts of language and society in the Bakhtin School canon, a reading that influenced an important article by Helen Rothschild Ewald in composition studies that called into question the value of work grounded in Bakhtin's middle-period work on language and the novel. Chapter 8, "Architectonics, Rhetoric, and Poetics," builds on the ground cleared by that refutation an account of the radical implications of the Bakhtin School's early work for re-describing rhetoric and poetics and rethinking their close relations to one another. Chapter 9, "Aristotle's *Rhetoric* and Bakhtin's Discourse Theory," draws out the implications of a Bakhtinian rhetorical theory against the dialogizing background of Aristotle's authoritative account of the art. Stepping outside the institutional contexts that delimited the ends of Aristotelian rhetoric and recalling specific prior utterances that situate the rhetorician's discourse rather than the objectified topics Aristotle offers, Bakhtin lets us imagine a rhetoric of performing utterance more fundamental than Aristotle's rhetoric of finding available means. Chapter 10, "Rereading the Place of Rhetoric in Aristotle's *Poetics* in Light of Bakhtin's Discourse Theory: Rhetoric as *Dianoia*, Poetics as an Imitation of Rhetoric," recovers a Bakhtinian poetics within Aristotle's *Poetics* by following out the full implications of Aristotle's referral of *dianoia* or thought to his *Rhetoric*. "Chapter 11, "Liberal Education, Writing, and the Dialogic Self," my earliest piece on Bakhtin and the teaching of writing that grew out of the CCCC session in which I participated in 1984, situates itself in relation to expressivist and social constructionist composition theories and imagines undergraduate students in the situation of Bakhtinian rhetors who cannot take for granted a "given" disciplinary discursive site but may, if encouraged and supported, discover the mutual bearings of the disciplines in a dialogic liberal education.

My engagement with the opposing though intimately interconnected perspectives that the two parts of the book contain has proceeded from dialogics to architectonics while Bakhtin's own development went the other way, and I have been at pains to preserve what I admire in his later work even as I have tried to register the force and distinctiveness of the earlier. The "fit" between the early dialogic last chapter and the late chapters that precede it bears out their compatibility. I have set myself against critics who find the early work authentic and undialogic and the later work a somehow tainted compromise with the social and the political. I have tried to hold his thinking and my own together across the shifts of vocabulary and the additions and alterations of terms. Reading over my own work of three decades as I have gathered and organized it here for the first time, I find an unfolding inquiry and argument that I hope will be apparent to readers who may be familiar with one or another of these pieces but not with the trajectory they mark out together. Though they were shaped to many different occasions and are responsive to a wide range of other thinkers, though by no means to all the consequential person-ideas of a time, culture, community or discipline I once hoped to address, they stand here as a whole utterance re-articulated by my arrangement and reaffirmation of them. I have learned from gathering and assembling them, and I hope my readers will help me learn more with that outsideness that only they can bring to them.

Part I. Dialogics, Rhetoric, Criticism

2. Dialogics as an Art of Discourse

Aristotle begins his *Rhetoric* by distinguishing between our spontaneous discursive activities and the arts of discourse that rationalize them. He claims that all of us use both dialectic and rhetoric, even if we use them all our lives without knowing it. We all try to "sift or support theses" or to "defend or attack persons" with or without recognizing what we are doing, and some of us succeed, whether "quite at random, or else merely with a knack acquired from practice." The art of rhetoric, like the art of dialectic, investigates the causes of success in these discursive activities and reduces them to self-conscious practices. Aristotle assumes that what was done by accident or knack can be done better by art and, furthermore, that it can be taught (*Rhetoric* 1354a). He goes on to distinguish the ends of rhetorical discourse and to catalog its means, in a treatise that has profoundly shaped the discursive practices it rationalizes.[1]

Giving a name and a shape to some discursive practices changes for better or worse the unrationalized activities in which the aims of the arts were discovered. Once we have distinguished between sifting or supporting theses in dialectical arguments and defending or attacking persons on rhetorical occasions, we are likely to try to place any discursive activity in one or the other of these categories; we will try to separate the dialectical interest in theses from the rhetorical respect for persons. When we are concerned with dialectical discourse, we will not consider who holds the thesis and who needs to be persuaded to hold it, for we will be trying only to support it and to establish its logical relations to other theses. When we turn to rhetorical discourse, we will subordinate the logical implications and grounds of theses to the beliefs a given audience holds that can be used to shape its judgment of us and of what or whom we are talking about. Any discursive activity that involves both persons and theses is likely to fall anomalously outside the domain of the arts of discourse or to be placed forcefully within one or the other: persons will become a convenient figure for theses in dialectic, or theses will become contingent functions of persons in rhetoric.

For those trained in these arts, as many generations in Western culture have been, there is no way of returning to unrationalized discursive activities that do not make these distinctions. Whether producing or interpreting discourse, most participants in this culture have chosen either the rhetorical or the dialectical mode and the characteristic questions and terms of that mode to construct or construe the work before them. However much the arts of dialectic and rhetoric have disputed with each other for dominance and enjoyed shifting prestige in different ages and places, they have divided between them the allegiances of most practitioners of discourse in most areas of inquiry and argument in the West.[2]

Against this cultural background I want to ask two questions. First, does Mikhail Bakhtin's account of dialogic discourse discover a discursive practice distinct from the practices that rhetoric and dialectic have rationalized? If so, could an art of dialogics based on Bakhtin's discovery have sufficient power to guide our reading and writing practices as the classical discursive arts have done? Affirmative answers to both questions would have important consequences for all fields of discourse whose practice draws on rhetorical or dialectical models; in this chapter I take my examples from literary criticism and philosophy.

The terms I have drawn from Aristotle to set up the opposition between the dialectical and rhetorical arts, of course, ignore the rich history of contending voices that each of these arts has involved. It is not just that rhetoric and dialectic have contended with each other at least since Plato's *Phaedrus* and *Gorgias* but that each has been itself an object of contention among its advocates and practitioners. We may even claim that Aristotle himself, in elaborating both arts, complicated the opposition he began with. Yet Aristotle's initial distinction remains sufficiently authoritative and familiar to orient my discourse rhetorically, and its opposition of thesis-centered and person-centered arts of discourse provides an especially appealing dialectical opening for a Bakhtinian art, because Bakhtin's dialogics is founded in the inseparability of thesis and person.

In his chapter "The Idea in Dostoevsky," Bakhtin declares that in Dostoevsky's art "the image of an idea is inseparable from the image of a person, the carrier of that idea" *(Problems* 85), and he adds that the idea thus understood "begins to live, that is, to take shape, to develop, to find and renew its verbal expression, to give birth to new ideas, only when it enters into genuine dialogic relationships with other ideas, with the ideas of *others*"(italics in the text, 88). In such dialogic relations, ideas cannot be separated from their holders for dialectical examination as theses, nor can persons be rhetorically manipulated in isolation from the ideas that shape their discourse. Bakhtin's synthesis of person and idea is perhaps the idea with which he most consistently identifies himself,[3] but one must wonder what alternative to Aristotle's person-centered rhetoric and idea-centered dialectic can follow from Bakhtin's compound person-idea. When we lose the distinction between theses to test and persons to defend or appeal to, have we also lost the distinction of purposes on which an art can be founded?

I think not. In my account dialectic concerns impersonal relations among terms that are independent of those who hold them—relations of confirmation and contradiction, antithesis and synthesis, and the like. Rhetoric concerns relations of practical agreement and disagreement among persons—relations that may be effected, despite ideological differences, in the formation of consensuses among divergent interests and parties. Dialogics concerns the relations among persons articulating their ideas in response to one another, discovering their mutual affinities and oppositions, their provocations to reply, their desires to hear more, or their wishes to change the subject. To make these distinctions in another, related way, I would say that dialectic aims at discovering the truth of ideas or theses, rhetoric at determining the decisions of people, and dialogics at articulating people's ideas, our own and those of others. As dialectic strives for conviction on a question and rhetoric for persuasion of an audience, dialogics strives for comprehensive responsiveness and responsibility to the consequential person-ideas of a time, culture, community, or discipline—that is, for the fullest articulation of someone's ideas with the actual and possible ideas of others.

Bakhtin praises Dostoevsky in language that specifies this aim of dialogic discourse in its widest cultural context. Dostoevsky, he says:

> ... brought together ideas and worldviews, which in real life were absolutely estranged and deaf to one another, and forced them to quarrel. He extended, as it were, these distantly separated ideas by means of a dotted line to the point of their dialogic intersection. In so doing he anticipated future dialogic encounters between ideas that in his time were still dissociated. He foresaw new linkages of ideas, the emergence of new voice-ideas and changes in the arrangement of all the voice-ideas in the worldwide dialogue. (*Problems* 91)

Dostoevsky is a paragon of dialogic practice because he takes the widest purview for the dialogue he imagines, because he hears the mutual bearings of ideas that do not yet hear one another, and because he presses the characters who embody those ideas to further articulation that alters the conversation from which he has drawn them. As practitioners of dialogics we would resemble both Dostoevsky and his characters, striving both to recognize the mutual bearings of diverse voices and to answer them from our own perspectives.

But we may imagine dialogics as a practice distinct from dialectic and rhetoric without being able to reduce that practice to an art. Though we may gain power over our practice simply by distinguishing dialogic aims from rhetorical and dialectical ones, an art of discourse would require some understanding of the principles that follow from dialogic purposes and of the genres that fulfill those purposes.

A first principle might be that every topic can be taken as a place where specific person-ideas address one another. For Aristotle, both dialectic and rhetoric work by erasing the images of specific former advocates of ideas and substituting topoi. Dialectic replaces these images with formal argumentative possibilities and abstract oppositions of terms, and even rhetoric, otherwise focused on the persons of the audience, the speaker, and the accused or eulogized, reduces the ideas of previous speakers to the generic ideological repertoires of different kinds of audiences. Though rhetoric may sometimes draw on ideas associated with admirable or reprehensible sources, it more often appeals to "commonplace" ideas whose lack of specific ownership makes them available for building new alliances without the encumbrance of old personal associations.

Dialogics, in contrast, would try to re-create the image of specific persons who voice their ideas in specific texts and contexts; it would situate an utterance historically or imaginatively in a field of other persons' utterances rather than topically in a field of dialectical terms or rhetorical commonplaces. Both historical and imaginative placements would be important, because the continued productivity of dialogue depends on our discovering mutual bearings among person-ideas that have not yet engaged one another as well as on our reconstructing the mutual bearings of those that have. Dostoevsky's achievement, after all, was not just to depict the ideological interplay of his age but to anticipate, extend, and provoke it. He brought together person-ideas that had not yet found one another, and he made them provoke one another to further discourse.

A corollary principle is that there is no systematic or historical limit to the voices that may find a place in a given dialogue. While dialectic expects its thesis to have a formal antithesis or consequence and rhetoric addresses itself to a historical audience in a given case, dialogics would open its exchanges to any voices its participants can feel the force of. Such voices may not offer an antithesis to a given thesis or an answer to a proposed question but may introduce another way of talking that challenges the very language of the present interlocutors; instead of appealing to the audience at hand, these voices may intrude the claims of other persons, those excluded from that audience who are nevertheless affected by the issues it is considering. An opening dialogic move, then, is to situate an utterance in a field of other specific utterances, but an always available dialogic move is to introduce another voice into that field.

The best generic model for this kind of discourse is the symposium. Unlike the dialectical genre of the treatise that tends to reduce prior voices to transcended theses and unlike the rhetorical genre of the argument that offers all the considerations it can find to establish its position against opposing claims, the symposium represents a series of voices differentiating themselves from one another and open to new voices. This genre may be imagined to report the interplay of ideologically characteristic utterances provoked not only by the topic but by what those who have already spoken have said about it. As literary forms, representations of such symposia would be not mere anthologies of essays, dialectical forced marches, or rhetorical prosecutions of cases but narrations or inventions of interactions open to further responses and perhaps designed to provoke them.[4] This genre's openness to new voices and its power to situate them among those who have already spoken impressed me forcefully in an undergraduate assignment I once had, one that asked me to place a contemporary psychologist's essay on love among the speakers of Plato's *Symposium*. David Orlinsky found his place around the table with Phaedrus, Pausanias, Eryximachus, and the rest, revealing both his meaning and theirs with the new force and nuance produced by their dialogic relations.

The dialogic genre of the symposium, however, can be organized to dialectical or rhetorical purposes, and other genres can be turned to dialogic purposes or include dialogic aspects. Indeed, nothing prevents the utterance of a single person from functioning as the dialogic intersection of several voices; a dialogic perspective leads to taking solo utterances in just this way. In the final analysis the dialogic reader would regard even a purportedly monologic voice, whether rhetorical or dialectical, as a response to other voices, though the response may be to reduce them or to shut them out or to overcome them. And the dialogic reader would also treat chinks in monologic unity—dialectical inconsistencies and rhetorical indecisions—as openings for further discourse.

To read others dialogically, then, would be to read for an opening in the discussion or a provocation to further discourse, and if such reading errs, it would not be likely to do so in the same ways as dialectical or rhetorical readings do. Dialogic reading would not generally reduce others to consistent dialectical counterparts, or dwell on the inconsistencies in their positions, or transcend them in higher syntheses. Nor would it minimize others as rhetorical opponents by attempting to discredit them. Instead, dialogic reading would assume the right to represent others in terms they might not have anticipated or acknowledged.

The dialogic reader would revoice the discourses of others in pursuit of his or her theme, and there is no guarantee that the tendencies of the reporting and reported discourses would be, in Bakhtin's terms, "unidirectional" *(Problems* 199), sharing the same language and values. Dialogic reading would strive, however, not for an impossible coincidence of the reader's and the other's languages but for revealing and answerable representations of the one in the other. Bakhtin describes the value of such representations in the following remarks, which Caryl Emerson reports and translates from his early essay "Author and Hero in Aesthetic Activity":

> "[O]ne can speak of the absolute aesthetic need of one person for another, for the seeing, remembering, gathering, and unifying activity of the other, which alone can create his externally completed personality; this personality will not exist if the other does not create it." . . . However abounding or lacking in love, this activity is always beneficial because it always "formally enriches" the object, fixing it in time and space from a point of view fundamentally inaccessible to the object itself. "What would I have to gain," Bakhtin asks, "if another were to *fuse* with me? He would see and know only what I already see and know, he would only repeat in himself the inescapable closed circle of my own life; let him rather remain outside me." (Emerson 70)

As readers sophisticated by an art of dialogics, then, we would self-consciously represent the voice-ideas of others and involve others in dialogues they had not anticipated, but we would also self-consciously expect unexpected replies and foresee unforeseen uses of our own words and ourselves by others. We would be more likely than others to recognize how even an admirer's repetition of our words may embarrass us and how another's reformulation of our meaning in the most alien terms may convert us.

Our discourse, in any case, is always subject to appropriation by others who do not share our precise standpoint. Even when we let ourselves wish that others would hear us exactly as we hear ourselves, we are acknowledging that our meaning is not for us alone to determine. Indeed, just as all of us have engaged in rhetorical and dialectical discourse without knowing it, so all of us have participated willy-nilly in dialogic discourse, defining ourselves and others in response to what others say and being ourselves defined by their responses to us. The point of naming this activity "dialogic" and cultivating it as an art is not just to learn to do it better and to teach it to others but also to give it standing among the verbal activities traditionally recognized as arts. Bakhtin's formulation of dialogic principles points toward a deliberate verbal practice that can contest the ground long held by rhetoric and dialectic and reshape our expectations in the verbal works we create and re-create.

I would like to turn now to considering a few of the ways that such an art might reshape the practice of literary criticism. Many Anglo-American critics have professed dismay at the diversity of voices in literary criticism and theory. Looking at both the tradition of critical theory and the contemporary arguments surrounding any given text or author, these critics have taken the spectacle for a "chaos," a "scandal," an embarrassment before the eyes of their more rigorous colleagues.[5] Critical theory has felt this embarrassment in the face of a dialectical standard of truth to which it has not been able to rise; it has had to settle for a kind of validity inferior to what it has imagined as philosophic truth. But critical practice has also felt the embarrassment before the more pragmatic rhetorical standard of choice; critical discourse seems unable to settle anything, to persuade anyone to take a poem one way rather than another, to resolve interpretive questions by decision if not by logical compulsion.

I do not imagine that an art of dialogic criticism would end these embarrassments for literary critics and theorists, since the dialogic critic could not rule out as irrelevant the dialectical struggle for truth or the rhetorical urge to decision. Dialogics as I have represented it has no a priori defense against powerful voices, however apparently distant their concerns or different their subject matters. The only dialogic defense, as some of Dostoevsky's heroes make clear, is an active, articulate defensiveness that reveals embarrassment at not living up to other people's standards even as it tries to answer their claims and define its identity in terms other than theirs.

But I do imagine that dialogically self aware critics may learn to orient their discourse specifically and productively instead of responding to rhetorical shibboleths like "scientific validity" or even to dialectical alternatives like my "rhetoric" and "dialectic." Such critics will be likely to respond to the ideas of particular challenging voices instead of posturing before Bacon's idols of the marketplace or the theater. They would also approach the diversity of critical and theoretical voices not as an issue to be settled or a problem to be resolved but as a conversation to be constructed and entered.

The dialogic critic would also recognize that many of the voices in that yet-to-be-constructed conversation have themselves proceeded along rhetorical or dialectical lines, defining themselves in reference to commonplace points of departure or dialectically opposed positions without working out their relations to the specific voices that have preceded or shared the field with them. The dialogic critic can find work not only in responding to those diverse voices but in inventing the responses they have not made to one another. The perception of chaos among these many critical voices has been conditioned, in part at least, by the unarticulated relations among them. They are all talking, but no one has bothered to work out what they have to say to one another. A dialogic criticism will not try to decide among their competing claims or to synthesize their opposing theses but will try to imagine and enter their unrealized conversations. The chaos might not become a cosmos and scandals would not disappear, but the disorders and shocks would tend to be more precisely situated and more interestingly nuanced than those that have provoked the familiar dismay.

Although dialogic conversation does not have the order of a rhetorical decision on a question or of a dialectical hierarchy of terms, it is not a chaos either. Those who take their turns speaking and listening, representing others and being represented by them, learn not just who these others are but who they themselves may be, not just what others may mean but what they themselves may mean among others. Whether the purview of such a conversation is a discipline, a culture, or a world of diverse cultures (and the boundaries among these purviews are not fixed and given in any case), the dialogic participants will both make it what it is and be made by it, conferring identities on their fellows and their communities, even as they receive identities from them.

Up to this point, much of my discourse has situated itself in relation to the dialectically opposed terms *rhetoric* and *dialectic,* though I have drawn them from Aristotle and tried to use them dialogically. But the topic of dialogic criticism, like all other topics of discourse, already brings together individual contemporary voices and ideas that bear on it, and my practice would be completely out of keeping with the art I am promoting if I did not try to respond to some of these influences.

I have chosen two interestingly parallel texts that present complex and revealing interactions of voices on the question of dialogic criticism—Tzvetan Todorov's recent essay "A Dialogic Criticism?" published in both France and the United States in 1984, and the final chapter of Merle Brown's 1980 book *The Double Lyric,* "The Idea of Communal Creativity in F. R. Leavis's Recent Criticism." Both essays are deeply informed by theories of dialogue that neither mentions explicitly: Todorov in his English essay draws on Bakhtin's work without invoking it (though Bakhtin figures more openly in the French version); Brown's chapter is informed by his earlier work on Giovanni Gentile's theory of internal or transcendental dialogue.[6] Todorov and Brown have sufficiently internalized the views of their philosophic mentors, whose voices they take for granted, to make their dialogues with their predecessors implicit rather than overt.

Each essay is a conversion narrative that tells how a major twentieth-century critic has discovered a dialogic critical practice and formulated its principles. Todorov recounts his own movement from his training in dogmatic criticism in Bulgaria through his participation in what he characterizes as the relativist and immanentist project of structuralist criticism to his discovery of dialogic criticism. The realization that his "frame of reference was not a finally revealed truth . . . but the result of certain ideological choices" (68) is the turning point in this account. Brown traces F. R. Leavis's development from the dogmatic rhetorical criticism of the *Scrutiny* years to the discovery, articulation, and stylistic realization of a fully collaborative criticism in the later work. Like Todorov, Brown sees the crucial shift as a reversal of the critic's identification of his own mind with a single, objective standard, a "literary mind" to which divergent individual minds must learn to conform (214). Todorov's structuralist phase, with its commitment to "neutral instruments, purely descriptive concepts" (67), and Leavis's relentlessly evaluative criticism in the *Scrutiny* period both appear to have involved such a totalitarian, or perhaps we should say monologic, identification. As Todorov recognizes in comparing Bulgarian dogmatic evaluation with fastidious structuralist neutrality, these opposed critical discourses share an unexamined single-mindedness that unduly limits the alternatives in critical theory and practice.

In both essays, the agents of the hero's conversion are persons with whom the hero identifies and whose criticisms of his ideas therefore carry special force. Todorov tells two revealing anecdotes of exchanges with uprooted intellectuals like himself, Isaiah Berlin and Arthur Koestler, whose commitment to ideological and political questions led him to realize that "literature consisted not merely of structures but also of ideas and of history" and that "there were no 'objective' reasons for the decision to renounce the exercise of freedom" (66). Brown imagines Leavis's responses to the criticisms of rival British practitioners of literary studies, F. W. Bateson and Raymond Williams, as leading Leavis to reject "the notion of a single given field, the literary, to be known possessively by the single right mind" (215) and to recognize "that a communal freedom and creativity of language depends as much on diversity in the way persons listen to speech as on diversity in the speech itself" (220).

So far I have emphasized the parallels between Brown's and Todorov's narratives, but just as their starting points were different and the voices that influenced their heroes were different, so the dialogic criticisms in which their narratives issue have different bearings on the art I am trying to promote. Two phrases may be taken to represent the difference of greatest consequence, though both texts complicate these phrases in developing them. For Todorov "criticism is dialogue, . . . the encounter of two voices, author's and critic's, neither of which is privileged over and above the other" (71). For Brown, Leavis recognizes the "communal creativity" he has been striving to articulate when he speaks of the "collaborative exchange" of criticism as "a manysided real exchange" in which the work under discussion comes into being among the diverse minds involved in discussing it (216).

For Todorov the exchange between critic and author is "one link in a continuous chain" of such binary exchanges, in which the critic becomes an author, who, in turn, provokes a future reader to engage in dialogue. Authorship and its accompanying authority pass down this chain in a series, "since the author was writing in response to other authors, and since one becomes an author oneself starting from this moment. The very form of a critic's text is therefore not a matter of indifference, since it must authorize response and not mere idolatry" (74–75).

Though Todorov goes on to question "succession" as a model of intellectual history, he does not question it as it appears in his model of critical discourse.

Even when he extends the sequence of exchange to introduce a moment concerned with establishing the author's "meaning" and a subsequent moment for discussing the "truth" of what the author says, Todorov does not explicitly admit any additional voices to the exchange. He speaks of addressing himself to Diderot or Constant or Stendhal or Rousseau instead of merely talking about them, but in this essay on dialogics he does not speak of addressing himself to the many others who have also spoken to or about his authors. He writes as if even the author's voice were ultimately dependent on the critic's attention alone, for he notes that "the writer's text is closed, whereas the critic's can continue indefinitely. For the game not to be fixed, the critic must loyally make his interlocutor's voice heard" (72). In this game there seem to be no other players who might speak up for the author and share the critic's responsibility for reviving the author's words, nor does the author retain any independent capacity to talk back. The rule is that the critic cannot authoritatively question the truth of the author's position without first speaking for the author.

The same rule appears to guide Todorov in the preface to his book on Bakhtin. There he says that he refrains from engaging Bakhtin in a dialogue before he has offered an exposition of Bakhtin's views. He also declares that he refrains from taking into account the numerous responses that others have made to Bakhtin—except to dismiss almost all of them authoritatively as "(excusable) misunderstandings." Finally, he declares his intention not to construct the dialogic relations between Bakhtin's work and the work of successors, thus sparing Bakhtin's work the burden of "further association of ideas" *(Mikhail Bakhtin* xiii). But such a "burden" for Bakhtin is both the inescapable burden of all objects of discourse and the necessary condition for the production of further discourse.[7]

Todorov's dialogic theory and his declared intentions thus reduce the multiplicity of voices gathering around an author to an orderly sequence of authorized interpretation followed by authorized dialogue about the truth of the author's ideas. For Todorov the discovery of the dialogic is not the discovery that the critic's voice must engage the many other voices already surrounding the object of discourse but the discovery that the critic's voice may take its turn after giving the voice of the object its due. Todorov's dialogics of successive authorship seems to exclude many voices from the dialogic exchange and to privilege both the original author and the critic who abides by the authorized rules of reading him.

Offering a contrast to this model of successive authorship, Brown highlights in Leavis's later criticism the image of a "many-sided real exchange" (216) that produces the contemporary life of an author's voice in the mutually responsive minds of readers of the author's works. Brown also emphasizes that in this exchange the author's voice is as autonomous as the readers' minds and voices. "A genuine poem," Brown writes, "like a living person, cannot but be troubling, resistant, probing the reader as he probes it" (211). For Brown, the poem brings readers' minds together—they meet in it—and their meeting consists in exchanging judgments of the poem that variously qualify, correct, add to, refine, or shift one another's emphases. Leavis calls this activity "a collaborative exchange, a corrective and creative interplay of judgments" (216).

In the most serious moments of such an exchange, the "self-worlds" (a phrase that carries some of the implications of my "person-ideas") of participants may impinge on one another, enabling each to sense another "who is radically other than himself" (205). Brown declares that

> human creativity depends upon one's developing as a self-world, a person, in such a way that he is openly expectant that he will be impinged upon by other persons. The wonder of such an encounter is the very heart of great poetry and the experience of reading it; in a derivative way, it is also the very heart of literary studies, as Leavis conceives of them and practices them. (213)

This moment of encounter with another person, felt radically as an other, would not be the moment to raise the dialectical question of whether the other's views are indeed "true" according to some ultimately shared standard of truth. Even as what Todorov calls "a regulatory principle of exchange with others" ("Dialogic Criticism?" 70), such a standard of truth would reduce the sense of radical otherness to an as yet unsolved problem and would direct further discussion to locating the higher principle that would synthesize the difference one had stumbled on. A more truly dialogic move would be to recognize the difference and try to characterize it, opening oneself at the same time to being characterized by the other in terms alien to those one might be pleased to acknowledge. Brown celebrates the recognition and articulation of alien self-worlds as "moments of full humanity," but the surprise and wonder and awe those moments hold cannot be separated from the vulnerability to others they reveal.

Todorov does not privilege such dialogic moments of recognition. For him the partialities and local determinations they reveal are subject to a dialectical inquiry into truth that seeks to transcend them ("Dialogic Criticism?" 70). Because his emphasis falls more on a truth that transcends partial views than on a dialogue that articulates them, I want to answer the question of his title "A Dialogic Criticism?" with the reply "No, still a dialectical criticism."

Further inquiry into Todorov's question might lead us to additional places where the term "dialogic" covers already familiar discursive practices as well as to other places, like Brown's essay, where unfamiliar names like "communal creativity" touch on the central principles of a dialogic practice. Such an inquiry would also find places where the familiar names "rhetoric" and "dialectic" have been expanded to include the dialogic practices I am trying to differentiate from them and still other places where those arts are at work without hearing "the sound of their own names."[8]

The problem of distinguishing these elusive practices is nicely epitomized in Donald N. McCloskey's title "Rhetoric Is Disciplined Conversation" (483); for dialectic is also disciplined conversation, and dialogics, were it to become a self-conscious discursive practice, would be disciplined conversation, too. The issues are what sort of disciplined conversation we will choose to participate in and whether we wish to clarify the different sorts of disciplines that are possible or to lose their differences in an undifferentiated formulation like McCloskey's "disciplined conversation" or Richard Rorty's "conversation of mankind" or "ordinary conversation" (PMN 322, 389).

Rorty, to whose philosophy of discourse I turn now, emphasizes a common, undifferentiated conversation to challenge the special standing accorded to philosophical or scientific discourse—what I would call dialectical discourse, though Rorty uses the word only once, adverbially, in a footnote (392). He tries to show that philosophical and scientific discourses are not essentially different from other sorts of practical discourse, or "ordinary conversation." Rorty describes this "ordinary conversation," however, in disciplinary terms reminiscent of the distinction among the branches of classical rhetoric—forensic, epideictic, and deliberative. "Ordinary conversation" for Rorty thus concerns itself with "the blameworthiness of an action, the qualifications of an office seeker, the value of a poem, the desirability of legislation" (322), and the "decisions about guilt and innocence in jury trials" (324). His alternatives to scientific and philosophical "truth" are the rhetorical ends of "agreement" and winning the argument. At one point he does speak of rhetoric explicitly when he writes that "rhetoric about the importance of distinguishing sharply between science and religion, science and politics, science and art, science and philosophy . . . has formed the culture of Europe . . . [and] made us what we are today" (331–32). He does not, however, feature the name of this art in his account of "ordinary conversation" nor does he acknowledge the extent to which his conception of such conversation has been predisposed by rhetorical categories and habits of mind.

Rorty thus ignores the names of the traditional arts of rhetoric and dialectic that shape his account of philosophical discourse and its ordinary alternative, but he does make distinctions of aim and emphasis within "ordinary discourse" between epistemology and hermeneutics, "normal" and "abnormal" discourse, and "systematic" and "edifying" philosophy. His characterizations of the last term in each of these distinctions resemble what I have been calling "dialogics," but, as I shall demonstrate, important differences arise in each case.

The epistemologist for Rorty aspires to "the role of cultural overseer who knows everyone's common ground . . . knows what everybody else is really doing whether they know it or not, because he knows about the ultimate context," whereas the hermeneuticist takes the role of "the informed dilettante, the polypragmatic, Socratic intermediary between various discourses. In his salon . . . hermetic thinkers are charmed out of their self-enclosed practices. Disagreements between disciplines and discourses are compromised or transcended" (317). Dialogics almost recognizes itself in this image of the hermeneuticist but balks when it also recognizes in the image the rhetorical aim of compromise and the dialectical goal of transcendence of differences. Dialogics seeks neither agreement nor transcendence of differences but rather articulation of them. Dialogics also finds in Rorty's image of epistemology a resemblance to its practice of characterizing others in its own terms, even if it does not claim that such characterizations can say what the other is "really doing." Dialogics does, as Rorty's hermeneutics does, "pick up the jargon of the interlocutor rather than translating it into one's own" (318), but it does not hold back from characterizing the other's jargon as jargon and distancing its own language from the language it picks up. Dialogics not only preserves the discourse of the other but also revoices it. Dialogics nearly finds itself in Rorty's characterization of hermeneutic understanding as "more like getting acquainted with a person than like following a demonstration," but it holds back again when the process of understanding, which begins when "we play back and forth between guesses about how to characterize particular statements," ends when "we feel at ease with what was hitherto strange" (319). There is no dialogic guarantee that improved understanding of others' ideas will leave us at ease with them or less estranged from their advocates. One does not feel at ease with a Raskolnikov or a Stavrogin once one gets to know him.

Rorty's extension to discourse in general of Thomas Kuhn's distinction between "normal" science and "abnormal" or revolutionary science produces other dissonances when dialogics is placed, as Kenneth Bruffee has suggested, in the category of "abnormal" discourse (216). For one thing, dialogics as I have characterized it aspires to be an art or disciplined practice, but for "abnormal discourse" "there is no discipline which describes it, any more than there is a discipline devoted to the study of the unpredictable, or of 'creativity'" (PMN 320). Dialogics may, in this context, be more like hermeneutics, which "is the study of abnormal discourse from the point of view of some normal discourse—the attempt to make some sense of what is going on at a stage where we are still too unsure about it to describe it" (PMN 320–21). But this formulation reveals the main problem from a dialogic standpoint about this way of dividing up discourse; it presumes as a norm the dominance of a highly specialized and monologized kind of discourse that for Bakhtin is the exception rather than the rule, and it calls "abnormal" that condition of dialogized heteroglossia that Bakhtin takes as the norm. Kuhn's paradigm posits a specialized knower perfectly acculturated to a univocal knowledge community and poses the problems of reacculturating such a knower to a different knowledge community or of mediating the relations among such knowers and communities. Bakhtin, however, posits a writer confronting "the socially heteroglot multiplicity" of "names, definitions and value judgments" associated with an object of discourse in an internally divided community, and he poses the problems of such a writer's producing a social identity in response to that multiplicity and of making that identity answerable to the others with whom it shares the world (DI 278). Rorty's extension of the Kuhnian model of normality perpetuates the point of view from which the present state of literary critical (and cultural) discourse looks like a transitional chaos that needs to be ordered (whether by agreement or truth) at some subsequent stage. It privileges the formation of dialectically grounded disciplines or rhetorically established knowledge communities over the articulation of extant dialogic diversity.

Rorty's third distinction between systematic and edifying philosophic practices invents in the notion of edifying philosophy a standpoint outside both dialectical unity and rhetorical community that comes closest of the three distinctions to characterizing dialogics and Bakhtin. Dialogics, as I have elaborated it, does resemble what Rorty calls "'edification' . . . the 'poetic' activity of thinking up new aims, new words, or new disciplines, followed by . . . the inverse of hermeneutics: the attempt to reinterpret our familiar surroundings in the unfamiliar terms of our new inventions" (PMN 360). Thinking up a new discipline under the new word "dialogics" with new aims distinct from those of our more familiar arts of discourse does open up just such a reinterpretation of those arts. And Bakhtin does share with Rorty's edifying philosophers the desire "to keep space open for the sense of wonder which poets can sometimes cause—wonder that there is something new under the sun, something which is *not* an accurate representation of what was already there, something which (at least for the moment) cannot be explained and can barely be described" (PMN 370).

But Bakhtin does not, as Rorty says edifying philosophers do, "dread the thought that their vocabulary should ever be institutionalized, or that their writing might be seen as commensurable with the tradition" (PMN 369). Bakhtin's contribution to classical poetics, for example, does not overthrow that poetics as a revolutionary systematic philosopher would do, or dog its heels like one of Rorty's edifying philosophers. His *Problems of Dostoevsky's Poetics* is structured as a full-scale rearrangement of Aristotle's hierarchy of plot, character, thought, and diction that devotes chapters to developing the importance of character ("the hero"), thought ("the idea"), and diction ("discourse") and to displacing plot and plot-governed classical genres like tragedy with the multi-voiced and open-ended genre of the Menippean satire. Bakhtin does not merely deconstruct Aristotle's hierarchies by making marginal Aristotelian topics central or replace Aristotle's terms with a new paradigm; he articulates a world of artistic practices beyond the boundaries Aristotle established in the same terms and with the same thoroughness with which Aristotle settled the territory within those boundaries. Bakhtin brings into focus a "classical" tradition of anti-classical discursive practices, analyzes their principles, and offers terminology for describing them, doubling the field covered by poetics instead of undermining its ground. Similarly, the dialogic art I have been proposing does not overthrow the arts of rhetoric and dialectic or resist institutionalization as an art itself. Rather I am trying to institutionalize it and to define its distinctive purposes in contradistinction to the purposes of those other arts, aiming thereby to extend and enrich the field of distinctive verbal arts and to avoid reducing them to a generalized conversation whose only aim is to continue itself.

Another attempt to use "conversation" in general as a model for more specialized cultural practices is Hans-Georg Gadamer's construction of the hermeneutical conversation, the "conversation that is the understanding of texts," on the model of "conversation proper" (TM 341). Rorty, who appeals to Gadamer's authority for his notion of edification, ignores more fundamental differences between his and Gadamer's interpretation of "conversation." We have seen that Rorty implicitly specifies "conversation" in terms that resemble Aristotle's art of rhetoric; Gadamer, on the other hand, models "conversation" explicitly on a dialectical art associated with Plato's depiction of Socrates. Indeed, Gadamer introduces the art of dialectic in terms of Plato's contrast between dialectic and a sophistic art of rhetoric, which aims "to win every argument," whereas dialectic in its search for truth may come "off the worse in the argument in the eyes of those listening to it." Further recapitulating Plato's case against the sophists, he also writes, "Dialectic consists not in trying to discover the weakness of what is said, but in bringing out its real strength. It is not the art of arguing that is able to make a strong case out of a weak one, but the art of thinking that is able to strengthen what is said by referring to the object." Gadamer's Platonic model of dialectical art, Socrates, is not merely Rorty's "polypragmatic intermediary between various discourses" but Plato's "person who desires to know," committed to the opinions expressed by his interlocutors for the sake of "the immanent objective logic" of the discourse through which "the logos" "emerges in its truth" (TM

330–31). Georgia Warnke is clearly right that Gadamer "remains closer to a foundationalist enterprise" than Rorty admits.[9]

Gadamer's equation of "the art of conducting a real conversation" with "dialectic," as "the art of questioning and seeking truth," appropriates "conversation" in general to the exclusion not only of Rorty's antifoundationalist rhetorical account of conversation but also of Bakhtin's dialogic model of conversation. Real conversation for Gadamer proceeds "first of all" on the condition that "the partners do not talk at cross purposes" (330), whereas dialogic conversation presupposes cross purposes and aims to clarify what is involved in their intersections and oppositions. True conversation for Gadamer furthermore aims to understand "not a particular individual, but what he says. The thing that has to be grasped is the objective rightness or otherwise of his opinion, so that they can agree with each other on the subject. Thus one does not relate the other's opinion to him, but to one's own views" (347). Dialogics, on the other hand, is interested in opinions modified by the individual inflections, emphases, and subject positions of specific persons and never imagines that it could abstract claims and opinions from their concrete expression and maintenance by particular individuals. For Gadamer, "every conversation presupposes a common language, or it creates a common language" (341), but for dialogics language is always, at the beginning and at the end of conversation, self-divided and only partially possessed and partially shared by diverse interlocutors. Though Gadamer acknowledges what Bakhtin also asserts, that "languages [are] views of the world" (TM 364), Gadamer holds that in hermeneutical conversation "reason rises above the limitations of any language . . . escapes the prison of language, and . . . is itself constituted linguistically" (363), whereas Bakhtin emphasizes those double-voiced verbal phenomena in which the mutual representation of intransigently diverse languages liberates readers and speakers not from language itself but from the perspectival confines of a single language, from what Bakhtin calls "the dungeon of a single context" (DI 274).

Gadamer's application of his dialectical model of conversation to the hermeneutical "conversation with the text" (331) that "has come down to us by the way of linguistic tradition" (351) presents a complicated contrast with a dialogic model of conversation. Bakhtin, like Gadamer, recognizes the "authoritativeness of tradition" (DI 344) as one kind of authoritative word that bears on "the ideological becoming of the human being" (DI 341), and he classifies relations between voices in prose discourse in terms that parallel Gadamer's classification of hermeneutic dialogues, but his account of the model he shares with Gadamer expands Gadamer's account of the possibilities of hermeneutical experience and challenges Gadamer's interpretation of those possibilities.

Gadamer characterizes three types of "hermeneutical experience concerned with what has been transmitted in tradition" (321) in terms of three types of relation between an I and a Thou. The one who has the first type of experience treats the "Thou" as an object, objectifies tradition as typical of "human nature" and "confronts it in a free and uninvolved way, and, by methodically excluding all subjective elements, . . . discovers what it contains [and] . . . thereby detaches himself from the continuing action of tradition" (322). Tradition taken in this sense would correspond in Bakhtin's terms to "objectified discourse" maximally distanced from the one who objectifies it and maximally characterized by "socio-typical determining factors." In such discourse, what Bakhtin calls "ultimate semantic authority" is entirely preempted by the one who characterizes or objectifies, and no dialogic interaction takes place between that authority and its objects (PDP 199).

Gadamer's account of the "second mode of the experience of the 'Thou'" is the most complex and must be quoted at some length. In this mode,

> the "Thou" is acknowledged as a person, but . . . despite the involvement of the person in the experience of the "Thou," the understanding of the latter is still a form of self-relatedness. This proceeds from the dialectical appearance that the dialectic of the "I-Thou" relation brings with it. This relation is not immediate but reflective. To every claim there is a counter-claim. This is why it is possible for each of the partners in the relationship reflectively to outdo the other. One claims to express the other's claim and even to understand the other better than the other understands himself. In this way the "Thou" loses the immediacy with which it makes its claim. It is understood, but this means that it is anticipated and intercepted reflectively from the standpoint of the other person. Because it is a mutual relationship, it helps to constitute the reality of the "Thou" relationship itself. The inner historicality of all the relations in the lives of men consists in the fact there is a constant struggle for mutual recognition. This can have very varied degrees of tension, to the point of the complete domination of the one person by the other. But even the most extreme forms of mastery and slavery are a genuine dialectical relationship of the structure that Hegel has elaborated. (TM 322–23)

In this Hegelian characterization, two self-involved persons encounter one another, reflect one another's claims from their own standpoints, assimilate the other into their own vocabularies, compete with one another for dominance, and struggle with each other for recognition. This mode of experience of the "Thou" corresponds with Bakhtin's category of "discourse with an orientation to someone else's discourse," for in this category particular selves are invested in both the discourse that is doing the talking and the discourse toward which it is oriented. One self may imitate, parody, or reflect the discourse of the other, and the range of relations between the two discursive selves may range from near identification (minimum tension in Gadamer's terms) to destructive parody (maximum tension). The whole mode of discourse collapses, however, if the two individuals become totally assimilated to one another or if they separate into two independent discourses, one of which is no longer reflected in the other (PDP 199).

Gadamer's account of this mode of experience of the "Thou" gives more emphasis to the possibility of domination than to that of identification and more weight to one person's anticipation of the other's meaning than to one person's desire for the other's recognition of his own meaning. His application of this model of experience to the hermeneutical conversation with tradition turns this emphasis into a reduction of the mode, for he reads the hermeneutical equivalent of this mode as the "historical consciousness" that claims to transcend its own limitations completely in its knowing of the other as a person, "not [as] the instantiation of a general law but [as] something historically unique" (323). Gadamer's image of the consciousness characterized by this mode of experience does not take itself to be involved in the mode's essential struggle for mutual recognition but imagines that it can recognize the other without being recognized in turn. In "seeking to master, as it were, the past" (323), this historical consciousness imagines that it transcends the dialectical struggle for mastery characteristic of this mode of experience and, in Bakhtin's terms, resumes the standpoint of objectified discourse, this time not the "socio-typical" variety but the kind that objectifies "individually characteristic determining factors" (PDP 199). From Bakhtin's point of view, and I think even in his own terms, Gadamer's identification of this mode with a self-deluded "historical consciousness" has reduced the hermeneutic version of this second mode of experience to a variant of the first mode.

Gadamer's reductive application of his second mode of experience of the "Thou" to the hermeneutical conversation with tradition leaves open the question of what an adequate application would be like. I think it would approximate Bakhtin's model of dialogic discourse, emphasizing the encounter with tradition that is also an encounter with the competing voices that claim to represent the texts of that tradition in the present, a struggle among voices that represent one another and the voices of the past in the language of the present. In the hermeneutical conversation thus characterized it would not be the case, as Gadamer, like Todorov, claims, that "one partner . . . , the text, is expressed only through the other partner, the interpreter" (349), for this model of the conversation would recognize, as Bakhtin does, the clamorous chorus of other interpreters who have already spoken, predisposed the interests of the present interpreter, and threatened to answer his reading if he differs with them or fails to acknowledge (recognize) them. Gadamer at an earlier point in his argument sees that "our historical consciousness is always filled with a variety of voices in which the echo of the past is heard. It is present only in the multifariousness of such voices; this constitutes the nature of the tradition in which we want to share" (252–53), but he leaves this multiplicity of contemporary voices out of account when he bases his model of the types of hermeneutical experience on the dyadic model of I-Thou relations, and he strives to transcend this multiplicity when his hermeneutics moves "despite the multifariousness of ways of speech" toward a "unity of understanding and interpretation" (TM 364).[10]

The third "and highest" (324) type of experience based in Gadamer's model of conversation grounds the openness to tradition in an openness to the "Thou," a commitment to "experience the 'Thou' truly as a 'Thou,' i.e., not to overlook his claim and to listen to what he has to say to us." "Not to overlook," however, soon becomes "the acknowledgment that I must accept some things that are against myself, even though there is no one else who asks this of me," and the parallel in hermeneutical experience becomes the imperative to "allow the validity of the claim made by tradition, not in the sense of simply acknowledging the past in its otherness, but in such a way that it has something to say to me" (TM 324). What is finally acknowledged here is not "the text as an expression of the life of the 'Thou,' but . . . a meaningful content detached from all bonds of the meaning individual, of an 'I' or a 'Thou'" (TM 321), "the text . . . understood [not] as a mere expression of life, but taken seriously in its claim to truth" (TM 264). In terms of Bakhtin's classification of modes of discourse, this mode of hermeneutical experience acknowledges tradition as a "direct, unmediated discourse directed exclusively toward its referential object, as an expression of the speaker's [in this case tradition's] ultimate semantic authority" (PDP 199). This mode of discourse is properly the opposite of Bakhtin's category of objectified discourse because it takes the opposite point of view from that category, accepting another's objectification instead of presuming to objectify another for oneself. Neither, in Bakhtin's terms, is a dialogic mode of discourse or experience; both "have in fact only one voice each. These are *single-voiced discourses*" (PDP 189).

Gadamer's account of hermeneutical conversation, then, like his model of conversation proper, is primarily dialectical and monological, though his second type of hermeneutical experience could be developed to encompass a fully dialogic conversation. Bakhtin's category of discourse with an orientation to someone else's discourse elaborates the possibilities of that second type of experience in ways that prevent its reduction to the first type or its transcendence by the third. Bakhtin thus would lead us to recognize productive relations to tradition not just in an open acknowledgment of its semantic authority but also in an active resistance to that authority, not just in "a subordination to the text's claims to dominate our minds" (TM 278), but in a polemical response to them. Bakhtin's typology of the ways in which one person's discourse can be oriented to someone else's discourse includes the possibilities of admiring imitation and continuation that Gadamer values, but that typology also calls attention to parodic reformulations of and polemical responses to the other's discourse that do not reduce that discourse or its speaker to an object but rather preserve their individuality in the act of representing or resisting them. The objectifying or actively polemical "vari-directional" forms of double-voiced discourse do not keep "the claim of the other person [or of tradition] at a distance" (TM 323), but they acknowledge the force of that claim by parodying or opposing it. On the other hand, the admiring or submissive "uni-directional" forms of double-voiced discourse do not fully assimilate themselves to the previous discourse they admire but preserve their identities as imitations, stylizations, or continuations by an other.

These intermediate discursive forms neither detach themselves "from the continuing action of tradition" (TM 322) nor "allow the validity of the claim made by tradition" (TM 324) by treating tradition as either pure objectified discourse or direct unmediated discourse. Rather, they exemplify various impure and indirect interactions with tradition that reveal the continuing power of its claims and the present impossibility of submitting completely to them. In Gadamer's terms, these discursive forms could be read as the signs not of a reflective superiority to tradition nor of an idealized openness to it but of an inescapable and active "living relationship to tradition" (324). They fill in dialogic possibilities in Gadamer's second mode of hermeneutical experience that his own dialectically predisposed imagination does not recognize, and they counteract conservative implications of his third mode of hermeneutical experience that his classically predisposed imagination too easily accepts.[11]

Gadamer's dialectical model of conversation, then, tends to exclude the middle that Bakhtin's dialogics articulates. Rorty's account of "ordinary conversation" tends toward the rhetorical, though his account of edifying philosophy has some affinities with dialogics. "Conversation" in both cases names not a given practice we all recognize and understand but a topic of discussion contended for by parties who, either dissatisfied with the arts of rhetoric and dialectic or still loyal to them, are deeply influenced by authoritative models of the traditional arts. The possible disciplines or arts of conversation, the ends they serve, and the means they mobilize, are themselves the objects of a conversation whose name—"criticism"? "philosophy"? "theory"?—and whose appropriate discipline—rhetoric? dialectic? dialogics?—remain under discussion.

Of these disciplines, however, dialogics would seem to be the only one that resists the appropriation of "conversation" in general as the name for a common-sense rhetorical consensus or for an idealized dialectical essence. For dialogics, the conversation about conversation, like the conversation about all other topics, has already begun, and the previous history of that conversation has left its marks on the present contributors to it. As my readings of Rorty and Gadamer have shown, the twenty-five hundred year history of the trivium in Western culture has left its marks even on those contemporary thinkers who would like to return to an artless or pre-disciplinary conversation. Dialogics would bring out the marks of rhetoric and dialectic in the discourse of current theorists in order to articulate its differences with them. It would, as I have tried to do here, sharpen its own distinctive identity as a verbal discipline by sharpening the identities of other disciplines and their practitioners. Against Rorty's undifferentiated and lax figure of the "ordinary conversation," dialogics offers the "living, tension-filled interaction" in which one speaking being encounters the words of another and articulates them both (DI 279). Against Gadamer's more demanding, essentialist figure of "real conversation" in search of the truth, dialogics offers a range of discursive practices in which one voice can define itself in relation to another without surrendering itself or objectifying the other. Dialogic conversation thus reveals itself not as a name for conversation in general or in essence but as a kind of conversation among others, a way of talking especially capable of distinguishing itself as it recognizes others.

3. Booth, Bakhtin, and the Culture of Criticism

In an essay in *PMLA*'s centennial number, Geoffrey Hartman portrays the present "culture of criticism" as "within historicism, reacting to the expanded horizon of fact it has brought about, now integrating by an impossible embrace and now violently throwing off the burden of multiplying and fragmenting perspectives" (372). Hartman assumes in the essay the impossible task of integrating the diverse and self-divided culture he imagines, embracing the German, French, British, and American cultures of criticism, and sublimating the violence of the "knowledge explosion" within his own cosmopolitan cultivation of acquaintance with more than one hundred fifty scholars and critics from Aarsleff to Zumthor.

At one point in his argument, Hartman asks whether Bakhtin's dialogics can help criticism cope with its "burden of multiplying and fragmenting perspectives." Hartman thinks that Bakhtin's "dialogic principle" "exposes a constitutive unintelligibility" in both the modern novel and human relations, and he asks whether such a principle can sustain us without our resorting to other powerful structures of thought and discourse: "Can we tolerate such ambiguity, such unresolved diversity," he asks, "without structures of domination or dialectic?" (389). Hartman fears that we cannot, but his commitment to survey the whole present culture of criticism does not permit him to pause and consider the question. I take it up in this chapter as part of an inquiry that asks whether a deliberately cultivated dialogic criticism can stabilize and clarify our culture of criticism without giving in to the alternatives Hartman fears.

When Hartman recognizes "domination or dialectic" as alternative practices that threaten to undermine Bakhtin's dialogics, he draws upon powerful Western cultural paradigms. He calls to my mind, for example, the paradigm of political regimes in the eighth book of Plato's *Republic*. There the democratic regime is threatened from below by the temptation to escape from its unresolved diversities into the domination of the tyrant's single voice, the "sinister unifying" Hartman fears (389). But it is also threatened from above by the dialectical philosopher's push to transcend diversities and subordinate them in an ideal scale of forms. In terms more pertinent to my argument here, Hartman's alternatives also recall how easily we can slip from the relatively unfamiliar and unrationalized practices of dialogic thought and discourse back into the familiar cultural tracks worn by the traditional verbal arts of rhetoric and dialectic.

Rhetoric, after all, may be understood as the great storehouse of strategies for imposing "structures of domination." In one of its persistent forms, it teaches its practitioners how to shape their discourse to "win over others," whether the phrase implies persuading them or just plain beating them. Dialectic, I have argued in Chapter 2, cultivates techniques of manipulating ideas rather than people, teaching its practitioners to organize and overcome ideas without reference to the people who hold them. Because rhetoric resembles dialogics in its concern with the relations among people in a given community and dialectic resembles dialogics in its concern with the relations among ideas, the dialogic figure of the hyphenated person-idea, the ideologist-hero, easily reduces, without a deliberate art of dialogics, to a rhetorical person struggling for domination or a dialectical idea contradicting, subsuming, or being subsumed by another idea. Dialogics is always at risk for breaking down into the rhetorical and dialectical arts that oppose it and each other.

But the issue is really more complicated than this dialectical formulation allows, because the arts brought forward under the names *rhetoric* and *dialectic* are not all of a piece, and the modes of opposition and cooperation among their advocates and the advocates of dialogics are not uniform. A dialogic survey of some of the many projects for criticism in recent years that have explicitly identified themselves with either rhetoric or dialectic would disclose friends, opponents, and even practitioners of dialogics flying the banners of both the other arts and calling on Bakhtinian dialogics to account for itself in a variety of terms. In this survey, neither domination nor dialectic would maintain a single identity as an alternative to dialogics, but each makes its appearance not only among those who represented rhetoric and dialectic for Bakhtin but also among others who now represent these arts in Anglo-American criticism.

Domination is a significant motif for the writer who most often represents rhetoric in Bakhtin's writings, Victor Vinogradov, a contemporary of Bakhtin's and an influential figure in Soviet stylistics.[12] Vinogradov, who views the novel as a rhetorical genre and analyzes its devices "from the point of view of their effectiveness as rhetoric" (DI 42), helps to shape Bakhtin's zero-sum image of the art. Bakhtin writes in his late notebooks, "In rhetoric there is the unconditionally innocent and the unconditionally guilty; there is the complete victory and the destruction of the opponent. In dialogue the destruction of the opponent also destroys that very dialogic sphere in which the word lives" ("Extracts" 182). Such remarks about rhetoric take on dialogic force in the context of the continuing dialogue Nina Perlina documents between Bakhtin and Vinogradov. She writes,

> Where Bakhtin states that any individual discourse act is internally a nonfinalized, open-ended rejoinder, Vinogradov demonstrates that even a real-life dialogue is built by a set of clear-cut monologic procedures. Where Bakhtin finds dialogic reaccentuation of another person's utterance, the hidden multivoicedness, or the polyphonic "word with the loop[hole]," Vinogradov discovers the speaker's attempt to muffle the voice of the opponent, to discredit his speech-manifestations, and to advance his own monologic pronouncement over the dialogic reply of another person. . . . Within the framework of Bakhtinian poetics, a speech-partner is the protagonist of the idea. Within the framework of Vinogradov's poetic system, a speech partner is the rhetorician whose main intention is to make his oratory the only effective and authoritative speech manifestation. For Bakhtin, the individual utterance is born between the speech partners, in the immediacy of discourse; for Vinogradov, a dialogic rejoinder is generated by and belongs to its absolute owner.

With Vinogradov in the background, Bakhtin associates rhetoric with "style determined by demands for comprehensibility and clarity, that is, precisely those aspects that are deprived of any internal dialogism, that take the listener for a person who passively understands but not for one who actively answers and reacts" (DI 280). As opposed to the seriocomic genres Bakhtin links with the dialogic, the classical rhetorical genres are one-sided, serious, rational, univocal, and dogmatic (PDP 107). Though rhetoric does represent the voices of others, rhetorical double-voicedness does "not extend to the dialogical essence of evolving language itself; it is not structured on authentic heteroglossia but on mere diversity of voices; in most cases the double-voicedness of rhetoric is abstract and thus lends itself to formal, purely logical analysis of the ideas that are parceled out in voices" or to polemically "erecting *potential* discourses for the accused or for the defense (just such free creation of likely, but never actually uttered words, sometimes whole speeches—'as he must have said' or 'as he might have said'—was a device very widespread in ancient rhetoric)" *(*DI 353–54*).*

Enter, at last, Wayne Booth, a frequent user of this device, probably the best-known rhetorical critic of literature in the Anglo-American culture of criticism in the last half of the twentieth century. His *Rhetoric of Fiction* is the most significant American analog of Vinogradov in the critical dialogue with Bakhtin. Just as Vinogradov strengthens Russian formalist poetics by accommodating the novel under the heading of rhetoric, so Booth strengthens Chicago Aristotelian formalist poetics by the same move.[13] In his Aristotelian framework, Booth conceives the rhetoric of fiction as focused on techniques of domination, on "the rhetorical resources available to the writer . . . as he tries to impose his fictional world upon the reader" or on "the author's means of controlling the reader" *(Rhetoric of Fiction* xiii). Booth assumes the end of imposing a unified fictional world of a given kind—such as the tragic, comic, or horrific—and concerns himself with advocating the unrestricted use of all rhetorical means to impose that world upon the reader.

Within Booth's argument for the author's use of all available technical means in imposing a fictional world on the reader, his polemical emphasis is on the uses of the author's voice. He shows the usefulness of direct authorial commentary, and he argues that even when such commentary is lacking and the author resorts to the "hundreds of devices that remain for revealing judgment and molding response," "the author's voice is still dominant in a dialogue that is at the heart of all experiences with fiction" (272). Booth's account of the novel at one point as dialogue among the author, narrators, characters, and readers (55) suggests Bakhtin's dialogic model of novelistic discourse, but his repeated insistence on the dominance of the author over narrators, characters, and readers links him more firmly with Vinogradov's monologic rhetorical theories of the novel than with Bakhtin's dialogic account of the Dostoevskyan novel.

Bakhtin's account of the Dostoevskyan novel in *Problems of Dostoevsky's Poetics* gives us an idea of how its ends differ from more familiar tragic or comic or rhetorical ends that Booth prefers. Bakhtin traces Dostoevsky's generic sources along several lines of what he calls the "serio-comic" or carnivalized genres. In all these genres, he writes, "there is a strong rhetorical element, but in the atmosphere of *joyful relativity* characteristic of a carnival sense of the world, this element is fundamentally changed: there is a weakening of its one-sided rhetorical seriousness, its rationality, its singular meaning, its dogmatism" (107). The "stylistic unity . . . of epic, the tragedy, high rhetoric, [and] the lyric" is replaced by mixed styles in the seriocomic genres

(108), as "the epic and tragic wholeness of a person and his fate" is replaced by self-division in which the hero "ceases to mean only one thing" (117). Carnival familiarization suspends the usual hierarchies of social values and destroys "epic and tragic distance" (124). "Deeply ambivalent" responses to fundamental contradictions replace the clarified responses of separate tragic and comic genres; promiscuous participation replaces the conventional "division into performers and spectators" (122).

This highly compressed summary of the seriocomic genre shows how Bakhtin gives *positive* character to a literary effect that Booth reads as a *lack* of the "clarity of distance" provided by the "traditional forms" *(Rhetoric of Fiction* 331). To Booth, who argues for the reader's right to know whether to "approve or disapprove, laugh or cry" (331), Bakhtin's "joyful relativity of all structure and order" (PDP 124) and his "ambivalent laughter" (166) are a challenge to fundamental distinctions of literary effect. The clarification of response one seeks in Aristotelian tragedy and comedy, and the determinate decision aimed at in some Aristotelian rhetorical genres depend upon the audience's recognition of the hero's standing and the audience's distance from the hero's situation, but the participatory response Bakhtin envisions puts the hero and the audience in a carnivalized proximity to one another that replaces definitive judgment with mutual vulnerability and responsiveness.

In such a fictional world, the author does not design characters to provoke laughter, tears, or admiration but to provoke articulate response. Instead of issuing in a nonverbal recognition or feeling or attitude or decision, the unfinalized interplay of value-charged discourse in the dialogic work continues in the diverse verbal responses it provokes in its readers. Booth's rhetorical emphasis on determinate and generally nonverbal effect leads him to call "the critical disagreement" provoked by stories "a scandal" *(Rhetoric of Fiction* 315). For Bakhtin, that unsettled controversy can be a mark of success in a work designed to dialogic rather than rhetorical specifications.

Although Booth's rhetoric of fiction appears to share a perspective with Vinogradov's that makes their work appropriate to the monologic novel, I shall resist the temptation to set up their monologism in rhetorical or dialectical opposition to Bakhtin's dialogism, because the dialogic perspective finally does not allow for such an opposition in critical theory any more than in novelistic practice. Though Bakhtin himself, despite his dialogic principles, habitually makes use of this heightened opposition, he writes in the essay "Discourse in the Novel" that "even in those places where the author's voice seems at first glance to be unitary and consistent, direct and unmediatedly intentional, beneath that smooth single-languaged surface we can nevertheless uncover prose's three-dimensionality, its profound speech diversity, which enters the project of style and is its determining factor" (DI 315).

For Bakhtin, then, neither "monologic" novelists nor critical theorists would "mean only one thing" any more than does the hero of the Dostoevskyan novel, and even rhetorical discourse, Bakhtin concedes, "once [it] is brought into the study [of the novel] with all its living diversity, . . . cannot fail to have a deeply revolutionizing influence [in revealing] the internally dialogic quality of discourse" (DI 269). While monological arguments, then, attempt to reduce their participants to representing single meanings, dialogic criticism recognizes the impossibility of such reduction and remains alert to what remains to be said from the unfolding positions of its concrete participants.

Booth's several engagements with Bakhtin's work reveal a more ambivalent dialogue than the reductive opposition between monologic and dialogic would allow. In the afterword to the second edition of *The Rhetoric of Fiction* (401–57), Booth singles out Bakhtin's dialogic poetics of the novel as especially impressive on the topics of language and style, historical and implied authors and readers, objectivity and technique, and ideology and form. Booth's acknowledgment of Bakhtin in his afterword is remarkable for its willingness to see Bakhtin as a challenge on the same issues that *The Rhetoric of Fiction* raises rather than to quarantine him as a theorist of some other critical mode with its own distinctive but unrhetorical questions. In this he shows the effects of the responsive and open-ended pluralism he invents in *Critical Understanding*. But in his introduction to Caryl Emerson's translation of Bakhtin's *Problems of Dostoevsky's Poetics*—an essay he sees as spilling over from the afterword to his own book—Booth combines this stance with the more defensive pluralism of his 1968 essay "*The Rhetoric of Fiction* and the Poetics of Fictions." He generously acknowledges Bakhtin's challenge to his rhetoric of fiction but also isolates that challenge in a critical mode distinct from his own.

Booth begins his introduction by establishing a common ground between his Chicago school Aristotelianism and Bakhtin's dialogism on the question of ideology and form, claiming that both positions reject the opposition between abstract form and ideological content for an idea of form charged with value or ideology. Booth distinguishes his Chicago Aristotelianism, however, for its focus on the distinction between the effects authors intend in their ideologically charged formal unities and the technical means they use to achieve them. According to the Chicago premises Booth worked with in *The Rhetoric of Fiction,* "authors," he writes, "were . . . in charge of created unities that consisted of choices exemplified and judged" ("Introduction" xviii).

Booth's introduction presents Bakhtin's position, however, as if it transcended the whole question of fictional techniques and their relation to artistic ends. Bakhtin's challenge, he writes, "has nothing to do with the author's effort to produce a unified effect. Its subject is not the ordering of technical means toward certain effects so much as the quality of the author's imaginative gift—the ability or willingness to allow voices into the work that are not fundamentally under the 'monological' control of the novelist's own ideology" (xx). As Booth recognizes, he has assimilated Bakhtin's position to Longinus—the alternative to Aristotle that the Chicago school has long acknowledged—an alternative concerned to demonstrate the presence of genius or greatness or sublimity in the author rather than to articulate the functioning of parts in the whole in a given work (xx, xxvii). Booth repeatedly emphasizes Bakhtin's transcendence of mere technical concerns for more profound and important issues (xx, xxiv-xxv, xxvii), making his challenge to the rhetoric of fiction seem more like a moral and spiritual challenge to its questions than a technical and artistic challenge to Booth's answers to them.

Booth thus diminishes his direct encounter with Bakhtin by conceding him the high ground and holding onto the low, but, as we have seen, dialogics and the rhetoric of fiction challenge one another more directly on the common grounds of the author's chosen artistic task and the technical means of realizing it than Booth's account of Bakhtin allows. While Booth repeatedly posits a dialogue in which "the author sees more deeply and judges more profoundly than his presented characters" (*Rhetoric of Fiction* 74), Bakhtin explicitly examines the novel in which not the author's superior consciousness but the hero's self-consciousness is the dominant of representation (PDP 49–50). Booth might see such a move as a shift in technical devices that "turns the character whose mind is shown into a narrator" (*Rhetoric of Fiction* 164), but Bakhtin's self-conscious hero is not a "center of consciousness" through whose perspective a story is told but the object of representation itself. The hero's discourse in its response to discourses of the other characters *and* the discourse of the author is, for Bakhtin, the novel's principal object of representation (PDP 63–65, 266).

Bakhtin's dialogics of fiction thus reopens the question of what is means and what is end in the novel and suggests that in some cases at least the choices Booth advocates as technically effective would not serve the end Bakhtin imagines. If the hero's self-consciousness is to be the dominant of representation, the author's position must be shifted from the finalizing and judging role Booth defends to an actively dialogic interchange with the hero. "Only in the light of this artistic project," Bakhtin writes, "can one understand the authentic function of such compositional elements as the narrator and his tone . . . and the . . . narration direct from the author" (PDP 64). This is not the critical language of someone unconcerned with "unified effect" and the "technical means toward certain effects" (Booth, "Introduction" xx), but that of someone who posits a different kind of effect, one that calls for a radical reconsideration of fictional means and ends. In Bakhtin's seriocomic genre, as we have seen, it is not, as Booth says, that the characters "defy any temptation the author may have to fit them into his superior plans" ("Introduction" xxiii) but rather that, as Bakhtin says, "the freedom of the character is an aspect of the author's design" and "is just as much a created thing as the unfreedom of the objectivized hero" (PDP 64–65). Bakhtin has not forfeited an interest in artistic design and the technique that serves it but has radically enlarged the field of such designs, and so has not only shifted the possible functions of techniques but also shifted the very boundaries between technique and design.

Booth's linking of Bakhtin to the Longinian tradition may be seen not just as an evasion of this fundamental conflict over the means and ends of fiction but also as part of another agenda. Booth's book on the ethics of fiction shows him less interested in the technical issues of the rhetoric of fiction than on the evaluative ethical issues. Even in *The Rhetoric of Fiction* itself, Booth opens the question of "the moral, not merely the technical, angle of vision from which the story is told" (265), and his identification of Bakhtin's argument with that "more profound" question may serve to acknowledge Bakhtin's challenge where it matters most to him, rather than to deflect it from the issues of the rhetoric of fiction in which he is no longer engaged.

Booth's and Bakhtin's divergent accounts of the novel are not without implications for the discursive practices of the culture of criticism, but this issue can be joined more directly through examining Booth's *Critical Understanding: The Powers and Limits of Pluralism,* in which he explicitly addresses his version of Hartman's problem of "multiplying and fragmenting perspectives" in criticism. Though Bakhtin's relevant work was not available in translation when Booth wrote *Critical Understanding,* its argument nevertheless bears upon Booth's discussion and complicates the potential relations between Booth's rhetoric and Bakhtin's dialogics. Booth there imagines what he calls the problem of "critical variety and conflict" (3) in characteristically rhetorical terms that produce images of "chaos" (7) and "warfare" (37), but he also gestures repeatedly in the course of his inquiry toward dialogic formulations that would reconstruct his initial rhetorical image of "the immensely confusing world of contemporary literary criticism" (3). Booth's argument shifts from the rhetorical to the dialogic in another sense when he turns from generating potential discourses about poems and pluralism to engaging at length the words and works of three specific pluralist thinkers, all of whom have persuaded him of their diverse views.

Booth's opening formulation of the problem of "critical variety and conflict" envisions a characteristically rhetorical situation of diverse rhetors brought to a given occasion of discourse to mobilize, display, and distinguish their rhetorical resources. Booth imagines a dozen critics given W. H.

Auden's "The Surgical Ward" and asked to say what they think is the most important point to be made about it, and he further imagines, in a characteristic hyperbole, that "an infinite number of possible interpretations" of "unlimited variety" would result (1–2). Following something like I. A. Richards's protocols in *Practical Criticism,* Booth's imaginary experiment brings diverse critical rhetoricians to a given occasion and asks them to produce their discourses in isolation from one another without mentioning a context of prior discourse on the poem. In accord with Bakhtin's account of the practices of rhetorical genres, Booth's experiment produces what Bakhtin calls "*potential* discourses" of hypothetical critics instead of using the "actually uttered" words of published critics, and it issues not in what Bakhtin calls "an authentic heteroglossia" but only in "a mere diversity of voices" (DI 353–54). To the "unlimited variety" of that "mere diversity," Booth adds the diverse potential judgments of his critical readers and thus produces his image of "the immensely confusing world of contemporary literary criticism" (3). This confusing world to which he offers his pluralism as the best response, however, is a function of the monologic rhetorical rules by which he constructs his image in the first place rather than a necessary or adequate portrait of the literary critical world itself.

A dialogic criticism, for its part, would emphasize the artificial isolation of Booth's hypothetical critics and offer the counter-model of the prose writer who

> confronts a multitude of routes, roads, and paths that have been laid down in the object by social consciousness. Along with the internal contradictions in the object itself, the prose writer witnesses as well the unfolding of social heteroglossia *surrounding* the object, the Tower-of-Babel mixing of languages that goes on around any object. . . . For the prose writer, the object is a focal point for heteroglot voices among which his own must also sound; these voices create the background necessary for his own voice, outside of which his artistic prose nuances cannot be perceived, and without which they "do not sound." (DI 278)

Bakhtin's account of this situation may still seem like confusion, but these other voices are many, not infinitely numerous, and they "sound" against the background of each other as the isolated voices of Booth's imaginary experiment do not. Furthermore, they belong to a "social heteroglossia" that makes their various utterances reflect the finite, if heterogeneous, possibilities of critical discourse in a given time and place, developing those possibilities, revealing new ones, and making the participants recognizable to one another in their developing concrete diversity. The problem for dialogics is never what to make of the confusing multiplicity of voices and evaluations in general but always what to say in response to the differences among this particular set of actually or potentially interrelated voices.

Booth's initial vision of the production of critical discourse shares a model of the determinants of that discourse with R. S. Crane's response to the questions, "'What *ought* I to say?' or 'What is *important* to say?'": it depends only on "the kind of problem you are interested in and . . . the resources of your 'language'" (43), in effect the Aristotelian rhetorical "given case" and the "available means" to address it. Bakhtin's image of the prose writer would not only add to these determinants *who* has already spoken and *whom* the critic is addressing but would also reinterpret both the "interests" and the "language" of the individual critic as already derived from and implicated in the social discourses that entail the interests and languages of others. Even critical rhetors called to display their critical resources and interests in response to a given literary work speak from a prior conversation and to unnamed mentors and opponents, share or oppose their interests, and revoice their languages.

Booth, however, at another point in his argument, reaches a position very similar to Bakhtin's. He writes,

> No critic makes himself; every one of us discovers his own voice only by listening or mis-listening, to those before us who seem to have spoken best. This much is seldom denied. What seems to be forgotten is that, even after I have begun to speak what I mistakenly call "*my own* critical truth," my continued vitality as a thinking critic . . . depends on my continuing capacity to take other voices into account. My life, indistinguishable from the life of my critical tribe, requires that my thought be an exchange among "selves" rather than a mere search for ways to impose what I already know. (*Critical Understanding* 223)

Note here Booth's departure from a rhetoric of imposition and domination toward a dialogics of mutual determination through exchange. A different emphasis on these same relations might bring out, in addition, the way in which "my thought" is an "exchange among selves" from the start and "my critical tribe" is already, as Booth elsewhere puts it, "inherently and irreducibly plural" (40). My vitality is not just at stake in my continued engagement with other voices outside my tribe but in its continuing articulations of the conflicts within my tribe and within "myself." And my investment in those conflicts always orients me to the discourse of my tribe and the discourses of other tribes (to which I may in other ways also belong) and shapes my sense of "What I *ought* to say" and "What is *important* to say."

I never encounter a situation, then, in which the critical world is all before me and the choice of critical interests and languages is entirely open, nor do I ever display my critical resources as if no one else had already spoken, or encounter the display of others' resources as if I had never heard of them before. Even utter neophytes in professional critical discussions arrive with investments in critical terms and human relations from familial, religious, political, and other social contexts that permit preliminary orientation to those discussions, recognition of their participants, and investment in their stakes. At the beginning of my own critical training, a schooling in the texts of American democracy attracted me to Wordsworth's vision of the poet as "a man speaking to men," though feminism had not yet called my attention to how that phrase sounded from a different social location. Similarly, the religious predispositions of some of the New Critics drew them to Coleridge's notion of the god-like poetic imagination. Both the transcendental mystifications of some schools of criticism and the demystifying gestures of others are continuous with discourses in the pre-critical culture in which we are steeped, and our interests in the critical sophistications of these discourses are predisposed, though not wholly determined, by our investments in these discourses themselves.

From Crane's dialectical point of view (see Olson), these predispositions may appear as mere "prejudices" that account for any given critic's arbitrary departure from the ideal universal critic, who could disinterestedly entertain all interests and disinterestedly choose the appropriate critical mode of pursuing each interest (*Critical Understanding* 43), but Booth's rhetorical commitments make him aware of both the difficulty of separating critical modes from the individual critics who practice them (28) and of the problem of distinguishing critical modes themselves (94). He approaches a dialogic reinterpretation of Crane's philosophically distinct critical modes when he identifies the modes we have learned with the "'school' we were trained in" (254) that constitutes our intellectual dispositions, sets our agendas, enables our inquiries, and involves us in a historical conversation, but he returns in conclusion to a rhetorical reinterpretation of "critical modes not as positions to be defended but as locations or openings to be explored—in the traditional rhetorical terminology, as topoi or loci" (339).

As topoi or commonplaces, however, the diverse critical modes lose not only the philosophical discreteness of Crane's dialectical formulation but also the individual, historical recognizability of the dialogic person-ideas involved in the cultural discourses of schools of thought. Although Booth characterizes a topic as "an inhabited place in which valued activity can occur among those who know how to find their way in" (339), it has lost the historical specificity of a "place" like the Chicago School, inhabited by R. S. Crane and

Richard McKeon and engaged with such figures as M. H. Abrams and Kenneth Burke, all of whom constitute the dialogic agenda of Booth's inquiry into pluralism. Both rhetorical *topoi* and dialectical modes have a generality that appears to transcend what Booth calls the "historical accident" (201) of specific affiliations and encounters. Booth wishes he could justify his decision to discuss Crane, Burke, and Abrams as topically or even dialectically representative of *"kinds* of pluralism," but he cannot escape his admission that "my life encountered these lives at such and such moments, and the personal force of these men strengthened the impact of their pluralisms" (201). *The Rhetoric of Fiction,* which distances itself from Chicago Aristotelian poetics by shifting its ground to Aristotle's rhetoric, directs itself against the predominant consensus about fiction in the wider culture of criticism, but *Critical Understanding* is dialogically preoccupied with powerful person-ideas affiliated specifically with the Chicago School. It self-consciously abandons the high ground of philosophical universality maintained in Crane's dialectical pluralism, but its rhetorical pluralism, under the powerful influence of Crane's voice, still ambivalently aspires to transcend the accidents of historically contingent rhetorical community and the violence of aggressively competitive rhetorical domination.

Booth's preoccupation with that violence colors much of *Critical Understanding* with the heightened diction of critics' killing and being killed, annihilating each other, battling, destroying, violating, and living only at the cost of others' death and defeat. Bakhtin's vision of rhetoric's intent "to bring about the destruction of the opponent" is right at home in this rhetorical battlefield. It would be fair to say that Booth strives to formulate a version of what Bakhtin calls "the dialogic sphere in which the word lives" as an alternative to this rhetorical scene of carnage ("Extracts" 182), and it is interesting that Booth makes his closest approach to Bakhtinian dialogics in his sections on the value of vitality. But it would also be fair to observe from our present perspective that the powerful habit of thinking in terms of the opposition between the familiar arts of rhetoric and dialectic limits the alternatives available to him. Booth resists the dialectical reduction of discourse to the "transpersonal" adjudication of "rival propositions" (28–29) just as he wishes for a better world than the bloody rhetorical battle of rival critics, but he is apologetic about using the word "dialogue" (237), deeply invested in the dialectical pluralism of modes he resists, and habituated to turn to rhetoric—in both theory and practice—when all else fails.

The book's most vital and provocative moments for me—its section on the value of vitality (220–23) to which I have already referred and its chapter on "overstanding" (235–56)—reach beyond the familiar alternatives and Booth's avowed affiliations to break new ground. Booth himself recognizes and dramatizes the novelty for him of his thinking in that chapter (236). In it he not only defends the imposition of alien terms and questions on a text ("overstanding") against his own powerful commitments to submit to the author's intentions but also recognizes that the repertory, as he puts it, of questions and responses we might bring to any text "will in large part depend on how many other texts we have respected and absorbed in the past" (242–43) and also on the "'school' we were trained in" (254). Booth's closing "image of the reader we seek to propagate" provides a powerful image of the mode of intelligibility of the dialogic self: such a reader "is one who is so active, so broadly experienced, so thoroughly 'possessed' by texts previously understood that his very individuality, no longer idiosyncrasy, will teach us not only something about himself but something about the text and the world" (256). Such readers individualize in their own texts the possibilities and conflicts of prior texts and thereby realize in themselves possibilities of the social world that are not simply peculiar to them but recognizable to others who are both inside that social world and outside that particular individual location in it. Booth's slightly embarrassed notion of "a kind of conversation or dialogue between a text and a reader" recognizes their participation in a common culture just as his affirmation of overstanding (Todorov translates a related Bakhtinian word as "exotopy") recognizes their inalienable alienation from one another.

The combined effect of these two recognitions would be to rule out the model of isolated critical rhetors from which *Critical Understanding* begins and to open the way to a dialogic model of "critical variety and conflict" that would resist both domination and dialectic for the sake of continuing the lives of historically diverse communities and historically diverse selves. Though a dialectical reading of Booth might expose the *contradictions* between his rhetorical and dialogic premises in order to refute them, and a rhetorical reading might try to exploit the *inconsistencies* between these premises in order to defeat him, a dialogic reading would try, as I have, to identify such divergences as productive sites for further conversation with him and to honor them as vital conflicting identifications within his exemplary life of ideas.

4. Rhetoric, Literary Criticism, Theory, and Bakhtin

I remember the day in 1972 or 1973 when the young man with an MA from Yale presented his deconstructive reading in Wayne Booth's seminar in rhetorical criticism at the University of Chicago. Despite our having been disciplined in pluralism and in understanding before "overstanding," our aggressive incredulity was palpable. In what sense was this rhetorical criticism at all? How could a rhetorical criticism, in which we had learned to read for implied authors' guiding our decisions about characters, issue in indecision, with authors out of play and language working its inevitable aporetic effects? What was this stuff and where did it come from? We roughed him up pretty badly, but little did we realize how thoroughly his school would take its revenge on us. We would find ourselves dated, marginalized, left behind nearly as completely as our Chicago School Aristotelian predecessors had been outflanked and obscured by the deconstructionists' New Critical forebears. This time, though, instead of winning poetry and poetics, they would carry off rhetoric. Like our Chicago forebears, most of us would remain convinced that we were right, but that would not stop the world from passing us by and adopting the radically simplified, easily reproduced, language-centered, impersonal and sublime rhetoric Deconstruction would offer. We had our day in that seminar, but we were going to be had. Almost. If the winners always get to tell the history, and I'm presenting myself as one of the losers, how am I still here to tell this story? How has one of the losers managed to survive in the field and manage to say in print, however belatedly, where rhetoric in literary criticism and theory are today, how they got here, and where they might go from here? Perhaps I have exaggerated both the victory of Deconstruction and the defeat of my Chicago School. Everyone knows that Deconstruction suffered a severe setback with the scandals surrounding the revelation of Paul De Man's wartime journalism, though its principal practitioners survived that defeat and have continued to invest de Man's legacy. And we know that "theory"—which was for many in the 1970s and 1980s the same as Deconstruction, which was for many the same as rhetoric—is now talked about in the past tense, having been at least twice supplanted by New Historicism and Cultural Studies, though it is still widely discussed and taught.

It is less widely known but still discoverable that some Chicago-trained rhetorical critics fled the center of "theory" thus understood to take over narrative theory from the flagging structuralist narratologists, while others (actually maybe just one of us—myself), engaged deconstructive rhetorical criticism on its flank, where it had appropriated Wordsworth's poetry, and simultaneously tried to outflank it by assimilating what had been Chicago School rhetorical interests into Bakhtinian dialogic terms—a move with which some of my Chicago colleagues, including Booth himself, also flirted but did not finally make. The rule of Deconstruction was never so complete that it shut out all opportunities to practice rhetorical theory and criticism of other kinds; it never dominated all the journals, presses, and hiring committees in a field where dominant critical fashions in a few key institutional sites change much more rapidly than faculty, curricula, editors and readers across the field as a whole. So I'm here to tell the tale nearly forty years into a career professing rhetoric in literary theory and criticism and in composition and aware that the graduate student I helped to assault in that seminar represented something more powerful than any of us then knew but not something so powerful that its later revenge was the end of me.

In terms of the well-known opposition that De Man posited between trope and persuasion (*Allegories*), deconstruction concerned itself with the former, Chicago with the latter, and both could easily dismiss what the other school was doing as not rhetorical criticism at all. The rhetoric of trope treated rhetoric as that figurative capacity of language that produces undecidable possible meanings that cannot be reduced to grammatical univocality or determined one way or another without violence; the rhetoric of persuasion treated rhetoric as a transaction between language user and receiver, implied author or narrator and implied reader or reader, usually concerned to affect the latter's epideictic evaluation of characters, subordinated, in good Aristotelian terms, to their poetic function in plots.

The deconstructive critics drew upon what Genette called a "restrained" rhetoric derived from a French tradition of Fontanier and grounded in a few passages of Nietzsche's, outside his lectures on rhetoric, that concentrated on tropes and figures. In these terms they could find persuasion irrelevant to rhetoric and see rhetoric in all language. The Chicago critics never talked about tropes and figures as such (it was a topic Aristotle's rhetoric didn't explicitly broach), though it has recently become clear that the "authorial intrusions" Booth sought to justify were, as Fahnestock has suggested, figures of thought. The first edition of the *The Rhetoric of Fiction* calls attention to these figures without ever naming them or identifying their provenance in Quintilian (the second edition makes a blanket gesture in his direction). Booth recognizes that provenance for the trope/figure irony to which he devoted a whole book in hopes of stabilizing the vertiginous irony of deconstructive reading, but deconstructive readers limited themselves to what Quintilian recognized as irony as a way of life, or at least a way of reading, without returning to classical sources or taking an interest in any of the trope/figure's more limited uses.

Both schools drew selectively from rhetorical theory to develop reading practices that offer distinctive satisfactions to those who participate in them, and as pedagogies of reading they are likely to continue. Chicago readers can account for how they are affected by representations of characters and actions in narrative; deconstructive readers can be impressed by the sublime workings of language that their readings reveal. But like New Criticism, in relation to which both these projects in different ways developed, both schools generate readings that exemplify their practices and produce arguments that elaborate and justify them but neither could be said to foster a research program. Chicago inquirers have already constructed more and more finely distinguished accounts of narrators, authors, implied authors, and readers, and though there are more books to read closely in these terms, there are not new problems to be addressed by those readings. Deconstructive readings will continue to appeal to those who find the allegories they generate compelling, but, like all allegorical readings, they have their interest only for the sect or church that is pleased to find its beliefs repeatedly confirmed by making unlikely texts turn out to bespeak already expected allegorical results; such readings have little appeal to non-believers.

Looking back on both these projects as in some sense finished, I see them both as rhetorical in a stipulative sense, not in a traditional or a fully theorized one. Let rhetoric be those "figural" features of language that trouble univocality or let rhetoric be those features of narratives that orient readers to the moral qualities of characters relevant to their fulfilling their roles in plots, and we will generate these kinds of rhetorical criticism. There is little point in quarreling with such stipulations as such, for they simply underwrite projects and direct attention to the features they have named. The appropriation of the term "rhetorical" by both schools set them in apparent conflict with one another, but they were good examples of the pluralist alternatives the Chicago School sometimes tried to treat as equally valid alternatives. The two critical modes consciously and deliberately defined their key term differently and so did different work with it. The deconstructionists may have been wiser on this point than their Chicago counterparts, for the Chicagoans felt compelled to argue with actual or hypothetical versions of deconstructive rhetorical criticism, but the deconstructionists just ignored the Chicago critiques and went on thinking the way they had set out to do. It was their confident monism that kept provoking the Chicago critics, who would have left them alone to play out the implications of their definition if they had just been willing to admit it was one definition among many.

The term "rhetorical" is not, however, a neologism that is simply available for any school to define as it pleases; it is, and was when these schools appropriated it, already a word in wide circulation with a long history, various authoritative instantiations, and quite a few current institutional claimants. It is not surprising that some of those claimants were indignant at what seemed to them to be misappropriations of a term of which they had some claim to ownership and understanding. Brian Vickers, for example, waxed wroth at De Man's claim to the term and ignored the Chicago School's work altogether, not even mentioning *The Rhetoric of Fiction* in a whole chapter on rhetoric and the modern novel—the sad fate of the losing side. His *In Defence of Rhetoric* limns what could be a fruitful line of inquiry that links the rhetorical practices of authors with what they learned in their rhetorical educations—a correlation that brings us down as far as James Joyce and Randall Jarrell and applies with equal or greater aptness to writers of the Renaissance, eighteenth century, and, as I have helped to show, to the Romantics, who are somehow supposed to have left this education behind, and touches, too, on the writing of colonized people who were subjected to rhetorical training in their Western educations. It would be a project that turned away from the opposition between historical knowledge and criticism that has been with us since the New Critics (and still with us in the Chicago and deconstructive projects) and instead historicized critical appreciation in part through the teaching of how past writers learned to write and read by studying rhetorical treatises and exemplars.

Vickers revives the lore of the figures not as a generalized troping undistinguished from a generalized figurality but as a historically catalogued repertoire of numerous figures of speech and thought as well as tropes distinct from them that writers learned to use to a variety of salient effects. He goes a considerable way to meet the call Jonathan Arac issued in *Critical Genealogies* to "repluralize the figures"—a call that recalled the philological knowledge that Auerbach and Curtius and some of their followers brought to their criticism. But in his zeal to show the deniers of rhetoric how much it has to bring to the critical task, Vickers falls into the scholarly habits that have made the task of recovering the rhetorical tradition as a live working tradition a difficult one. He cites too many variations in too many classical and modern sources of definitions of the figures, names too many figures in their Greek and Latin variants, and illustrates their presence in too many works, none of which he reads to the level of a serious contribution to its criticism. He leaves his readers—few of whom would have considered themselves critics or theorists anyway, for he is mainly preaching to the rhetorical choir—with the impression that defensive pedantry rather than functional criticism can issue from recovery of the resources that the rhetorical tradition supplied to the writers we have subsequently separated into the literary tradition.

Here, it seems to me, there is still room for a significant project of historical and theoretical inquiry into rhetorical criticism, and for a rhetorical inquiry, too, into how best to make the fruits of that project widely recognized and used. What Vickers has somewhat hastily and polemically adumbrated is a potentially rich and relatively under-explored area of investigation. It has not yet been pursued widely as a shared project in part at least because rhetoric as a field of inquiry has been twice separated from literary criticism in the U.S.—once through the formation of rhetoric departments that abandoned literature departments to focus on the art in its civic, political manifestations, and again by the appropriation of rhetoric to composition studies within English departments, where the focus on production rather than reception has often exploited rhetoric for only half of its potential. Literary criticism has been othered in both these appropriations of rhetoric, just as rhetoric has been removed from and othered in the literary part of English studies. At the same time literary study itself has to some degree recently been superseded by cultural inquiries, some of which bring back civic rhetorics close to those used in departments of communication. This institutional history has meant that a full-scale inquiry into the rhetorical underpinnings of what only recently has been fractioned off as "literature" has not yet been undertaken, even though most writers marked as "literary" in all but the last century or so were schooled in rhetoric and saw what we take as their literary work within a rhetorical frame of reference. There have been specialized studies of particular writers and particular periods—especially the medieval and early modern (e.g., Payne, Tuve, Joseph, Armstrong)—in relation to their rhetorical educations, and there have been gestures toward writers in other periods (e.g., Needham and Bialostosky), but the problem of learning to read earlier literary writers with critical terms and expectations informed by the rhetorical habits and understandings they wrote with has not been comprehensively addressed or recognized as a theoretical resource across the boundaries of literary periods. Neither has the question of whether or how rhetorical criticism informed by the long tradition of rhetorical theory and rhetorical writing might transfer to those writing and reading in the wake of that tradition (but see Bender and Wellbery).

To address this unfinished business, let me raise some of the questions that might be fruitful to ask, mention some of the recent work that might be called on to help answer them, and note some of the cautions that might be observed in addressing them.

What difference does it make to literary criticism that most of the writers for most of the Western literary tradition were schooled, directly or indirectly, in rhetoric and wrote what we have come to call literary texts in a context of rhetorical ends and rhetorical resources? What aspects of their work should we look to as evidence of their learning of rhetoric, and given that they learned it, what kinds of appreciation of their work would our recognition of it enable? It is not enough to point to their use of tropes and figures or their conformity to a pattern of arrangement and say that they were rhetorically trained and that rhetoric is therefore important. What otherwise anomalous features could we account for by recognizing their rhetorical provenance? What points could we take, what turns could we follow, what discoveries could we make about what they expected their readers to know and value that we might otherwise have missed?

What can we learn about rhetoric when we find it poetically embodied, and what do we make of poetry, and literature more generally, when we recognize it as an embodiment of rhetoric?

What difference does it make if we understand the rhetorical tradition itself, as Jeffrey Walker teaches us to do, as more fundamentally literary than its earlier historians have taken it to be? A literary scholar writing the history of rhetoric, Walker has found epideictic rhetoric, which has closest affinities with poetic utterance, more fundamental and continuous in the history of rhetoric than the deliberative rhetoric that has been the center of the art for historians concerned with its civic praxis. Starting from Walker's history, rhetoricians with literary critical interests need not see themselves poaching on poetic territory owned by others but can boldly venture into a province of rhetoric where poetic works are and always have been and where much rhetoric has much in common with those works. How might this epideictic provenance orient the reading of literature?

How much common ground is there among the rhetorical training writers through the ages received, and where is that common ground best represented? What parts of that training, what terms and distinctions and notions of their use, were most consequential in shaping writing over time? How could those parts be most fruitfully represented and acquired in contemporary criticism as a repertoire of critical terms and expectations? These are crucial questions if the history of rhetoric is to become a functional resource for rhetorical criticism of literature. Though the place and shape of rhetoric has varied significantly through time, though different rhetorical treatises shaped to different purposes have been available to writers at different times, though rhetorical terms have been variously defined, is it possible to construct a non-trivial (or perhaps we might better call it "post-trivial") version of rhetorical functions and participants, patterns and moves, that could serve contemporary readers as a rhetorical toolkit for reading literary works across time? Such a toolkit would not have tools to fit every particular work, shaped as they were under various versions of rhetoric. It can't have so many varied tools that one doesn't know where to look for one that fits the case, nor can the toolkit be reduced to a one-size-fits-all tool that lacks capacity to discriminate interesting functional features across a sufficient range. The art of rhetoric itself has considerable experience in organizing itself within parameters like this, sorting topics and figures and argumentative patterns to address the likely situations to which orators using them might be called, but scholarship on the art has tended to accumulate variants, multiply entities, and lose touch with functional delimiters. It may be helpful to think of the rhetorical critic of literature we are arming as a rhetorician who draws from the history of rhetoric rather than as a scholar of that history; then we can set out to shape an account of the commonplaces of rhetorical criticism to that rhetorician-critic's task of discriminating and appreciating a wide array of literary works.

How can we name, define, and mobilize the resources of the rhetorical tradition—not just tropes and figures but other stylistic distinctions, as well as other kinds of distinctions including topics, modes of argument, patterns of arrangement, issues of delivery in written texts—for the use of contemporary literary critics and students of literature? Perhaps the best example we have of a successful attempt to do this, concerned, however, not with literary criticism but with critical-rhetorical appreciation of scientific argument, is Jeanne Fahnestock's *Rhetorical Figures in Science*. Fahnestock's introduction provides a thoughtfully reduced history of rhetoric aimed at deriving some functional definitions of figures that can be of service in appreciating their use in both the invention and presentation of scientific arguments. She reviews traditional definitions of tropes and figures and related enthymemes (though not all of them) and criticizes them with an eye to clarifying the features they can discriminate in use. She suggests alternative ways of thinking about the troubling and interesting category of figures of thought and offers analogs from contemporary speech-act theory and pragmatic linguistics for thinking about them. She delimits a subset of figures appropriate for her critical task and devotes the remainder of her book to examining their working in specific writers and writings. Though she goes further into the history of rhetoric than she needs to for the purposes of her work in rhetoric of science, she treats the extra history she provides in a way that makes it functionally available for other rhetoricians of science and even for rhetorical critics of other genres. My own mobilization of traditional distinctions concerning arrangement and figures of thought to address some anomalies in the interpretation of Wordsworth's *Prelude* moves in a parallel direction, governed by similar critical rather than historical priorities (Bialostosky 1992).

Are there contemporary vocabularies available in other inquiries into language and argument that offer ways not only to redescribe but to rethink these rhetorical resources? Fahnestock's brief turns toward speech act theory and pragmatics to open lines of inquiry that might issue in fruitful redescriptions, even reconceptualizations, of traditional rhetorical terms and distinctions in contemporary theoretical vocabularies. With a critical project governing these turns, we need to be careful, as we have already been with historical scholarship, to rein in theoretical over-elaborations of categories and definitions. The point of seeking more recent vocabularies is to make traditional rhetorical distinctions more readily available for current use and perhaps to articulate their relations in memorable frames of reference that might let us understand them better and deploy them more thoughtfully.

This is a question to which I would like to propose an answer by pursuing a possible line of redescription drawn from the Bakhtin School, contrasting it to an elaboration of Fahnestock's undeveloped suggestion that we think of figures of thought in terms of speech act theory, and showing that Bakhtin's terms capture her insights better than J. L Austin's. Fahnestock finds the rubric "figures of thought" misleading, because the paradigmatic instances Quintilian cites "have less to do with the content than with the context." She suggestively renames figures of thought "interactional devices" and says that such moves are "more like gestures, ways of marking in speech or constructing in written texts the intentions, interactions, and attitudes among participants." The "energy of interaction," she goes on, "resembles the twentieth-century notion of the speech act either intended or accomplished by an utterance." Elaborating further in a long note, Fahnestock concludes that "many of the figures of thought . . . specify interactions between speaker and audience and reciprocal intentions and effects" (197 n. 5). Fahnestock's emphasis on the way figures of thought embody or imitate the interactions among participants in the discursive situation fits the terms of the Bakhtinian rereading of the figures I will elaborate in a moment, but first I want to consider her suggestion that figures of thought might be understood in terms of speech act theory.

The basic distinction in speech act theory between constative and performative utterances parallels Quintilian's distinction between unfigured discourse, which directs attention to the matter, and figures of thought, which artfully enact or act out some transaction among the participants in the discursive situation. It does help to think of the figures of thought as performative and to recognize that even straightforward narration and proof directed toward the matter—included on Cicero's list of figures but not on Quintilian's—are kinds of performance, just as, it turns out for Austin, constative utterances are kinds of performance. It may also help to recognize that figures of thought may bring into being the discursive interactions they enact, just as performative utterances may issue in new relationships among the parties to them.

Austin's positing of the categories constative and performative is part of what J. Hillis Miller recognizes as the primarily grammatical or logical rather than rhetorical bent of his thought (39–40), and the interests he has in classifying verbs of discursive action or clearly distinguishing performative from constative utterances are not the interests of a pragmatic, pedagogically oriented rhetorical criticism concerned with modeling what happens in literary discourse for the sake of reading it better. So while speech act theory may offer the performative as a helpful way of thinking about figures of thought in general, a contemporary rhetoric of the figures of thought could be diverted from its purposes—if it let itself get caught up, as rhetorical theorists repeatedly have done in the past—in logical or grammatical disputes over mutually exclusive definitions of categories, the classification of the figures in those categories, or even the ultimate collapse of the distinction between them.

Bakhtin's dialogic theories offer a more rhetorically useful way to capture Fahnestock's insight and resituate the classical figures of thought in currently available terms, because it has a comprehensive account of the participants interacting in discourse that helps organize the figures of thought and a powerful account of speech genres that helps to reinterpret them. The Bakhtin School's account of discourse from its earliest essays posits that *"any locution actually said aloud or written down for intelligible communication . . . is the interaction of three participants: the speaker* (author), *the listener* (reader), *and the topic* (the who or what) *of speech* (the hero)" (DLDA 105, italics in original), and it adds in later work the additional premise that the topic or hero or object of discourse is always "a focal point for heteroglot voices among which [the speaker or writer's own voice] must sound; these voices create the background necessary for his own voice . . ." (DN 278). The hero, that is, has always already been spoken of and spoken for so that the current speaker's voice must always find its place among those that have already had their say about it. This model of the participants interacting in a discursive event permits us to see the figures of thought as foregrounding or acting out the current writer's or speaker's relations to all participants—to precedent speakers or writers on the subject, to the hero as evaluated object or potential speaker, to the listener's or reader's previous or potential utterances, or to the speaker's own utterance in progress.

For example, the paradigmatic figure of response to precedent utterance is the prosopopoeia, or attribution of words, to another of which quotation is a literal species. The model figure of address to the hero is the apostrophe, which turns from the listener to speak to the hero or sometimes to personify the topic of discourse. The representative figure of address to the reader is the anticipation of his or her objection or concurrence with the speaker. The figure of the speaker's reference to himself or herself as producer of the utterance currently in progress that brings such gestures into view is the self-interruption, but any first-person enacting of discursive actions—announcing the sequence of topics or saying "in conclusion I . . ." or apologizing for going on at too great length—brings the speaker figuratively to the fore. The Bakhtin School's account of interactions among discursive participants thus permits us to stabilize and enlarge Fahnestock's insights, allowing us to go beyond her emphasis on interactions of speaker and audience to identify four main types of interactions among four discursive participants.

Bakhtin's account of speech genres enables another fruitful rethinking of the figures of thought. He defines primary speech genres—typifiable utterances that bespeak typifiable relations among the participants in discursive interactions in everyday exchanges—as the constituents of secondary speech genres—the more elaborate, usually written, utterances that characterize scientific, business, political, military, and literary communication in institutionally organized spheres of communication. Figures of thought, in these terms, I suggest, "play out," as Bakhtin puts it, "various forms of primary speech communication" (98). "Quite frequently," he elaborates, "within the boundaries of his own utterance the speaker (or writer) raises questions, answers them himself, raises objections to his own ideas, responds to his own objections, and so on. But these phenomena are nothing other than the playing out of speech communication and primary genres. This kind of playing out is typical of rhetorical genres . . . but other secondary genres (artistic and scholarly) also use various forms such as this to introduce primary speech genres and relations among them into the construction of the utterance (and here they are altered to a greater or lesser degree for the speaking subject does not change. Such is the nature of secondary genres" (72–73). Though Bakhtin does not use the rhetorical term "figures of thought" in this discussion, he has both enumerated key figures and redefined them fruitfully as the incorporation of primary speech genres, which stand on their own in everyday discourse, into secondary genres where they function as the parts of more complex utterances that interrelate to one another in some ways as the primary genres interrelate in everyday dialogic exchange.

The radical conclusion that follows from this redefinition of figures of thought is that all secondary genres, including all literary genres, are *composed of* primary speech genres; such figures, understood as primary genres enacted within the compass of more highly elaborated utterances, are the building blocks of those genres. Any text, therefore, should be analyzable into a sequence of such figures; we should be able to resolve it into a series of interactions with precedent utterances, its topic or hero, its audience, and the utterance in progress. Every text, in these terms, can be understood as built up as a sequence of figures of thought, and our effort to critically appreciate complex secondary utterances like literary works should attend to their sequencing and their interactions.

Let me illustrate how we follow in a challenging poem the sequence of interacting internalized speech genres—or figures of thought—involving several discursive participants by describing in these terms a piece of Milton's "Lycidas" that unfolds as a series of internal questions, answers, self-corrections and corrections from others. Milton's speaker at line 50 first asks a question that functions as an accusation—"Where were ye, Nymphs, when the remorseless deep / Closed o'er the head of your loved Lycidas?" He then builds his case against the nymphs, enumerating the places where they weren't, places from which he imagines they might have been able to prevent Lycidas's drowning. But then he catches himself, responds to his own words, and withdraws his own accusation: "Ay me, I fondly dream had ye been there!" For he realizes and explains that if the Muse herself couldn't save that first poet Orpheus from his pursuers, how could he imagine that these lesser nymphs could have done anything for Lycidas? But their failure and the Muse's failure to help prompts another question from him: What good does it do to serve the thankless Muse and tend the trade of poetry? If the Muse can't save you, why not, he goes on, give up the discipline of learning to write and instead enjoy dallying with pastoral maids? Again he answers himself, that fame is the reason why, but then objects to his own answer that just when you are hoping to achieve fame, you die, and what then? This time another voice intervenes to correct him, Phoebus, who reminds him that fame is not a worldly good but a heavenly one, judged by Jove and not subject to mortal terminations. The speaker then invokes pastoral waters to bring his song back from the "higher mood" of Phoebus's song to his own pastoral note, and next begins an account of a coroner's inquest in which he listens to the representatives of the sea deny responsibility for the shipwreck in which Lycidas died, blaming it on his boat. I think I have gone far enough to illustrate the way the poem internalizes a series of familiar types of utterances, enacts interactions among several participants, and builds one figure upon the other as answer to question, question prompted by conclusion, objection prompted by the next conclusion, or self-reflexive fresh start taken after another voice has put in its oar in the internalized conversation. And this has taken us far enough to see how classical rhetorical categories like the figures of thought might be made critically functional if redescribed in the contemporary critical idiom of Bakhtin's theories.

One consequence of reinterpreting figures of thought within Bakhtin's account of speech genres is that the figures become recognizable as an artificial technical specification of a universal vernacular phenomenon. The art of rhetoric as Quintilian elaborated it may have initially codified figures of thought and tried to set apart their deliberate, even insincere, use as a mark of art, but Quintilian recognized in Cicero's account a broader understanding of the figures of thought as a set of noticeable discursive moves, and Fahnestock has driven that point home, calling figures "better but not unique ways to achieve certain discourse functions" (23). If we use Bakhtin's account of speech genres to articulate a derivation of figures of thought from primary types of utterance, then the use of those "figures" need not be a sign of knowledge of the art. The discursive moves to which the art has given technical names can be used by writers innocent of those names and innocent of the art itself. Though artistic practice might highlight and cultivate and direct the use of figures of thought, it has no monopoly on their use. This re-placement of the figures (and potentially of other rhetorical terms and distinctions) as artificial selections from a natural discursive repertoire raises further questions that a fresh inquiry into rhetorical criticism might address.

Just how technical are the resources that the art of rhetoric has codified? Have the technical names by which rhetoricians have learned and taught them obscured their vernacular origin and their pervasiveness in ordinary language use? Which, if any, of them are strictly artificial, available only to the rhetorically schooled, and what is the relation of these artificial resources to the workings of ordinary language? How has schooling in them affected their deployment? What are the most important artificial practices contingent on specific rhetorical sources that shaped the work of particular authors or periods? How can they best be discovered and made available to critics focused on those specialties? On the other hand, to what extent can technically named rhetorical devices and patterns be recognized in practices of unschooled discourse or discourse schooled without formal rhetorical training?

What implications do our answers to this last question have for criticism of writers of the last century or so who learned to write without reference to formal rhetorical training, or at least to formal rhetorical training linked to classical education? To what extent have they nonetheless learned what we can call rhetorical moves, either from their everyday availability, from study of earlier authors who were formally schooled in them, or for modern versions of rhetorical education conducted under other names? To what extent can the historically underwritten rhetorical criticism we have been imagining here fruitfully address itself to that part of the history of literary production, "post-trivial" literature, as it were, that was not shaped by formal rhetorical training? To what extent can we draw upon rhetorical formalizations of discourse moves as an open-ended generic vocabulary that can help us notice moves that pre-existed their formalization and that exist whether or not those formalizations are explicitly taught? If the extent is considerable, we will have opened the way to articulating a rhetorical criticism grounded in what can be learned from the history of rhetorical theory and practice but not restricted to seeking explicit correlations between literary productions and historically specific rhetorical educations.

I hope I have raised enough questions to prompt others to consider further elaborating and contributing to the project of historical and theoretical inquiry into rhetorical literary criticism that I am proposing. Consequential critical projects are not the work of single critics but of groups engaged with deploying the same critical resources and advocating for their program under a recognizable banner. New Criticism and Deconstruction both represented collective projects, however internally diversified, and both achieved a proper nominalization that made them objects of adherence, opposition, and representation. There are introductions to, bibliographies of, anthologies on them. There are books exemplifying their practices for wider audiences. They have afterlives in histories of criticism as my "Chicago" School, metonymically identified with its institution of origin, does not.

As rhetoricians, we should be well prepared to undertake the advocacy required. What would we call the criticism I have been desiderating? Just "Rhetorical," hoping to recapture the word? "New Rhetorical," hoping to try the well-worn gambit that has served New Critics and New Historicists alike (though Howell has already used the phrase otherwise in the history of rhetoric)? Or is there a neologism like "deconstruction" waiting to be recovered from rhetoric's great storehouse of Latin and Greek technical terms? Whatever we call our toolbox of rhetorical terms, we will have to present the acquisition of it as an attractive project, not dry-as-dust or lifetime-consuming antiquarian work, but as work functional from the start in improving our understanding and enjoyment of literary works. It needs to come not just with good name recognition and advertising but with an effective user's manual, a pedagogical sequence that helps new users get immediate use from the toolkit and build toward more complicated, less scripted uses. The New Critics did not neglect this part of their program; indeed, they attended to it more assiduously than to theoretical defense, while my Chicago predecessors published an enormous tome of rigorous scholarly argument and critique that persuaded few beyond the Midway (see Crane). Booth's intervention into discussion of fiction, less formidably written and focused on a genre not well developed in New Criticism, found a wider following. Deconstruction's advocates took an interesting tack, professing rigor and courting difficulty, but also building an aura of sublimity, inevitability, and European sophistication around their work. Their following did not spread as far or go as deeply into the educational system as New Criticism (and it depended in part on New Criticism for its appeal), but practiced by a relatively small coterie, it achieved a prestige out of proportion to its size.

The account I have been offering of rhetorical criticism of literature is obviously one shaped and limited by the peculiar corner of the field from which I have come. It omits significant lines of inquiry, rhetorical hermeneutics, feminist rhetorics, Burkeans, and others that would be important if someone else were telling the tale. But I would like to think of this intervention as also a contribution to "literary history" in the broad sense that Francis Bacon treats it in his *Advancement of Learning*. He surveys the state of learning and the learned in his time to highlight what appears cultivated and what lies fallow, aware of the need to promote collective labors to bring fallow fields under the plow. My chapter of recent "literary history" tells a story of a branch of learning at least partly from outside the self-serving stories of its sects, attending to "their inventions, their traditions, their diverse administrations and managings, their flourishings, their oppositions, decays, depressions, oblivions and removes, with the causes and occasions of them" with the goal of making us better at managing these affairs of learning and perhaps enabling us deliberately to intervene to improve them (*Advancement* 70). I have found rhetorical criticism and theory of literature "deficient," as Bacon would have put it, but not without some suggestive and hopeful resources and possibilities, among them a Bakhtin School redescription of classical figures of thought. Such surveys of the state of learning and suggestions for new directions are inescapably presumptuous and quixotic, but they are also occasionally fruitful, as I hope this one will be.

5. Bakhtin and Rhetorical Criticism

While most rhetorical critics of literature from both the Chicago and the deconstructive schools took note of the emergence of Bakhtin School translations in the 1980s, neither school was much deflected from its established interests by what it found there. Rhetorical critics in composition, on the other hand, found challenges in Bakhtin's denigrations of rhetoric but also potentially fruitful resources in his general theories of language and society. In 1990 two then beginning scholars who have since published important monographs on Bakhtin, Kay Halasek and Michael Bernard-Donals, invited me to respond to their papers on Bakhtin and rhetorical criticism at a session of the Discussion Group on the History and Theory of Rhetoric and Composition at the Modern Language Association convention, and our exchange, supplemented by an additional essay by one of the readers for the journal, James Zebroski, was published in *Rhetoric Society Quarterly* in 1992. A timely exchange and something of a Burkean parlor conversation, our joint contribution was awarded the Charles W. Kneupper Award for Outstanding Contribution to *Rhetoric Society Quarterly*. The person-ideas Halasek and Bernard-Donals articulated remain interesting not only because these scholars, whose work has moved well beyond these early pieces, continue to be important in the field of composition but also because they both spoke at the time for something larger than themselves, schools of thought that shaped them and continue to be shared by others in the field.

First, I would like to offer here a dialogic analysis of their essays, which may also be taken as a rhetorical or tendentious characterization of them. If we begin with the two points of reference provided by the session's and this chapter's title, "Bakhtin" and "Rhetorical Criticism," I think we can say that Halasek identifies herself as a rhetorical critic or theorist who belongs to a still vital community of like-minded rhetorical critics and theorists, one that "brings together post-structuralist thought, social constructivism, and writing theory and pedagogy" ("Starting" 1–2). For them Bakhtin's vilification of rhetoric is a problem and an alternative Bakhtinian rhetorical tradition is an opportunity. Halasek can summarize the rhetoric Bakhtin attacks and distance herself from it as "not one to which rhetoricians today are likely to adhere," and she can appropriate as much more congenial to herself and her fellow rhetoricians the rhetorical tradition of oppositional genres and parodic discourse moves with which Bakhtin identifies the novel. She imagines Bakhtin's hostility to rhetoric as in relation to his hostility to the official languages of "Russia during his lifetime" and imagines herself and her colleagues as also opposed to a rhetoric "that is monologic and dogmatic in its defense of oppressive authority" but apparently not confronted with a similar authoritarian political situation. Instead of identifying herself exclusively with a "parodic rhetoric" opposed to an official monologic "polemic rhetoric," she posits a "dialogic rhetoric," which can contemplate the tensions between polemic and parodic rhetorics in the professional and pedagogical tasks of textual and cultural analysis. She finds that Bakhtin offers her a better way of doing what rhetorical critics like her were already doing (5).

Halasek welcomes Bakhtin's tension-filled genres and joyful relativity in a prose that is relatively free from tension and clear about where it stands. She can separate Bakhtin's vilification of rhetoric from his celebration of it, choose one side over the other, and even explain away Bakhtin's adherence to the side she rejects as a function of his particular historical situation. She is at home with the listeners she posits and brings them a Bakhtin they can use without having to change their minds about rhetoric or politics.

Bernard-Donals, on the other hand, writes a tension-filled and ambivalent prose in the name of escaping from relativism and uncertainty. He is not at one with what he takes to be the community of contemporary rhetorical theory but sees it as "plagued" by the collapse of a distinction between science and rhetoric that he wants to reassert (11). He persists in a commitment to theory or science or dialectic or history that he believes rhetorical critics like Fish and Rorty have subsumed under rhetoric, and he turns to Bakhtin not to assimilate him to the consensus in current rhetorical theory but to find a way out of what he takes to be the impasse of current rhetorical theory. The Bakhtin he needs for his purposes is not the celebrant of parody and joyful relativity but the theorist of the socially constituted subject who can provide rhetorical criticism with a scientific model for understanding "how subjects' consciousnesses are formed in language" (13). He draws more from the so-called "disputed texts" by Voloshinov and Medvedev written in Marxist idiom than from the indisputably Bakhtin-authored ones. In effect, he wants to substitute a Bakhtin School sociolinguistics of the subject for the psychology of the subject Plato calls for in the *Phaedrus* as the scientific foundation for a rhetoric that could then know, as he puts it, "which rhetorical strategies work to improve the placement of human subjects and which don't" (12). This formulation finesses, as I think the whole argument does, the difference between a scientifically grounded rhetorical technology that could tell which techniques work to move subjects from one place to another and a dialectically grounded philosophy of rhetoric that can tell which changes of subject position constitute "improvements," or movements in the direction of the good. It is my impression that Bernard-Donals would like both these questions to be settled authoritatively outside the domain of the contingent so that rhetoric could reliably bring about good social change.

For Halasek, then, rhetorical criticism is critical reading of texts informed by rhetorical categories, and Bakhtin offers terms that enrich and expand those categories without displacing them. For Bernard-Donals, I suspect, rhetorical criticism is really philosophical or scientific criticism of rhetoric, an exposé of the material contradictions that comprise the rhetoric of any utterance not grounded in material fact. The Bakhtin School offers him a way of expanding the domain of materialist scientific analysis and thereby shrinking the domain of rhetoric. I am not entirely persuaded by either of these programs for the future of rhetorical criticism, dialogic rhetoric or materialist rhetoric.

One thing I'd say to Halasek is that Bakhtin's negative account of rhetoric cannot be so easily disowned or dismissed as an accident of his peculiar political circumstances. Nina Perlina, whom I cite in Chapter 3, has shown that Bakhtin shaped a significant part of his view of rhetoric in response not to Soviet politics but to a contemporary formalist rhetorical theorist, Victor Vinogradov, for whom rhetoric is just the agonistic zero-sum game Bakhtin treats it as. For Vinogradov, Perlina writes, rhetoric entails "the speaker's attempt to muffle the voice of the opponent, to discredit his speech manifestations, and to advance his own monologic pronouncement over the dialogic reply of another person. . . . Within the framework of Vinogradov's poetic system, a speech partner is the rhetorician whose main intention is to make his oratory the only effective and authoritative speech manifestation" (15–16). Though an authorized Soviet voice, Vinogradov speaks not only as a mouthpiece of official Soviet propaganda but as a spokesman for a powerful and continuing tradition of competitive public rhetoric that has a powerful proprietary claim on the name "rhetoric." Bakhtin's account of the difficulties of appropriating other peoples' words would suggest that any effort to reclaim the name "rhetoric" for a more comprehensive theory of discourse that encompasses polemic as well as parody, dialogic utterance as well as monologic rhetoric, will need to acknowledge and contend with this version of rhetoric as a living contemporary possibility, not dismiss it as a historically surpassed moment in an alien polity. I'd cite Brian Vickers's *In Defence of Rhetoric* as a reassertion of this tradition and its characteristic practices in the English-speaking critical world, but I'd also suggest that we all ignore this version of rhetoric in our own practice at our peril.

If I would like to make it harder for Halasek to get rid of the rhetoric she doesn't like and to appropriate the Bakhtin she does like for what she wants to call "rhetoric," I would like to make it easier for Bernard-Donals to relax and learn to live with rhetoric without needing an appeal to something more certain. I don't understand why and in what sense he finds scientific knowledge is necessary for political action. I know that Marxism has claimed to make such knowledge available for the action it calls for, but Aristotelian rhetoric as I understand it organizes its resources to make decision and consequent action possible on those matters for which we lack scientific knowledge. If there is no "possibility of knowing which rhetorical strategies work to improve the placement of human subjects"—and I believe there is no way of knowing this in any sense that distinguishes knowledge from opinion—there are nevertheless many ways in which various groups of human subjects can decide to try to improve their "placement," as Bernard-Donals puts it, by using various expedient strategies from their various points of view. Those points of view are the discreditable "biases" he takes them to be only from the point of view of one who imagines a possible escape from limited points of view, but they are the starting points from which various groups decide what changes will be improvements, even if other groups think the same changes will be deteriorations. That's politics, as I understand it, and it's the domain in which rhetoric thrives. Claims to scientific knowledge need to pass through rhetorical maximizations and minimizations on their way to affecting persuasion, as we see in debates over global warming. Far from being necessary to the domain of praxis, claims to scientific knowledge (except as a technical expertise about means and consequences in limited domains) are subject to rhetorical treatment; they must make their way through rhetoric in the political domain, the domain of deliberation about things that can be one way or another, depending on how much we can be made to care about them, believe them, and act upon them.

Having said this, however, I would add that it makes a lot of difference to our rhetorical practice how we conceive of the communities in which we deliberate and the subjects with whom we deliberate about what to do. If we imagine those communities and subjects as monologic and monolithic, we will direct our arguments to those whose judgments we can already predict and reinforce values whose place is already established. If, however, we imagine communities and subjects as dialogic and internally divided, we will be more resourceful in inventing diverse means of persuasion and less sure of who can be brought to share in a judgment and join in a community until all the cases have been heard. We may even admit to being unsure of what we ourselves will decide or what communities we belong to until we have heard what the others have to say.

I would, then, go along with Bernard-Donals in finding Bakhtin's account of heteroglot communities and individuals useful for rhetorical practice, but I would see this usefulness not as a scientific advance over monologic versions of interpretive communities and subjects but as a belief more likely to produce inclusive communities, interesting arguments, informed judgments, and strange bedfellows. We may not need Bakhtin, however, to make this point. We might recall that Aristotle was no slouch when it came to imagining communities that took for granted conflicting premises. He documented long lists of conflicting beliefs from which he imagined rhetors might construct lines of argument, and though he sometimes showed philosophical contempt for this mess of mutually contradictory premises, he did not imagine that rhetoric had anything else to work with or anywhere else to turn. When Bernard-Donals hopes for a scientific or dialectical basis for rhetoric, he participates, as I have suggested, in a Platonic fantasy, not in an Aristotelian distinction between domains of rhetoric and science.

A rhetorical criticism convinced of the heteroglossia of communities and individuals would judge rhetorical practice by its ability to discover and appeal to the full range of different arguments and beliefs available in a given case. In the case before us, for example, it would ask those who seek to persuade us of Bakhtin's fruitfulness for the future of rhetorical criticism to touch upon the diverse available understandings of "rhetoric" as well as the diverse voices and resources associated with the name "Bakhtin." For example, Susan Wells's paper on "Bakhtin and Rhetoric," presented at the International Bakhtin Conference in 1989, articulated Bakhtin with Derrida and discovered a conflict between Bakhtin's exclusion of rhetoric from the realm of the dialogic and his inclusion of a monologized "rhetoric" as a necessary Other to the dialogized novel. Wells showed how Bakhtin's polemical image of rhetoric limits the deliberative, epideictic, and forensic genres of rhetoric to a forensic courtroom genre in which there are always winners or losers and the dialogue must end, and she asserts that neither of the other rhetorical genres would have provided the same foil for Bakhtin's open-ended dialogue. As Wells put it, in those two genres, "the situation of the discourse, even if punctuated or interrupted, does not end: further deliberations, further praise or further blame are always possible." Wells's revival of one of the large distinctions within traditional rhetoric permits a richer articulation of Bakhtin's views as already informed by rhetoric, even as her Derridean sophistication permits her to recognize Bakhtin's investment in rhetoric in his vehement rejections of it.

Other recoveries of terms from the rhetorical lexicon permit other recognitions of Bakhtin's appropriations and elaborations of rhetoric. One that especially interests me comes from a book that derives the most important dialectical philosophy of the last two centuries from rhetorical sources and, at the same time, gives us an aspect of rhetoric many of us have forgotten. John H. Smith's book, *The Spirit and Its Letter: Traces of Rhetoric in Hegel's Philosophy of Bildung,* shows how Hegel's *Phenomenology of the Spirit* projects onto a world-historical scheme the practices connected with *exercitatio* in the rhetorical training Hegel received in his gymnasium. *Exercitatio* is not glossed in Lanham's *Handbook* or defended in Vickers's *Defence of Rhetoric,* but it names a pedagogical practice crucial to any social understanding of the discursive subject. In this pedagogy, as Smith describes it, the student "'consumes' the great texts of the pasts [sic] by *lectio,* 'digests' them by *selectio* and *imitatio,* and transforms them creatively by a program leading from literal translation (*interpretatio*) to independent production (*aemulatio*)." *Exercitatio* is the process in which "the individual consciousness learns to treat external forms as part of itself as well as to treat itself as consisting of incorporated external forms. The formative acts of appropriating preexisting external forms to the self [constitute] a process of creative transformation (literally spiritual 'digestion')" (18, 20). Smith declares the importance of Bakhtin's work to his reading of Hegel in these terms but does not show how Bakhtin's account of individual ideological development in "Discourse in the Novel" follows the same model, even using the same metaphors of property and digestion. Bakhtin is as deeply rhetorical in these terms as Hegel, even more deeply rhetorical since he has refused to reify this heterogeneous and open-ended process of self-development into a dialectically determinate series. A critically fruitful and pedagogically powerful articulation of rhetoric and dialogics might well grow out of further excavation of the history and practice of *exercitatio* in combination with further reflection on the dialogic formation of the subject.

Still another way to see rhetoric differently and to see Bakhtin as rhetorical is to follow the hint that Patricia Bizzell and Bruce Herzberg give when they introduce selections from Bakhtin's "The Problem of Speech Genres" into their anthology *The Rhetorical Tradition.* They write, "It would not be wrong to think of the speech genres . . . as rhetorical situations and to see Bakhtin's argument as a way of extending rhetoric's gaze to every act of speaking or writing." They add, however, impressed by Bakhtin's explicit attacks on rhetoric, that "to be sure, Bakhtin takes his approach not from rhetoric but from linguistics and semantics" (926). But I would not be too sure. Bakhtin's definition of speech genres as types of utterance with relatively stable thematic content, style, and compositional structure that perform recognizable functions in typical situations of communication, mobilizes the hallowed rhetorical distinction among invention (thematic content), style, and arrangement (compositional structure) and insists, as rhetoric itself sometimes did, that all three of these aspects of utterance be shaped to the functions of utterances in the kinds of situations to which they are addressed. Bakhtin is expanding the range of situations from formal occasions of public discourse to all possible occasions of social communication, but in doing so he enriches rhetorical criticism even as he depends upon some of its most widely repeated traditional categories.

I have already developed in Chapter 4 one more way that Bakhtin's work can inter-illuminate traditional, though in this case neglected, rhetorical categories. Quintilian's distinction between figures of thought and figures of speech has almost disappeared from current usage in the general meltdown of distinctions between tropes and figures, but the category of figures of thought takes on new interest in the light of Bakhtin's emphasis on the way in which utterances respond to prior utterances, anticipate subsequent ones, and comment upon themselves. Many of the figures of thought Quintilian enumerated, among them apostrophe or diversion of address from the judge, self-correction, impersonation of the speech of another, and many more, are also signs in discourse of dialogue with others. They are the gestures formalist critics once called narratorial intrusions. They call attention to the discursive situation into which the utterance intervenes, to what has already been said or might be said about the topic (even what has already been or might be said by the speaker), to what the audience may say, to what the hero said or would say. Quintilian listed them to make them available for artificial and deliberate use in rhetorical discourse, but a dialogically engaged reader may turn to his list for help in naming the kinds of discursive moves that reveal hidden or overt dialogue in double-voiced discourse. In this case Bakhtin helps us find a new use for a neglected but rich set of rhetorical distinctions with fruitful application to everyday discourse as well as to poetry, drama, and the novel.

If Bakhtin is to continue to enrich rhetorical criticism and rhetorical criticism is to illuminate our reading of Bakhtin, I agree with Halasek that we need to work through Bakhtin's unfruitful attacks on a polemically limited version of rhetoric (though I would add that we should not forget the truth of that version or cease to struggle with it), and I agree with Bernard-Donals that we need to pay attention to the implications for rhetoric of Bakhtin's theory of the heterogeneous, socially formed subject (though I would add that we must also recall Bakhtin's emphasis on the creative subject who reforms the givens of social language and works through them to produce fresh and productive words). Rhetoric, in its traditional terms, and in its diverse contemporary manifestations, is richer than Bakhtin's polemical images of it, and Bakhtin is more richly invested in it than those images of it will let us recognize. From what I take to be a fruitful perspective for further investigations—one that redefines rhetoric as "rhetoricality" and makes it central to postmodern intellectual work and cultural life—John Bender and David Wellbery write that "Bakhtin's works, deeply influenced by those of Nietzsche, could be read as virtual treatises on the nature and functioning of rhetoricality." I will say more about this reconfiguration of rhetoric and Bakhtin's relation to it in the next chapter.

6. Antilogics, Dialogics, and Sophistic Social Psychology

Much of what went by the name of "literary theory" in Europe and North America at the end of the last century can be recognized as a revival of orientations that belonged to the arts of the medieval trivium, the verbal liberal arts of grammar, rhetoric, and dialectic or logic. I. A. Richards ("Introduction"), Paul de Man (*Resistance*), Colin MacCabe, Robert Scholes, and Nancy Struever are among those who have recognized or called for the revival of the "trivial arts" in modern literary studies. The medieval institutional division into faculties of grammar, rhetoric, and logic or dialectic has been lost in our organization of departments by national language and literature, but it takes only some creative re-indexing to discover divergent dialectical, rhetorical, and grammatical orientations among, say, members of an English department, or convergent grammatical orientations among, say, narratologists in French, English, and Slavic departments.

It also takes only a little creative re-indexing of Bakhtin's work to discover its critical engagement with all three arts of the trivium. Several scholars, Michael Holquist and A. C. Goodson among others, have reminded us of Bakhtin's critique of Saussurean grammar and the structuralism it underwrote. John H. Smith has shown us Bakhtin's affinities with and Peter Zima has shown us his departures from Hegelian dialectic, and Marxist dialectical theorists like Fredric Jameson have reframed Bakhtin's dialogics as dialectic (*Political Unconscious*). Chapter 4 has developed his relevance to rhetorical criticism and theory of literature. My argument so far has shown Bakhtin's interest in all three arts and posited a Bakhtinian art of "dialogics" that differs from both Aristotelian rhetoric and Aristotelian dialectic, opening the possibility of a fourth verbal liberal art that enables us to cultivate and critique the other three arts for our contemporary purposes.

This chapter concerns the relevance of Bakhtin's words to only one of those arts, the art of rhetoric, and it takes up that art and Bakhtin's words, too, in a context that calls into question the traditional divisions among the arts of the trivium. That context is not the post-philosophical (i.e., post-Platonic) verbal arts of rhetoric, dialectic, and grammar but the pre-philosophical verbal practice of the sophists. This practice is sometimes called "rhetoric," for that is what Plato and Aristotle called it, but its practitioners (with one exception) are not on record as calling it by that name (see Cole, Schiappa). They were more likely to call it simply logos, or "the word," as our English translations of Bakhtin's *slovo* call it, and it involved aspects of what heirs to Plato and Aristotle and the trivial arts are likely to call both rhetoric and dialectic, however anachronistic these now inescapable terms may be.

A number of late twentieth-century scholars and writers returned to the sophists, among them Robert Pirsig, who invokes them against the Aristotelian "Church of Reason," Richard Rorty, who acknowledges their anticipation of his pragmatism, Stanley Fish, who affirms their affinity with his understanding of rhetoric, Jasper Neel, who declares both himself and Derrida latter-day sophists, and Susan Jarratt, who revives sophistic moves for feminist purposes. My principal interlocutor in this essay is Michael Billig, who recreates what he calls a sophistic rhetoric to correct the limitations of current research paradigms in social psychology.[14] He joins this argument because what he calls sophistic rhetoric closely resembles what I call Bakhtin's dialogics, though Billig makes no reference to (and had no knowledge of, by his later testimony) Bakhtin when he wrote this book. This resemblance calls into question the distinctions I have made between a Bakhtinian dialogics and Aristotelian rhetoric and raises the question of Bakhtin's affinities with a sophistic understanding of verbal practice.

This way of contextualizing Bakhtin's work may require a more radical re-indexing than the context of the trivium, for students of Bakhtin have explicitly linked him to the sophists only in his interest in the novels of the second sophistic (see Morson and Emerson). Billig's version of sophistic rhetoric provides a much more comprehensive perspective from which to reconsider Bakhtin's dialogics as a post-disciplinary reassertion of discursive practices that preceded the distinction of the disciplines of rhetoric and dialectic, to see Aristotelian rhetoric as an institutionalized limitation of dialogic potentialities, and to see a new sophistic rhetoric as an attempt to recover those potentialities from the institutions that have confined them. Billig's elaboration of the varied contexts, strategies, and circumstances of rhetorical activity also permits us to interrogate Bakhtin's dialogics about the identities of arguers and the contexts of arguments.

Through much of his career Bakhtin defined the dialogic in contradistinction to a monologic rhetoric that aimed to determine its audience's responses and close off further discussion. In *Problems of Dostoevsky's Poetics*, for example, he opposed the dialogic serio-comic genres to the one-sided, serious, rational, univocal, and dogmatic classical rhetorical genres (107). In his late notebooks he wrote, "In rhetoric there is the unconditionally innocent and the unconditionally guilty; there is the complete victory and the destruction of the opponent. In dialogue the destruction of the opponent also destroys that very dialogic sphere in which the word lives" ("Extracts from 'Notes'" 182). I have referred in earlier chapters to Nina Perlina's account of Bakhtin's opposition to Victor Vinogradov's advocacy of a monologic Aristotelian rhetoric. I, too, emphasized in Chapter 2 the difference between dialogics and rhetoric along similar lines, arguing that rhetoric one-sidedly strives to silence opposition and settle issues, whereas dialogics openly attempts to provoke responses and respond to multiple provocations.

Anyone who shares Bakhtin's image of rhetoric as the one-sided, monologic counterpart to a double-voiced or multi-vocal dialogics would be provoked by Michael Billig's identification of rhetoric with the sophist Protagoras's idea of "the two-sidedness of human thinking." "According to Diogenes Laertius," Billig writes, "Protagoras was 'the first person who asserted that in every question there were two sides to the argument exactly opposite to one another.'" From this Protagorean maxim Billig further derives the position familiar to Bakhtinians that "if there are always two sides to an issue, then any single opinion, or 'individual argument' is actually, or potentially, . . . a part of a social argument." Every individual utterance, or logos, in these terms, "could be matched by a counter-statement," or what Billig calls "an 'anti-logos,'" and every logos in its turn could be understood as itself an anti-logos or response to some other contrary opinion in the community in which it is uttered. "There is no absolute refutation," Billig writes, "because every 'anti-logos' can become a 'logos' to be opposed by a further 'anti-logos.'" "'Logoi' are always haunted," he goes on, "if not by the actuality of 'antilogoi' at least by their possibility" (41–46).

If this account of Billig's sophistic rhetoric sounds like Bakhtin's dialogics with perhaps an overtone of Hegelian dialectics, the resemblance does not end here. The practice of sophistic rhetoric, Billig goes on, "was designed to ensure that, far from logos being a powerful master, it would always be opposed by a rebellious anti-logos. If, by chance, the anti-logos managed to usurp the logos, in order to become the new ruling master, it too would be likely to face the revolutionary uprising of the anti-logos, eager to tear down the authority of the powerful logos." This counter-hegemonic alignment of sophistic rhetoric not only sounds more like Bakhtin's dialogics than like his image of rhetoric; it also appears to contradict well-known sophistic claims to use the power of logos to "command obedience by replacing argument with silence," the aim that Bakhtin ascribes to rhetoric. Billig, however, argues that such claims always are made with what Bakhtin would call a loophole. The sophist Gorgias's strongest claim for the power of logos to overwhelm restraints and compel submission, for example, his "Encomium on Helen," must be read not at face value but as "a defensive argument, opposing a prosecution who talks the language of personal responsibility and who claims Helen should have countered Paris's logoi with her own anti-logoi." In addition, Gorgias's one-sided exaggeration of the power of logos contains a "built-in qualification to the seemingly sweeping generalization [that 'logos is a powerful master']: logos only works its unopposed will over the feeblest of frames." Gorgias's apparently monologic assertion of the power of logos is itself an anti-logos to the prevailing view of Helen, and it contains a dialogic qualification within itself. Far from imposing their wills through speech and teaching their students to impose their one-sided wishes on others, sophistic rhetoricians in Billig's account stress the "two-sidedness of human thinking," aim to "develop a mental two-sidedness in their pupils," and exercise "not the power to command obedience by replacing argument with silence" but rather "the power to challenge silent obedience by opening arguments." Billig's sophists would seem to share Bakhtin's appreciation of the dialogic counterpoint to would-be monologic authoritarian discourse in their valuation of "the power of 'anti-logos' to question 'logos'" (47–49, 79).

The resemblance between Billig's sophistic rhetoric and Bakhtin's dialogics does not stop at the highly general images of and attitudes toward discourse and counter-discourse I have just gone over; Billig richly elaborates the implications of these images and attitudes along several lines that clarify the ground he shares with Bakhtin, articulate it in new ways, and compel us to reconsider it. Like Bakhtin, Billig sees that his two-sided and open-ended image of discourse has consequences for the identities of the subjects who participate in discourse and the status of institutionally delimited arguments within wider histories and communities of discussion.

Like Bakhtin, Billig focuses not just on utterances but on the identities of their speakers, recognizing, as Bakhtin does, that given speakers can discover what they think and believe only through the widest possible engagement with the opposing views of others, that the same speaker may express different attitudes under the provocation of different opponents and interlocutors, and that, given the impossibility of responding to all the others whose opinions differ from our own, "we can never fully know ourselves" (254). Billig, however, also counters this open-ended and ambivalent image of the discursive subject with a counter-image of the one-sided advocate, seeking to turn all available argumentative resources to the triumph of a cause, and unlike Bakhtin's dialogic subject, Billig's rhetor embraces *both* the roles of dialogic deliberator and monologic advocate, alternating between them in response to both internal dispositions and external circumstances. Our characterizations of some interlocutors as dogmatic and others as wishy-washy marks our awareness of different argumentative dispositions, but Billig shows that even dogmatic speakers may take the other side when provoked by a more extreme statement of their views and that speakers characterized by shifting between the one hand and the other may take firm hold of a position with both hands, when tone or the other position has been forcefully and publicly voiced by another.

Indeed, Billig recognizes that the dialogic or deliberative functioning of his rhetor requires the deliberator to be advocate of the competing positions between which she or he deliberates and that the full force of advocacy requires the advocate to know the alternatives to his or her position in order to counter them. Deliberation, then, like Bakhtin's genres of Menippean satire and the novel, sets competing monologic social languages off against each other and depends for its effectiveness on the full exertion of their single-minded powers. Advocacy, a kind of monologic discourse with a loophole, asserts its position not as if it were the only one but against opposing positions, acknowledging their power as well as the controversiality of the question.

A true monologic authoritative discourse would hardly be a discourse at all but rather a failure to acknowledge or respond to contrary positions, a smug silence or simple reassertion that marked those positions as inconsequential and took the case to be closed. As Bakhtin puts it, "Only by remaining in a closed environment, one without writing or thought, completely off the maps of socio-ideological becoming, could a man fail to sense [the] activity of selecting a language and rest assured in the inviolability of his own language, the conviction that his language is predetermined" (DI 295). The apparently single-minded advocate, then, pressing a case with all available means of persuasion, must be a two-sided participant in a two-sided forum, one whose very participation in that forum is an acknowledgment of the two-sidedness of the question and a response to the other side. There is no contradiction, then, between openness and advocacy, for the real contradiction lies between both openness and advocacy, on the one hand, and ignorance and silent repression, on the other. Even monologic utterances asserted in hidden dialogue with their anti-logoi participate in the struggle of logos with anti-logos, but closed minds and heavy hands do not.

Rhetoric, as Billig presents it, is thus never just the rhetor's attempt to persuade the audience but is always also participation in controversy. Indeed, like Bakhtin, and unlike classical rhetoric in the Aristotelian vein, Billig does not confine the shaping context of discourse to the audience of that discourse but gives precedence to the "counter-opinions" that the discourse must answer. And like Bakhtin, Billig draws the consequence of this precedence for the interpretation of utterances:

> to understand the meaning of a sentence or whole discourse in an argumentative context, one should not examine merely the words within that discourse or the images in the speaker's mind at the moment of utterance. One should also consider the positions which are being criticized, or against which a justification is being mounted. Without knowing these counter-positions, the argumentative meaning will be lost. (91)

In a formalized argumentative setting like the law court or the deliberative assembly divided between opposing parties, the counter-positions from which an utterance takes its argumentative meaning are evident enough. Billig shows that even in the epideictic forum of the celebratory utterance like the funeral oration, where there is no formalized opponent, there is still "a hidden argumentative context. . . . [T]he one-sided praises of the graveside can be seen as an implicit argument against the normal ambivalent estimations of everyday life." "Contesting, contradictory parties," Billig writes, "provide the necessary social context of argumentation, whereas a neutral audience is an optional extra" (89–90).

In denying the exclusive priority of audience, Billig also calls into question the discursive finality of decisions made by authorized listeners in institutional contexts set up "to cut a debate short and to produce a socially usable final word" (108). Aristotle had delimited these institutional contexts and the three genres of rhetoric that serve them by the purposes for which these authorized listeners had assembled, but Billig places these gatherings in the context of wider and continuing social controversies. Though these institutions can limit the issues under debate, the speakers who can participate in them, the arguments that can be introduced, and the judges who can decide, and though they can use the instruments of state or corporate power to maintain order in their chambers and enforce their decisions, they cannot forestall the anti-logoi that may be provoked by their logoi or prevent oppositional words in the inner speech of others. Susan Wells, arguing that Bakhtin's image of a rhetoric in which "there is the unconditionally guilty and the unconditionally innocent" is based upon the forensic rhetoric of the law court, contends that the other genres of rhetoric are more open to "further deliberations, further praise or further blame," but even courtroom rhetoric in the wider arena of continuing social discourse cannot silence further debate (15). As Billig says of an egregiously racist South African court decision, "In the courtroom the judge might have the power to impose a final word, but such powers are unable to still the momentum of controversy, which such a judgment inevitably sets rocking" (144). Even the death penalty, final with respect to the life of the one whose sentence is carried out, may not still the controversy over the justness of the conviction and might even provide the rallying cry of a martyr's name to a political movement. This possibility of reopening settled issues may cheer us when we don't approve of the settled judgment, but it too is a double-edged sword in which our cherished court decisions may provoke counter-movements that put judges in place to reverse them.

By thus imagining the institutional contexts that define the ends of Aristotelian rhetoric in the wider give and take of continuing social controversy, Billig's sophistic rhetoric joins Bakhtin's dialogics in treating official discourse as one kind of discourse, however locally and temporally powerful, that must hold its own over time against other discourses that criticize its decisions and challenge its authority. Though the Aristotelian genres of debate in the legislative assembly, prosecution and defense in the law courts, and official celebrations in ceremonial assemblies have powerful influence in societies in which they are institutionalized, they do not exhaust the field of discourse, nor can they control the ways in which their own discourse will be represented in the genres that stylize or parody their official voices or set them off against other voices, as Dickens, for example, does in *Bleak House*. For both Billig's rhetoric and Bakhtin's dialogics, the whole field of discourse in society and history is more comprehensive and fluid than the instituted debates and ceremonies upon which Aristotelian rhetoric exclusively focuses.

The contextualizing of official rhetorical institutions and their correlative genres in the wider field of social debate does not dissolve their identities or dissipate their power, but it does open their identities to argument and their power to question. A similar contextualizing of the institutions of the trivium—the once-established verbal liberal arts—would similarly ask what counter-positions led to their widespread disestablishment, and what further anti-logoi the subsequent establishment of *those* counter-positions has provoked. Asking such questions, we might discover that Billig's sophistic rhetoric and Bakhtin's dialogics are analogous interventions into analogous argumentative situations in the modern development of the verbal arts. For Bakhtin, modern linguistics and stylistics and, for Billig, modern social psychology have appropriated substantial areas of verbal practice and proposed to subject them to scientific disciplines that govern their empirical inquiries by the logics of univocal paradigms. Such appropriations of the verbal arts by more prestigious and powerful sciences during the past three hundred years—grammar by linguistics, dialectic by logic and "scientific method," rhetoric by stylistics and psychology—aimed to make the verbal liberal arts more rigorous and reliable but have also made them narrow, abstract, and irresponsible toward the practices that, as arts, they once not only studied but taught. In this context Billig and Bakhtin revive a dialogic field of discourse broader than the modern disciplines or the ancient ones of rhetoric and dialectic in order to open fields delimited by narrow logical paradigms to ambivalent genres and attitudes that those univocal paradigms cannot comprehend. Billig and Bakhtin situate themselves in an interdisciplinary forum where rhetoric can be brought to challenge social psychology or what Bakhtin sometimes calls metalinguistics can be brought to challenge linguistics.

They revive the trivium not by reinstating its once-established disciplines but by taking up a position among them marked by the name trivium itself, the place where three roads meet. They criticize the modern sciences of language not by reestablishing the traditional arts but by reopening the public forum for the debate about verbal practice, in which those arts and sciences must contend with each other for authority and answer the questions posed by an audience of diverse specialists and generalists. What Billig calls sophistic rhetoric and what I call Bakhtin's dialogics participate in what John Bender and David Wellbery have called "rhetoricality," a modern discursive situation that no longer trusts "the ideal of scientific neutrality" but does not return simply to "the classical rhetorical tradition . . . a rule-governed domain whose procedures themselves were delimited by the institutions that organized interaction and domination in traditional European society." "Rhetoricality," they go on, "by contrast, is bound to no specific set of institutions. It manifests the groundless, infinitely ramifying character of discourse in the modern world." It is not surprising that they should also write that "Bakhtin's works . . . can be read as virtual treatises on the nature and functioning of rhetoricality" (23–25, 37). Billig's *Arguing and Thinking* could also be read as such a treatise; its reinvention of themes that we associate with Bakhtin, and that Bender and Wellbery associate with modernity in general, reveals to us that Bakhtin's and Billig's arguments participate in a debate about the genres and institutions of language whose agenda participates in wider cultural movements than their individual interests or our own.

Part II. Architectonics, Poetics, Rhetoricality, Liberal Education

7. Bakhtin's "Rough Draft"

Helen Rothschild Ewald's 1993 essay, "Waiting for Answerability: Bakhtin and Composition Studies," attempts to consolidate and redirect nearly a decade's appropriation of Bakhtin's work in composition studies. Its ambition to provide an authoritative map of and a new direction to Bakhtinian composition studies has been fulfilled in both its original place of publication and in its republication as the culminating essay in the first collection of "landmark" essays on Bakhtin, rhetoric, and writing (Farmer). While demonstrating the widespread use of Bakhtin in the field, Ewald characterizes this work as predominantly social-constructionist and heralds a new ethical emphasis that might be drawn from his earlier work on answerability. With heavy irony she deprecates how "handy" (332, 337) Bakhtin's work has been to a range of social-constructionist writers but chooses not to undertake a direct refutation of their claims. Instead, she chooses to suggest some teaching practices as part of a general reorientation of composition studies that would "focus on answerability" and examine "our specific situational responses to ethical issues that arise when we engage in writing or the teaching of writing" (345). Connecting with a cross-disciplinary revival of inquiry into ethical issues, Ewald's intervention could have been taken to herald an important ethical turn in Bakhtinian composition studies.

Ewald necessarily drew her account of Bakhtin's early themes of ethics and answerability, as she acknowledged, from Gary Saul Morson and Caryl Emerson, Slavicists who had provided the most extensive and authoritative reading of Bakhtin to date and joined vigorously in the revival of ethical issues in literary criticism. She shares not only Morson and Emerson's emphasis in *Mikhail Bakhtin: Creation of a Prosaics* on the superior authenticity and ethical seriousness of Bakhtin's early work but also their impatience with readers of his work who have confined their interest to his socially oriented theories of dialogue and carnival. Like Morson and Emerson, she eschews refutation of these readers but identifies herself with a more serious and worthy future line of inquiry into "answerability in the ethical sense of individual accountability" as opposed to answerability in the dialogic sense of responsiveness to prior utterance (339). She implies, again with her Slavicist counterparts, that earlier uses of Bakhtin in the field have been opportunistic and collectivist rather than ethical and individualist, and she directs future studies based on Bakhtin away from his mid-career interests in dialogism, heteroglossia, and carnival to his earlier, and presumably more authentic, ethical inquiries. These tones and emphases urge scholars of composition to reorient their uses of Bakhtin, as Morson and Emerson urge scholars of literature and culture to do, chastening our early enthusiasms for his work on social language from an ethical high ground that one can criticize only at the risk of seeming to condone irresponsibility. These emphases, carried across disciplinary boundaries to composition studies, weakened the claims of what was at the time and continues to be a fruitful Bakhtinian paradigm for inquiry in our field in the name of a supposedly more authentic and authoritative early Bakhtin we had not then yet known.

These emphases also depend, I will argue, upon a reading of that early Bakhtin that forces his work into ethical terms that obscure its continuity with the texts on language we have invested in. Ewald's intervention, I believe, was premature to complain in 1993 of an "egregious omission" of the topic of answerability in earlier Bakhtinian composition studies (332) and too dependent upon Emerson and Morson's tendentious reading of a text that we can now but could not then examine for ourselves. An English translation of Bakhtin's *Toward a Philosophy of the Act* appeared only the same year Ewald's article appeared, and we can now tackle this challenging fragment for ourselves, weighing our reading against those by Morson and Emerson and Ewald that preceded its appearance.

Though Ewald does not cite Morson and Emerson's first summary of *Toward a Philosophy of the Act* in *Rethinking Bakhtin,* the claims and emphases she draws from their later work are most fully developed there and need to be met in their most elaborated form. Morson and Emerson's reading of Bakhtin's text there emphatically highlights Bakhtin's " formulations . . . concerning ethics" in *Toward a Philosophy of the Act,* and they tell us with equal emphasis that he "had evidently not discovered the controlling importance of language and had not yet arrived at his concept of dialogue, when he composed this early essay" *(Rethinking* 2). If "the center of Bakhtin's concern is clearly ethics" (6), they write, "language was *not* a central category in his thought" in this period (italics in the text, 5): language plays "at best a secondary role," (6) and the treatment of "the problem of language" in this text is "just about exhaust[ed]" by a few "rather unsubstantial observations" (14–15). Ethics, then, is his "main concern" in their account, and even when Bakhtin goes beyond it to offer a theory of "all human life," it is still "treated from an ethical standpoint" (6–7), if not always from the standpoint of the "ethical as it is usually understood" (8). Morson and Emerson even separate from their verbal provenance two topics central to the argument that seem to have strong associations with speaking and writing—tone and signature. They admit tone is "a feature of language," but they consider this "almost coincidental" and insist that it belongs to "a much broader category of life" than the linguistic. "For Bakhtin," they write, "acts have tone; speech has tone by virtue of being a form of action." They do not associate the topic of signature with writing at all. Their briefer summary in *Creation of a Prosaics*, the text Ewald cites, declares that "the verbal arts were originally quite peripheral to [Bakhtin's] project. The crucial concept was the *act,* which Bakhtin divided into acts of thought, of feeling, and of external deed" *(Prosaics* 69). These representations portray this early Bakhtin text as uninterested in, even opposed to, the emphases and topics that first engaged composition and rhetoric scholars, and many literary scholars as well, with Bakhtin's later work. Their emphases would discourage us from approaching *Toward a Philosophy of the Act* to pursue our inquiries into language, dialogue, and writing; instead they would lead us to approach it for ethical enlightenment, even chastisement, with our earlier interests in social language humbly suspended.

My argument here will contest this reading of Bakhtin's earliest work on both counts. I will argue first that it is *not* an ethical treatise in its own terms and that it is not helpful to represent it as one. *Historical* is a better key term than *ethical* for this work, but neither term encompasses its attempt to characterize a participative consciousness prior to all disciplines of knowledge. Second, I will show that *Toward a Philosophy of the Act* does not give the act precedence over the utterance but that it makes the utterance ultimately paradigmatic of the act. Finally, I will show that this fragment offers highly charged visions of action as publication of the written word and of established culture as prohibitive of authorship, visions that resonate with and help situate more familiar visions in composition and rhetoric.

Simply stated, my first claim is that *Toward a Philosophy of the Act* is not a treatise on ethics but a treatise on an unfamiliar field of inquiry Bakhtin calls first philosophy, architectonics, or, not much more helpfully, the phenomenology of participative consciousness. Bakhtin's inquiry into this field resists and criticizes in turn each of the three disciplines of the Kantian triad, epistemology, aesthetics, and ethics, insofar as each purports to offer theoretical universals under which individual cognitions, judgments, and obligations can be subsumed and fully accounted for,[15] and he sets against all of them what he calls participative consciousness—the uniquely situated, thoughtful, historically actual act of the individual, actual, living participant in the "unique unity of ongoing Being" (2). The abundance of adverbs and adjectives Bakhtin uses to characterize this consciousness marks the difficulty of distinguishing it from more familiar objects of inquiry. Struggling to define concrete actions of unique agents against the imperious universalizing laws of the disciplines including ethics, Bakhtin emphatically and repetitively, hyper-adjectivally, points to the unique, embodied "real, actual, thinking human being" (6) situated as a participant in life in relation to the world and other human beings. He makes this participating person the starting point for first philosophy prior to the disciplines of epistemology, aesthetics, and ethics. Bakhtin resists here, as he will always resist, the promotion of ideas independent of their thinkers to a position over and above the position in which embodied thinking persons think and articulate those ideas, ethical ideas being no more separable from the activities of their thinkers than cognitive or aesthetic ones.

But the pressures of Bakhtin's inquiry to get to activities and contexts prior to the disciplines of epistemology, aesthetics, and ethics takes its toll on both Bakhtin and his readers. He tries to modify the familiar terms of those disciplines, on the one hand, making the road hard going, and he slips into using their familiar terms to mean unfamiliar things, on the other, tempting readers to slip back into inappropriate understandings. The expectations shaped by the Kantian disciplines repeatedly tempt both his readers and Bakhtin himself to interpret first philosophy in their terms. Morson and Emerson almost consistently and Bakhtin occasionally identify first philosophy with the discipline of ethics or moral philosophy, where the "ought" belongs in the Kantian scheme of disciplines. Although Bakhtin sometimes slips into calling first philosophy moral philosophy (56), the argumentative energy of his fragment goes into *distinguishing* first philosophy from ethics (21–27), whereas the argumentative energy of Morson and Emerson's interpretation of the fragment goes into *identifying* its topic with ethics, only rarely distinguished from "ethics as it is usually understood." As Ewald's appropriation of their reading shows, their assimilation of Bakhtin's argument to one of the terms it attempts to modify and transcend encourages reduction of his unfamiliar line of thought to more familiar, habitual terms.

Such reductions are a risk in all explanations, but if I were compelled to choose a familiar epithet to explain Bakhtin's first philosophy by linking it to a more familiar domain of understanding, I would call it "historical" *(istoricheskoi)* rather than "ethical" and argue that Bakhtin himself makes much more use of this epithet than of the one Morson and Emerson have chosen to highlight. Witness the phrases translated as "a given act/activity and the historical actuality of its being" (2), "a performed act . . . [and] the whole concrete historicalness of its performance" (3), "the individual-historical aspect [of a thought] (the author, the time, the circumstances, and the moral unity of his life)" (3), "the historically individual, actual cognitional act" (6), "once-occurrent living historicalness" (7), "historically valuative uniqueness" (8), "living historicity" (8), "the answerable and individual historical act" (9), "the actual historicity of Being" (10), or "the historical being of actual cognition" (33). There are yet more instances. The epithet "historical" helps Bakhtin emphasize the concrete situatedness of participative consciousness among times, places, and persons with proper names, but it also creates problems for him with the expectations created by the *discipline* of history. Thus at the very beginning of this fragment he declares that "historical description-exposition" and "discursive theoretical thinking" both "establish a fundamental split between the content or sense of a given act/activity and the historical actuality of its being, the actual and once-occurrent experiencing of it" (1–2). So history as the discipline of historical description-exposition is separated from the concrete historical actuality of participative consciousness just as theory is, and the discipline of history will create interference with Bakhtin's understanding of historically situated consciousness just as the discipline of ethics interferes with his understanding of the act. Bakhtin nevertheless repeatedly risks the use of the epithet "historical" in *Toward a Philosophy of the Act,* but Morson and Emerson do not acknowledge it in their account of this text, and when they discuss historicity in Bakhtin, other texts are their sources. Their emphasis on Bakhtin's ethical inquiries in *Toward a Philosophy of the Act* goes along with their declaration that the text exemplifies his "lifelong dislike of Marxism" *(Rethinking* 2), but his extensive emphasis on historicity and the historical bring him closer to the historical materialism from which they attempt to separate him. His one remark on historical materialism in this text—not noted as far as I can observe in *Rethinking Bakhtin* or *Creation of a Prosaics* (part of it may not have been available in the text Morson and Emerson used)—is not hostile but more admiring than critical. It begins by acknowledging the attractiveness of historical materialism, "despite all its defects and defaults," to participative consciousness because of historical materialism's effort "to build its world in such a way as to provide a place in it for the performance of determinate, concretely historical, actual deeds; a striving and action-performing consciousness can actually orient itself in the world of historical materialism" (20). He does not choose in this context to develop fully his critique of historical materialism but declares that "what is important for us, however, is that it does accomplish [the] departure [from within the most abstract theoretical world and its entry into the living world of the actually performed deed], and that this constitutes its strength, the reason for its success" (20). Its besetting sin, named but not elaborated here, is shared, he is careful to note, with other attempts at formulating participative consciousness through the ages: "a methodological indiscrimination of what is given and what is set as a task, of what *is* and what *ought* to be" (20). We will return to Bakhtin's elaboration of this distinction later in *Toward a Philosophy of the Act*, where historical materialism is no longer explicitly in question; what needs to be said first is that no other school of contemporary thought is given credit for getting closer to what Bakhtin is after in his account of participative consciousness than historical materialism. His use of the epithet "historical" leads us to acknowledge not his dislike of Marxist thought but his affinity with it.[16]

It would not do, however, to conclude this line of argument by saying that *Toward a Philosophy of the Act* should be understood as a historical rather than an ethical treatise, for we would have to add again, not history as it is usually understood. Bakhtin is not concerned with disinterestedly interpreting past actions but with interestedly describing a phenomenology of action in general that would apply in past, present, or future, and his understanding of action is not external and disinterested but participatory and interested. Indeed, the hardest thing to get our minds around in *Toward a Philosophy of the Act*, shaped as we are by the cultural disciplines Bakhtin criticizes, is that it views all action, thought, and utterance as necessarily participatory and interested. Cognition, appreciation, and action; knowing, judging, and doing; science, art, and politics are all engaged with value from the start, all bound up with an "ought" not specifically moral, with "that which is yet-to-be-achieved" (33). The epithet "historical" gives us the concrete situatedness of what Bakhtin is getting at and the epithet "ethical" points toward how our participation in such concrete situations is saturated with values that oblige us to respond, but neither epithet alone nor both together, as they are usually understood, give us the predisciplinary or extradisciplinary reality Bakhtin is trying to get at.

Bakhtin, then, does not present *Toward a Philosophy of the Act* as a work about ethics, and we lose more than we gain in understanding it if we treat it as one. The question that remains for those of us interested in the verbal arts is whether it has anything to do with the emphasis on language as utterance that has been so fruitful to composition studies in Bakhtin's later works. I have already cited Morson and Emerson's depreciation of the importance of language in the argument of *Toward a Philosophy of the Act*. Their emphasis, it should be noted, is itself provoked by Holquist and Clark's earlier account of this text as already containing Bakhtin's later ideas on these topics. Morson and Emerson have denied that it has much to say about these matters to make room for a story in which Bakhtin's thought develops from early ethical inquiries to mid-career inquiries into language and literature and back again to those ethical preoccupations. I see closer connections between this first inquiry and the mid-career ones, though I do not see Bakhtin's later ideas already worked out here. *Toward a Philosophy of the Act* develops concepts the later works elaborate and raises questions that the later works answer, but it does not already have the answers.

Two points need to be made against the background of Morson and Emerson's account of the argument. First, Bakhtin's conception of the act includes not only "acts of thought, of feeling, and of external deed" *(Prosaics* 69), as Morson and Emerson claim at one point, but also *utterances* as kinds of acts, as they elsewhere sometimes recognize *(Rethinking* 14, 15). Second, Bakhtin's conception of the act is modeled on and inconceivable without the utterance. Tone is not coincidentally a feature of language derived from the properties of acts, as Morson and Emerson claim; it is a feature of language that he uses to define acts and make them intelligible.

First, then, Bakhtin's enumerations of what is included as an act include the word or utterance. He writes, "A performed act is active in the actual unique product it has produced (in an actual, real deed, in an uttered word, in a thought that has been thought . . .)" (26–27). Or here, where he adds "words" to the list of acts Morson and Emerson enumerate, he declares:

> The moment constituted by the performance of thoughts, feelings, *words,* practical deeds is an actively answerable attitude that I myself assume—an emotional volitional attitude toward a state of affairs in its entirety, in the context of actual unitary and once-occurrent life. (37, italics added)

This inclusion of the utterance as a kind of act means that whatever is said of the act can also be said of the utterance, which, it therefore follows, must be understood not as an instance of a theoretical generalization but as a response to a concrete situation. Here we are close to the dialogic, as Morson and Emerson at one point recognize when they write that "human will, like the dialogic utterance, is 'creatively active in the act, but in no sense does it generate a norm, a general proposition'" (14). An utterance, as one kind of act, responds then to *"these* individual unique persons . . . , *this* sky and *this* earth and *these* trees, and the time . . . , [and] the value, the actually and concretely affirmed value of these persons and objects" (30). The well-known scene in the Voloshinov essay "Discourse in Life and Discourse in Art"—where the word *well* uttered by one man to another in a room in Russia in May resolves their common knowledge and evaluation of their hero, the weather—comes to mind as an illustration of the utterance understood as a situated act.

There are other rich parallels between *Toward a Philosophy of the Act* and that Voloshinov essay; the one that helps develop my second point is that *intonation,* a key term, perhaps *the* key term, in both works, inescapably links the act to the utterance. The Voloshinov essay argues that intonation synthesizes word, referent, and evaluation in the utterance. Intonation, according to this essay, is not in the words as linguistics isolates them in a dictionary but in the speaker's utterance of words in concrete situations, in which they always express an evaluation of the referent and a potential for action toward it.[17] A note in *Toward a Philosophy of the Act* also recognizes the provenance of intonation as "the actually pronounced word" that "cannot avoid being intonated, for intonation follows from the very fact of its being pronounced" (32). To speak of the *act,* then, as having intonation, as Bakhtin does in this essay, is either to understand the act in terms belonging to the utterance or to think of acts as necessarily accompanied by actual or implied utterances that express their intonation. I think Bakhtin does both.

Bakhtin's most extensive account of language in *Toward a Philosophy of the Act* (30–37) comes up in answer to the question, how do the participants in acts or deeds orient themselves toward and understand their acts or deeds? "Does . . . he understand it logically?" Bakhtin asks rhetorically. "Not at all," he answers. The participant in the deed understands it concretely in relation to a specific situation of persons and objects and the "actually and concretely affirmed value of these persons and objects" (30). This "event as a whole," he goes on, "cannot be transcribed in theoretical terms," but that does not mean that the participant's understanding of it cannot be expressed at all. That understanding is not ineffable; it can be "uttered clearly and distinctly," because "language is much more adapted to giving utterance precisely to [the concrete] truth [of the act that the performer of the act sees and hears and experiences and understands]" than to giving utterance to "the abstract moment in its logical purity" (31). Again

I must take exception to Morson and Emerson's emphases in *Rethinking Bakhtin* where they treat this passage as isolated and unsubstantial (15). On the contrary, it opens a line of argument that both defends this account of language and explains that it is essential to any account of the act. Bakhtin first argues that language is suited to expressing the participant's understanding of the performed act because historically language developed to serve that function and only later was turned to abstract logical purposes. He goes on to elaborate the claim that "the expression of the performed act" requires "the entire fullness of the word," which includes "the word as concept," "the word as image," and "the intonation of the word" that expresses the "emotional-volitional aspect" of the act.

Here we arrive at a critical juncture in Bakhtin's argument. Intonation, understood as the expression of "the emotional-volitional aspect" of the act, unites the given and the yet-to-be achieved, the distinction Bakhtin says historical materialism gets wrong. This distinction marks two aspects of any event or object actually experienced by consciousness, the recognition of what is given and the desire or sense of obligation felt with respect to it. Bakhtin radically claims that nothing can come to consciousness that is not taken in *both* these ways, that there is no indifferent or disinterested consciousness. He writes, "An object that is absolutely indifferent, totally finished, cannot be something one becomes actually conscious of; . . . pure givenness cannot be experienced actually" (32). What comes to consciousness is also necessarily experienced as something that carries a value, that needs to be opposed or cherished, resisted or affirmed. All objects of consciousness are, as it were, not just topics but heroes.[18]

Intonation of "the living word, the full word" is the *expression,* uttered or actively thought, of the *ought* as such: "the word does not merely designate an object as a present-on-hand entity, but also expresses by its intonation my valuative attitude toward the object, toward what is desirable or undesirable in it, and, in doing so, sets in motion that which is yet-to-be-determined about it" (32–33). If, as Bakhtin writes, "emotional-volitional tone is an inalienable moment of the actually performed act" (33), and if emotional-volitional tone is expressed in the intonation of the living, full word, then expression, actual or thought, in the living, full word is an inalienable moment of the actually performed act. Tone in language is not coincidental and subordinate to the act, as Morson and Emerson claim, but essential and inalienable, then, and it is not accidental that when Bakhtin comes a few pages later to declare the "point of origin of the answerable deed and of all the categories of the concrete, once-occurrent, and compellent ought" (40), he does so in terms of the uttered word. At that point of origin is the implied declaration, "I, too, *exist* . . . actually—in the whole and assume the obligation to say *this* word"

(40). Here the paradigmatic act through which I take my place in Being and acknowledge its inescapable "compellent ought" is the utterance of a particular word the intonation of which expresses that obligation and makes my act intelligible. An act without an intonated utterance implied or declared is no act at all, and an utterance, implied or declared, is already an act. It is noteworthy that when, at the end of the fragment, Bakhtin offers to provide "a representation, a description of the actual concrete architectonic of value-governed experiencing of the world," he illustrates it with an emotionally intoned poetic utterance that enacts a speaker's futile attempt to claim fulfillment of a promise from a loved one who has died. This illustration from the "world of aesthetic seeing" is "in its concreteness and its permeatedness with emotional-volitional tone . . . closer than any of the abstract cultural worlds (taken in isolation) to the unitary and unique world of the performed act" (61).

The view of the utterance as act and the act bound up with utterance in *Toward a Philosophy of the Act* is reiterated in Bakhtin's later and more explicitly dialogic and language-centered work. In his analysis of the motif of the speaking person in the novel and other genres in "Discourse in the Novel," Bakhtin claims that the action of a character in a novel "is always highlighted by ideology, is always harnessed to the character's discourse (even if that discourse is as yet only a potential discourse)" (DI 334), and he claims that it is "impossible to reveal, through a character's acts and through these acts alone, his ideological position and the ideological world at its heart, without representing discourse. . . . [I]t is impossible to represent an alien ideological world adequately without first permitting it to sound, without having first revealed the discourse peculiar to it" (DI 335). What he calls publicistic discourse,

> when it analyzes an act[,] uncovers the verbal motifs, the point of view in which it is grounded, . . . formulates such acts in words, providing them the appropriate emphases—ironic, indignant, and so on. This does not mean, of course, that the rhetoric behind the word forgets that there are deeds, acts, a reality outside words. But such rhetoric has always to do with social man, whose most fundamental gestures are made meaningful ideologically through the word, or directly embodied in words. (DI 353)

In law, ethics, and politics, he goes on, "an independent, responsible and active discourse is *the* fundamental indicator of an ethical, legal, and political human being" (DI 349–50).[19]

The view of language elaborated in Bakhtin's later works, then, is theoretically central to *Toward a Philosophy of the Act,* but is there anything distinctive in the way Bakhtin thinks about the act in his earliest fragment that still has bearings for our interests in language and writing? Is there anything about emphasizing the act as utterance and the utterance as act that reaccentuates or reconceptualizes what we have learned from the later texts? Here I think Morson and Emerson point the way in their remark in *Prosaics* that when we "compare the idea of the architectonic act with the later (and more familiar) 'dialogic word,' what is remarkable about the act is its high degree of closure" and the relatively unproblematic way in which the author of the act signs for it (70). To think of the act as authored, not just responsively performed, as Bakhtin does when he speaks of the "actual act/deed and its author" is to evoke the metaphor of the act not just as utterance but as written work signed for and owned up to by an author. The language in which Bakhtin develops this metaphor seems sometimes even to specify the genre of the work in question as if it were the definitive treatise and not the novel, for Bakhtin imagines the answerable act as

> a final result or summation, an all-round definitive conclusion . . . [that] concentrates, correlates, and resolves within a unitary and unique and, this time, *final context* both the sense and the fact, the universal and the individual, the real and the ideal, for everything enters into the composition of its answerable motivation. The performed act constitutes a going out *once and for all* from within possibility as such into *what is once-occurrent*. (28–29)

It is not hard to imagine such a grandly conceived "composition" as a version of the "fair copy," through which one can effect a "unique act or deed" and "get out of the realm of endless draft versions and rewrite one's life once and for all," that Bakhtin contrasts, later in the fragment, to the "rough draft of possible actualization or an unsigned document that does not obligate anyone to anything" (44). I imagine in the tone of this latter passage its twenty-four- to twenty-six-year-old author's wish to "get out of the realm of endless draft versions," his frustration with his own work in progress, and his desire to make a claim and name with a finished work, as I imagine in the former passage a fantasy of conclusiveness and comprehensiveness, of magisterial summa writing, that would likely frustrate almost any would-be treatise-writer who tried to live up to it.

What seems hyperbolic here—surprising from the point of view of the later Bakhtin, and, I think, appealing from the point of view of Morson and Emerson's ethical reading of the text—is the finality of the act as presented in these passages, its repeated "once-and-for-all" character. Is this somehow the last act, the act that sums up all other acts, the act to end all acts? It sounds as if it were and as if, with its face turned first to all previously inconclusive and nondefinitive acts, it now concluded and finished them, and then with its face toward all subsequent acts it defied them to add anything, to do anything more or say another word. With our ears tuned to the later Bakhtin, this is the specter of the monologic authoritative word that tries to finish off the need for further words, and we are right to be puzzled if this is what we are finding in these key passages in *Toward a Philosophy of the Act*.

I do not believe, however, that this is the right way to read these passages. What does Bakhtin's hero, the act, turn its face toward that makes it come forward with such a triumphant conclusiveness in these passages? Not, I think, toward prior or subsequent *acts* by the author of this act or by others. Rather, the act turns toward the time of deliberation in which many acts would have been possible, the time of not yet having decided what to do or say, and its triumph is to have reached a decision. Thus in the earlier passage, the "answerable act surmounts anything hypothetical, for the answerable act is the actualization of a decision—inescapably, irremediably, irrevocably" (28). In the later passage, the fair copy ends the deliberation among rough drafts among "unacknowledged possible variant[s] of once-occurrent being" and expresses a " once-occurrent affirmation or non-affirmation of a possible sense or meaning" (44).

What is at stake here is not getting the last word but *saying something*, actualizing an answerable act or word and waiting for the answers to it rather than languishing in indecision among contingent possibilities of action and utterance. It is not that the paper we submit has said everything there is to say on the topic, or that it will leave the teacher or our colleagues with nothing to say in response, but that we have decided it is finished and ready to submit with our name on it, the "endless" rough drafts over. We have, to shift genres, put the letter in the mail and stopped agonizing over it; rather than preempting a response, we at last await one. The intonation of "endless" marks Bakhtin's desire to end deliberations, his frustration with deciding among possibilities, his wish to take a stand and take part, just as the intonation of the emphatic "inescapably, irremediably, irrevocably" in the earlier passage declares a desire for finality that is genuinely final. Having declared ourselves, we cannot not have done so. Even if we try to take back what we have done or said, all we can do is retract something already done and said; we cannot not have said it. If we say something else, it will be in the context of already having said what we said in the first place. If we say what we already said again, we will be reaffirming it or repeating ourselves, never doing the same thing in saying it that we did the first time.

In a phenomenology of participation such as Bakhtin is working out here, the passages I have been examining stand out as highly charged, vivid, and strongly intonated. In them Bakhtin participatively, with intonation that expresses his volition and evaluation, declares for joining in ongoing being over standing on the sidelines or sitting indecisively at the table. He declares his desire to make a *published* intervention, not to continue drafting indefinitely. The hyperbole of his declarations for participation is just what he is prepared to answer for against the background of both his own situation as an un-debuted author and his diagnosis of a contemporary cultural crisis, in which the weight of what is already known and established threatens to preempt individual authorship altogether.

In Bakhtin's stark account of this crisis, "the world of culture and the world of life" "have absolutely no communication with each other and are mutually impervious" (2). The world of life—the world of our active creating, cognizing, doing—does not recognize itself in the objectified cultural world of written knowledge and does not know that world as one produced by activities of living thinkers, creators, and cognizers. Published knowledge, moral laws, and prior aesthetic judgments are authoritative and alien, purporting to define or regulate all areas of our activities without revealing themselves as produced by those activities and subject to change through their continuation. They are embodiments of what, in the section of "Discourse in the Novel" most widely cited by compositionists, Bakhtin will later call authoritative discourse.

This crisis is not resolved but exacerbated, according to Bakhtin, by efforts from within the world of culture to impose "cultural values-in-themselves" on a living consciousness, which would then "adapt to them, affirm them for itself." In this conservative project, any living consciousness finds cultural values already on hand and given to it, and its whole self-activity amounts to acknowledging their validity for itself.

> Having acknowledged once the value of scientific truth . . . , I am henceforth subjected to its immanent law: the one who says *a* must also say *b* and *c,* and thus all the way to the end of the alphabet. The one who said *one,* must say *two:* he is drawn by the immanent necessity of a series. (35)

Bakhtin compares this view of culture's relation to individual consciousness, in which "at one time man actually established all cultural values and now is bound by them," with Hobbes's political theory, in which "the power of the people . . . is exercised at one time only . . . ; after that the people become slaves of their own free decision" (35). Or, as he later puts it describing authoritative discourse, "It is, so to speak, the word of the fathers. Its authority was already *acknowledged* in the past. It is *prior* discourse. It is therefore not a question of choosing it from among other possible discourses that are its equal" (DI 342).

Bakhtin rejects such conservative projects to impose an already evaluated culture as "radically unsound" and denies that "an actual consciousness to be unitary must reflect in itself the systematic unity of culture along with an appropriate emotional-volitional coefficient" that reflects a proper appreciation of authoritative cultural values. He affirms, on the contrary, that

> the emotional-volitional tone and an actual valuation do not relate at all to content as such in its isolation, but relate to it in its correlation with me within the once-occurrent event of Being encompassing us. An emotional-volitional affirmation acquires its tone not in the context of culture; all of culture as a whole is integrated in the unitary and once-occurrent context of life in which I participate. . . . Any universally valid value becomes *actually* valid only in an individual context. . . . This is not a universal valuation of an object independently of that unique context in which it is given to me at the given moment, but expresses the whole truth [*pravda*] of the entire situation as a unique moment in what constitutes an ongoing event. (35–36)

The integration of culture and life for Bakhtin is thus not to be achieved through the authoritative imposition of given cultural values on members of the culture and their cognitive and affective conformity to those values but rather through the acts in which uniquely situated participants in culture evaluate from their distinctive concrete positions the cultural values on offer to them in emotional-volitional tones expressive of the whole truth of their entire situations. Compositionists will recognize these acts as constitutive of what Bakhtin later calls internally persuasive discourse.

But such individual participative acts are just what are threatened with extinction or preemption in Bakhtin's hyperbolic vision of the hypertrophy of autonomous objective culture and the atrophy of authorship. The massive accumulation of authoritative knowledge provides what Bakhtin calls an alibi for Being that we might also see as an alibi for nonparticipation or an alibi for not writing. Morson and Emerson elaborate Bakhtin's account of this alibi in terms suggestive for our purposes (and suggestive of Bakhtin's theory of the utterance). They write:

> It is quite common, Bakhtin notes, for scholars to take knowledge itself as their alibi for being. . . . Bakhtin does not use a linguistic analogy to explain what he means, . . . but he seems to have in mind the sense that *znanie* [knowledge] is like a grammatical paradigm with many choices, whereas *priznanie* [acknowledgment] involves an actual choice among these alternatives, a bringing of knowledge toward one by attaching it to *(pri-)* one's self. . . . Real responsible

action, then, involves a choice among the possibilities made available by knowledge. In the world of unacknowledged knowledge by itself, there is no "I" and no true responsibility: "The world of meaningful content is infinite and self-sufficient, *its* power to signify makes *me* unnecessary, my act for it is accidental. It is the realm of endless questions. . . . Here it is impossible to start anything, every beginning will be arbitrary; it will drown in the sea of [possible but not actual] meaning. It does not have a center, and provides no principle of choice: everything that is, could both be and not be, or could be differently." *(Rethinking* 18)

The passage Morson and Emerson quote here from Bakhtin voices the anxiety of the non-participating writer, the one for whom knowledge is other and self-sufficient, the one who, not choosing a question to which his or her knowledge can be made to answer or a language in which to write, wanders in "the realm of endless questions," shuffling note cards in vain, in danger of drowning in a sea of meaning. But in the context of Bakhtin's argument, this writer is no inadequate or pathological or even inexperienced writer suffering from writer's block but a paradigmatic case of someone experiencing the crisis of consciousness in modern culture. In that culture, all must write against the backdrop of disciplines whose accumulated knowledge demands their acquiescence and threatens to silence or preempt them.

Bakhtin's whole argument in *Toward a Philosophy of the Act* situates itself with reference to this extreme vision of cultural crisis, and our ultimate response to his argument depends on our participation or nonparticipation in this vision. It is a familiar vision that resonates with Shelley's romantic vision of the "cultivation of the mechanical arts [and of scientific knowledge] in a degree disproportioned to the presence of the creative faculty, which is the basis of all knowledge" (503) and with T. S. Eliot's modernist vision, nearly contemporary with Bakhtin's, of Prufrock in crisis among "a hundred indecisions / And . . . a hundred visions and revisions" unable to "say just what I mean" (4, 7). It is also a vision that resonates with widely shared images of paradigmatic situations in composition studies—that of the freshman writer facing the accumulated knowledge of the university, of the novice writer in the disciplines facing their bodies of specialized knowledge, and even of our own field's academic writers facing the knowledge of the established disciplines from which we draw many of our concepts and methods.

This vision of cultural crisis underwrites a heroic existential narrative of self-assertive self-creation in the face of overwhelming odds. In it we risk and ask our students to risk writing about what we and they don't know enough about, and we make ourselves answerable as we would have them be answerable for acts of appropriation and evaluation beyond our and their expert competence. In this narrative, though we sometimes call ourselves a new discipline, we most often seek out spaces we call predisciplinary or postdisciplinary or interdisciplinary or antidisciplinary or transdisciplinary, where we cultivate our own and our students' "historically valuative uniqueness" (8) by actively appropriating for our own purposes the knowledge that the "real" disciplines would impose upon us and our students. In opposition to what we, like Bakhtin, perceive to be the dominant disciplinary regime of our time, we foster an outgunned guerrilla enterprise that we cannot surrender but cannot impose as a discipline on our students, because once it is just another imposable discipline it is no longer the active extradisciplinary intervention we want it to be (see Chapter 11).

And within the institutional context of the modern university, this heroic narrative provokes a counter-narrative. Where disciplines dominate and impose their catechisms on novices and admit only advanced students to the active work that lets students become authorities, a project that encourages beginning students to seize the authority to participate in the ongoing intellectual work and write the internally persuasive discourse of that participation will seem premature, irresponsible, shallow, undisciplined. There will be calls to subordinate it to recognized disciplines—to grammar, to classical rhetoric, or now, to an ethics that can keep the inescapably transgressive energies of intellectual appropriation and participation from going too far. It is not surprising that conservative Bakhtinians and compositionists who share their anxieties about the impious energies his later works have released might want to rein them in and might hope to find the ethical reins they desire in Bakhtin's own texts like *Toward a Philosophy of the Act*.

That text will not, I have argued, sustain their desire to authorize, in Bakhtin's name, an ethical circumscription of promiscuous verbal productivity, but it does celebrate and advocate a participation in that productivity that it does not enable. Focused as it is on distinguishing participatory consciousness from disciplinary knowledge and arguing that the former is fundamental to the latter, *Toward a Philosophy of the Act* offers no ways to mediate between the novice who would participate vitally in a discipline and the expert who would impose an inert discipline on the novice. Read as a fragmentary treatise on the philosophy of education, *Toward a Philosophy of the Act* poses a problem of art's (and science's) alienation from life without offering any way to reintegrate disciplinary knowledge into life work. The treatise sharpens the opposition between objective culture and the living subject, "the whole boundless world in its entirety that is capable of being cognized objectively, and my small personal life" (50), and magnifies the importance of the living subject's personal life compared to that of the intellectual world, but it does not point the way to an integrated *intellectual life.*

Toward a Philosophy of the Act could be said in these terms to recapitulate a fundamental opposition that composition studies repeatedly acts out, even as most Bakhtinian compositionists resist it, an opposition in which heroic liberated subjectivity, like that Peter Elbow celebrates, sets itself against academic disciplinary authority, like that David Bartholomae insistently points to—though Bartholomae invites novices to seize it. The debate between these scholars, who have long commanded the attention of the field, turns at the level of slogan between "writing without teachers" and "writing with teachers." As Bartholomae frames both his own position and Elbow's, "Students write in a space defined by all the writing that has preceded them, writing the academy insistently draws together: in the library, in the reading list, in the curriculum. . . . And yet, it is obvious that there are many classrooms where students are asked to imagine that they can clear out a space to write on their own, to express their own thoughts and ideas, not to reproduce those of others."[20] Bakhtin's fragmentary first treatise clarifies the stakes in this constitutive debate for composition and rhetoric and situates it as a moment in a longstanding and significant philosophical debate. It also lets us see Bakhtin himself, in his earliest work, closer to Elbow's position, while the Bakhtin we know from the later, more familiar work is closer to Bartholomae. In that later work, he also finds ways out of repeatedly reenacting the opposition between undisciplined life and disciplinary art (and science).

Toward a Philosophy of the Act clarifies the problem to which some of Bakhtin's later work can be taken as offering solutions, and that problem turns out to be one that compositionists continue to engage with benefit of his later work. His earliest work offers to composition studies, and to the many other scholarly inquiries that have found Bakhtin's later work productive, not an ethical alternative to the later social models but a philosophical formulation of the question to which those later works offer a variety of answers. *Toward a Philosophy of the Act* helps composition studies understand how its own participation in the large intellectual debates of this century has shaped its disciplinary debates and narratives, preparing it to find Bakhtin's work, early and late, pertinent and productive.

8. Architectonics, Rhetoric, and Poetics in the Bakhtin School's Early Phenomenological and Sociological Texts

The Bakhtin School's relevance to poetics and rhetoric has most often been gauged from the perspective of Bakhtin's works on the novel, *Problems of Dostoevsky's Poetics* and "Discourse in the Novel," where both rhetoric and poetry are explicitly mentioned and denigrated as foils to his full-blown dialogic theories of discourse.[21] His earlier unfinished works concerned with what he calls "architectonics" have provided less appealing starting places for investigation of the verbal arts. Morson and Emerson, among his most authoritative expositors, have discouraged pursuing such investigations, claiming that the early works were concerned with ethical and philosophical issues that overshadowed his later and less authentic interest in language and the verbal arts. I have shown in Chapter VII that they overstate the importance of ethics in his earliest fragment, *Toward a Philosophy of the Act,* and understate the importance of language, which is fundamental even to this early work. In that chapter, however, I did not consider what difference it might make to read this work and others by Bakhtin and Voloshinov related to it for what they add to our understanding of poetics and rhetoric. I propose to undertake that task in this chapter and to show that a fundamental rethinking of rhetoric and poetry is possible in their terms.

The task faces a difficulty at the outset, because "architectonics" is an uncommon term that Bakhtin himself struggles to define and defines differently in different contexts, always against the grain of its authoritative provenance in Kant's *Critique of Pure Reason*—the definition that has shaped most dictionary definitions of it. For Kant, "an architectonic . . . [is] the art of constructing systems. A systematic unity is what raises ordinary knowledge to the rank of science, that is, makes a system out of a mere aggregate of knowledge." A system for Kant is "the unity of manifold modes of knowledge under one idea. This idea is the concept provided by reason—of the form of a whole—in so far as the concept determines *a priori* not only the scope of its manifold content, but also the position which the parts occupy relative to one another" (653).

Bakhtin's most explicit formulation of a definition of architectonics echoes but radically transforms Kant's; Bakhtin *opposes* the architectonic to the systematic (TPA 72). He writes in "Author and Hero in Aesthetic Activity," "Architectonics—as the intuitionally necessary, nonfortuitous disposition and integration of concrete, unique parts and moments into a consummated whole—can exist only around a given human being as a hero" (AA 209). Bakhtin preserves the disposition of parts in a unified whole in his definition, but the parts are concrete and unique, not abstract and conceptually subordinate; there is necessity holding the parts together in both definitions, but it is rational and *a priori* in Kant, intuitional in Bakhtin. A rational concept stands at the head of a Kantian architectonic, while a valued hero stands at the center of Bakhtin's. Mathematical knowledge exemplifies Kant's architectonic; the "world of aesthetic seeing" in a lyric poem exemplifies Bakhtin's.

Bakhtin appropriates Kant's term to his own purposes, one of which is sharply to differentiate his position from Kant's. Bakhtin's account of "participative consciousness" in *Toward a Philosophy of the Act*, as I have shown in the previous chapter, sets itself against Kant's theoretical architectonic, against the priority of systematic knowledge and the subordination of our cognitive, ethical and aesthetic experience to first principles. Bakhtin tries to open space prior to the disciplines that systematize those principles for a "first" or "moral" philosophy that gives an account of "the architectonic of the actual world of the performed act or deed—the world actually experienced, and not the merely thinkable world." "It is this concrete architectonic of the actual world of the performed act that moral philosophy has to describe," he writes,

> *not* the abstract scheme but the concrete plan or design of the world of a unitary and once-occurrent act or deed, the basic concrete moments of its construction and their mutual disposition. These basic moments are I-for-myself, the other-for-me, and I-for-the-other. All

> the values of actual life and culture are arranged around the basic architectonic points of the actual world of the performed act or deed: scientific values, aesthetic values, political values (including both ethical and social values), and, finally, religious values. (TPA 54)

He sets out an account of "the common moments or constituents" of concrete act-performing consciousness—"I, the other, and I-for-the-other"—as prior to, more fundamental than, and a necessary condition for the creation and re-creation of the disciplines that cultivate systematic knowledges, and he calls "architectonic" not the rationalized forms of those knowledges but the "concrete plan or design" of once-occurrent acts that produce them.

Poetry, as I have said, provides Bakhtin's example in *Toward a Philosophy of the Act*

> of the actual, concrete architectonic of value-governed experiencing of the world—not with an analytical foundation at the head, but with that actual concrete center (both spatial and temporal) from which valuations, assertions, and deeds come forth or issue, and where the constituent members are real objects, interconnected by concrete event-relations in the once-occurrent event of Being (in this context logical relations constitute but one moment along with the concrete spatial, temporal, and emotional-volitional moments). (TPA 61)

"The world of aesthetic seeing" exemplified in the lyric poem "in its concreteness and its permeatedness with an emotional-volitional tone" is "closer than any of the abstract cultural worlds . . . to the unitary and unique world of the performed act" (61). Rhetoric makes no explicit appearance in *Toward a Philosophy of the Act,* but the fragment's concern with participation, evaluation, decision, and action, with what is given and available and what is made of it would seem to point toward rhetoric as another exemplification—perhaps, as we shall see, an even more suitable one. For if both poetic and rhetorical utterances can be understood as examples of evaluative consciousness at work in the world, rhetorical utterance would seem to have a special affinity with a word that "expresses by its intonation my valuative attitude toward the object, toward what is desirable or undesirable in it and, in doing so, sets it in motion toward that which is yet-to-be-determined about it, turns it into a constituent moment of the living, ongoing event" (32). Bakhtin here formulates something like the intimate connection Aristotle recognizes between epideictic arguments and deliberative ones, between evaluative discourse and the deliberative discourse that prompts to action.

However exemplary poetic or rhetorical discourse may be of "the actually performed act" (28), neither poetics nor rhetoric accounts for the act; both are specialized disciplines derived from the act and, as disciplines with their own laws, opposed to it.[24] What Bakhtin's *Toward a Philosophy of the Act* focuses on is a description of the act as the ground of all disciplines and of our participation in them and in the life they both derive from and stand against as autonomous cultural enterprises. What is striking to me, however, is how close the disciplines of poetics and rhetoric are to that ground, how intimate those arts are with the verbal activity that necessarily accompanies the act. These arts rationalize to different ends architectonic action that underwrites all institutions and rationalized cultural practices, and they can both help clarify the character of that action and refresh themselves by reflection on their close relations to it. In addition, their close relations to one another become clearer and more productive when their relations to the "actually performed act" are clarified. As arts, poetics and rhetoric both have tendencies to become conventional, technical, routine, and legislative, but when they are referred to the architectonic action that underwrites them, both can be reinvigorated.

Bakhtin's fragmentary text translated as *Toward a Philosophy of the Act* has four main parts, two of which are especially suggestive for my discussion of rhetoric and poetics. First, his text critiques the neo-Kantian disciplines of theoretical cognition, aesthetics, and ethics or practical reason from the perspective of a first philosophy centered on participative consciousness and the act (1–27). Then it elaborates a phenomenology of "the actually performed act" (28–54). At the end of that section, it offers the divisions of what it proposes as the whole inquiry into the architectonics of the actual world of the performed act in relation to the "crisis of contemporary action" (54–56). Finally, it takes up the first part of the proposed inquiry, "an examination of [the] fundamental moments of the architectonic of the actual world of the performed deed" (54), concentrating in the part we have on "a world permeated in its entirety with the emotional-volitional tones of the affirmed validity of values" (56).

When in this final section Bakhtin separates "my performed act and my self-activity of affirming and acknowledging any value" as two modes of participation in the event of Being (60), he distinguishes two aspects of his analysis that have strong relations to rhetoric and poetics respectively and that receive their fullest developments in his second and his final sections. The second section, on the performed act or deed, lays out the centrality of choosing and acting and the discourse that articulates them for participative consciousness in terms that repeatedly bring rhetoric to mind. The final section, on "value-governed experiencing of the world" (61), takes a poem as its exemplar and has close affiliations with the account of poetry he develops in "Author and Hero in Aesthetic Activity," another early fragment that appears to take up the second part of his proposed inquiry—"aesthetic activity as an actually performed act or deed, both from within its product and from the standpoint of the author as answerable participant" (51). I shall concentrate on these two sections of *Toward a Philosophy of the Act* in discussing rhetoric and poetics in relation to Bakhtin's architectonic of the act, drawing also from other sections and "Author and Hero," and beginning with rhetoric.

In its classical formulations by Plato and Aristotle and the traditions shaped by them, rhetoric has been defined by and against the backdrop of philosophic or scientific enterprises that posit systematic knowledge as paradigmatic and normative. Against this backdrop, as a counterpart of dialectic, the practice of rhetoric appears deficient, its auditors lacking in objectivity and unable to manage philosophical arguments, its arguments truncated and lacking in scientific certainty or dialectical universality, its rhetors appealing to irrational responses and partial interests, its language a dubious departure from the philosophical norm. Bakhtin's phenomenological effort to define a "first" or "moral philosophy" prior to systematic knowledge and grounded in the participatory consciousness of the actually performed act provides a different backdrop against which rhetoric sounds different. As I will show, the situation of participants in the actually performed act sounds like the classical rhetorical situation, and classical rhetoric sounds like the discourse of answerable participation, but framed in Bakhtin's terms rhetoric no longer appears to be a deprived (let alone depraved) discourse but rather one that requires "the entire fullness of the word" to give voice to the answerably performed act (31).

Participants in Being, according to Bakhtin, orient themselves to three "central emotional-volitional moments" that could be taken as ways of naming the three parties to the rhetorical situation, "I, the other, and I-for-the-other" (54). The "I" correlates with the position of rhetoric's speaker, the "other" with the speaker's topic or hero, I-for-the-other with the listener or audience in whose eyes or ears the speaker's discourse and gestures register. These three "common moments" in "the concrete architectonic of the performed act" are the points around which "all the values of actual life" are arranged (54).

Indeed, we can say that the relations among these "moments" or "points" are all necessarily and inescapably evaluative. "I" am conscious of the other and another is conscious of me never as "something simply given" but always "in conjunction with another given that is connected with those objects and relations, namely, that which is yet-to-be-achieved or determined" (32). That is to say, consciousness is always evaluative, always includes an ought or a desire or interest in connection with that of which it is conscious. "The mere fact that I have begun speaking" about something, Bakhtin writes, "means that I have already assumed a certain attitude toward it—not an indifferent attitude, but an interested-effective attitude." For, as he says a few lines earlier,

> an object that is absolutely indifferent, totally finished, cannot be something one becomes actually conscious of, something one experiences actually. When I experience an object actually, I thereby carry out something in relation to it: the object enters into relation with that which is to-be-achieved and grows in it—with my relationship to that object. Pure givenness cannot be experienced actually." (32)

In this architectonic, not neutral scientific or philosophical objectivity (themselves interested attitudes for Bakhtin) but "an interested-effective attitude" characterizes the relation of I and the other and I-for-the-other. It would, I think, be fair to say that "an interested-effective attitude" is also the attitude rhetoric takes toward its topic or hero and solicits from its audience; rhetoric would appear to be native to the architectonic of the actual world of the performed act, not alien to it.

The event in which participatory consciousness participates is not just evaluative but also concrete and particular. The participant in the act or deed "sees clearly *these* individual unique persons whom he loves, *this* sky and *this* earth and *these* trees . . . and the time; and what is also given to him simultaneously is the value, the actually and concretely affirmed value of these persons and objects" (30). And the evaluation is specific to the event and its concrete parts. "This is not a universal valuation of an object independently of that unique context in which it is given to me at the given moment, but expresses the whole truth [*pravda*] of the entire situation as a unique moment in what constitutes an ongoing event" (36). And the unique evaluation is the evaluation from the point of view of a uniquely situated participant. "There *is* no acknowledged self-equivalent and universally valid value, for its acknowledged validity is conditioned *not* by its content taken in abstraction, but by its being *correlated* with the unique place of a participant" (48). The values acknowledged in the situation, then, are the values of the participants in the situation, and an expression of those values or an appeal to them is not an unfortunate failure to acknowledge some universal values relevant to the situation but a necessary recognition of the specificity of values needed to resolve or determine this situation for those involved in it. Again rhetoric's partiality and its appeal to partial auditors belongs to this world.

Bakhtin characterizes the language that expresses the evaluations of concrete situations by participants in those situations in contrast to the "theoretical terms" of systematic knowledge (30). His argument warrants a long quotation:

> It would be a mistake to assume that this concrete truth [*pravda*] of the event that the performer of the act sees and hears and experiences and understands in the single act of an answerable deed is something ineffable, i.e., that it can only be livingly experienced in some way at the moment of performing the act, but cannot be uttered clearly and distinctly. I think that language is much more adapted to giving utterance precisely to that truth, and not to the abstract moment of the logical in its purity. . . . Historically language grew up in the service of participative thinking and performed acts, and it begins to serve abstract thinking only in the present day of its history. The expression of a performed act from within and the expression of once-occurrent Being-as-event in which that act is performed require the entire fullness of the word: its content/sense aspect (the word as concept) as well as its palpable-expressive aspect (the word as image) and its emotional-volitional aspect (the intonation of the word) in their unity. . . . One should not, of course, exaggerate the power of language: unitary and once-occurrent Being-as-event and the performed act that partakes in it are fundamentally and essentially expressible, but in fact it is always a very difficult task to accomplish, and while full adequacy is unattainable, it is always present as that which is to *be* achieved." (31)

Bakhtin may be taken here to give rhetoric its task in his terms, the task of giving adequate expression to Being-as-event and the performed act that partakes in it, and he authorizes its use of a full range of verbal work, the word as concept, as image, and as emotional-volitional intonation—closely parallel to the Aristotelian repertoire of logos (the concept), ethos (the image of the speaker in the speech), and pathos (the emotional-volitional) that rhetoric traditionally draws upon. Since Bakhtin sees language as having "grown up" as a function of participative thinking and performed acts, he is confident in its capacity to express them and make them "answerably aware" of themselves (31). Rhetorical discourse appears to have an essential and inescapable role in this world and to have the resources it needs to fulfill that role.

Of those resources, emotional-volitional intonation is most essential to expressing the "interested-effective" attitude of the participant in the act. The inescapably evaluative, "something-yet-to-be-determined" character of the act

> is intonated, has an emotional-volitional tone, and enters into an effective relationship to me within the unity of the ongoing event encompassing us. An emotional-volitional tone is an inalienable moment of the actually performed act, even of the most abstract thought, insofar as I am actually thinking it, i.e., insofar as it is really actualized in Being, becomes a participant in the ongoing event. Everything that I have to do with is given to me in an emotional-volitional tone, for everything is given to me as a constituent moment of the event in which I am participating. (33)

Close to Bakhtin's later dialogic insights, these formulations envision a situation in which participants encounter objects as already carrying the emotional-volitional tones of other participants' evaluations of them and need to determine the tone they will take toward those objects in response to already spoken tones. Rhetoric—in these performative terms alien to Aristotle—might be thought of as taking, in response to given tones, determinate tones that affect the tones taken by others, tones that either declare an attitude or motivate and answer for an action.

We might, then, further characterize rhetorical discourse in these terms as the emotional-volitional discourse of answerability. "Emotional-volitional tone," Bakhtin writes,

> is not a passive psychic reaction but is a certain ought-to-be attitude of consciousness, an attitude that is morally valid and answerably active. This is an answerably conscious *movement* of consciousness, which transforms possibility into the actuality of a realized deed (a deed of thinking, of feeling, of desiring, etc.). We use the term "emotional-volitional tone" to designate precisely the moment constituted by my self-activity in a lived experience—the experiencing of an experience as *mine*. . . . This relating of it to me as the one who is active has a sensuous-valuational and volitional—performative—character and at the same time is answerably rational. . . . The moment constituted by the performance of thoughts, feelings, words, practical deeds is an actively answerable attitude that I myself assume—an emotional volitional attitude toward a state of affairs in its entirety, in the context of actual unitary and once-occurrent life. (36–37)

The classical rhetorical name for what Bakhtin describes here is "persuasion," a word Bakhtin himself uses later in "Discourse in the Novel" when he talks about "internally persuasive discourse." Restating the passage in these terms will make it less opaque. Persuasion is an attitude or movement of consciousness that transforms possibility into actuality. It brings together reasons and evaluative emotions in the one persuaded, who takes ownership of the attitude and the acts that may follow from it, is prepared to answer and argue for them, and expresses that answering argument in a tone that conveys both the evaluation of the situation and a determined will toward it.

That determined will is a "decision or resolution" that issues in an answerable act, which is "the actualization of a decision—inescapably, irremediably, and irrevocably. The answerably performed act is a final result or summation, an all-round definitive conclusion. . . . The performed act constitutes a going out *once and for all* from within possibility as such into *what is once-occurrent*" (28–29). Rhetoric here would be both the discourse that attempts to persuade and the discourse that articulates a persuasion, the discourse that leads to decision and the discourse that answers for a decision and the action that follows it. Bakhtin's phenomenology of the actually performed act can thus be taken as a phenomenology of rhetoric and the world in which it operates, and rhetoric, thus understood, can be taken as the very discourse that prompts and accompanies our participation in Being-as-event.[23] Not a specialized political or institutional discourse or art, it would be in these terms the very discourse of active, decision-making participation in the world, the discourse of ethical, practical, future-oriented cherishing of what needs to be cherished, rejection of what needs to be rejected, neglect of what should be neglected, and pursuit of what remains to be accomplished. No act thus understood would be intelligible as an act without the accompaniment of rhetorical discourse, and rhetorical discourse itself would be an act as well as a prompting to further action.

Given this close affinity of rhetorical discourse to the actually performed act, it would be surprising that Bakhtin never uses the word "rhetoric" in *Toward a Philosophy of the Act,* if we did not already have in mind the many negative images of rhetoric that appear later in his work. Delimited as it was by the agonistic and zero-sum rhetorical discipline of his day, "rhetoric" for him is a term to be trumped with new terms, not one to be expanded and reinterpreted. By the same token, given the familiar delimitations and denigrations of poetry in his later work on novelistic discourse, it is surprising that he chooses to illustrate the architectonic of the act with a lyric poem, the form that later stands in for a monologic foil to the dialogic novel. But in the context of *Toward a Philosophy of the Act,* the poem, an example of "the world of aesthetic seeing" (61), has an exemplifying advantage over ethical-rhetorical discourse: it makes active evaluative consciousness and its evaluative determinations of its world available for contemplation rather than making claims on that world and other participants in it. In a revision of the final section of *Toward a Philosophy of the Act* included in "Author and Hero," Bakhtin characterizes

> the position occupied by the aesthetic *subiectum,* i.e., . . . the author and the reader . . . *outside* all constituents, without exception, of the inner architectonic field of artistic vision. It is this outside position that makes it possible for the first time to encompass the entire architectonic—the axiological, temporal, spatial, and meaning-governed architectonic—through a unitary, equally founding, self-activity. Aesthetic empathizing . . . —the seeing of objects and heroes from within—is actively accomplished from this *outside* standpoint where material obtained through empathizing, along with the matter of outer seeing and hearing, is integrated and shaped into one concrete, architectonic whole. (AA 212)

Aesthetic contemplation thus stands outside the heroes of the event it empathizes with instead of participating in that event. It closes the "yet-to-be-realized meaning" of the event and orders the event architectonically by "transposing the center of value from what-is-yet-to-be-achieved into what-is-given, i.e., into a given human being as the participant in that event" (AA 211). The author "extracts" the event "out of reality (cognitive-ethical reality) and frames it artistically" (AA 216), making it possible for readers to appreciate the hero's participation in the event without their being called themselves to participate in it. Or, as Nancy Struever puts a similar point, "The first and controlling poetic act is an act of wholesale deprivation: to divest behavior and events of their civil import, and subtract them from the current debate" (79). In Bakhtin's terms, the aesthetic "consumption" of the event embodied in the work is introduced "from a position which relate[s] this event to its given participants and [makes] the experiencing and striving itself the center of value from the standpoint of the one experiencing and striving, rather than the *object* toward which that experiencing and striving is directed" (AA 221). The scene represented on Keats's Grecian urn comes to mind here.[24]

The world of the act embodied in the poem as aesthetic artifact is "a world permeated in its entirety with the emotional-volitional tones of the affirmed validity of values" (TPA 56). Space and time and words take on value from the perspective of the speaker or hero of the event[25] as do the things given and things to be accomplished in their world. Mortal time not mathematical time, inhabited space not geometric space, determinate persons not just anybody, determinate circumstances not open possibilities, utterances not grammatically possible sentences, characterize the world in which the hero, the center of values, speaks and acts. What the poem as aesthetic object reveals, as it were, is the determinate valuative charge on everyone and everything in the world of the poem, but the contemplator can recognize those values without being directly connected to them, insulated from the charge that might, in a direct utterance in life, shock him or her into action.

The intoned evaluations of everything in the situation of the speaker in the world of the poem are encompassed by "the formal intonation of the author/reader" (AA 213) who cherishes or celebrates it and distances it. The world of the poem, Bakhtin writes,

> is the world of the affirmed existence of *other* beings; I myself—as the one who affirms—do not exist in it.... These others are *found* by me; I myself, the one and only I, issuing from within myself—I am fundamentally and essentially situated outside the architectonic. I partake in it only as a contemplator, but contemplation is the active, effective situatedness of the contemplator *outside* the object contemplated.... Aesthetic activity is participation of a special, *objectified* kind; from within an aesthetic architectonic there *is* no way out into the world of the performer of deeds, for he is located outside the field of objectified aesthetic seeing. (TPA 73)

Aesthetic activity situates action in progress in terms of present effort rather than future outcome and as the other's action rather than my own or one that implicates me. Even in lyric poetry, where the poet and the speaker/hero are sometimes the same person, the poet stands apart from himself as speaker and appreciates his action and passion as if they were those of another.

Poetics, in these terms, then, might be seen as studying the aesthetic isolation, consummation, and contemplation of rhetorical acts in the broad sense we have given "rhetorical" in the previous section. Bakhtin never makes this point in just these terms, both because "rhetoric" for him always remains the name for a specialized disciplined discourse, not the name for discourse of active participant consciousness in general, and because he initially must contend with the formalist account of poetics that follows from Aristotle and treats language not as the verbal embodiment in concrete utterances of evaluation and choice but as the linguistic material out of which poems are made. I have shown above that it is reasonable to extend the term "rhetoric" to name the discourse that prompts and accompanies the act, but I need to show here how Bakhtin struggles with the formalists for ownership of the word "language."

When he lets the formalists have the word and lets it represent the material out of which the poem is made, he says things like "the author's creative consciousness is not a language-consciousness (in the broadest sense of the word); language-consciousness is merely a passive constituent in creative activity—an immanently surmounted material" (AA 194). When he takes ownership of the word, language comes close to being not the material but the content and form of poetic representation: "Every word not only designates an object, not only calls forth a certain image, not only sounds in a particular way, but also expresses a certain emotional-volitional reaction to the object designated, and this reaction finds its expression in the intonation of the word when it is actually pronounced" (AA 214). In narrative in particular, the literary mode that will later replace the lyric poem as paradigmatic for Bakhtin, "the word . . . is always the author's word and, consequently, it also expresses the reaction of the author, even if certain words or a whole complex of words may be placed *almost* totally at the disposal of the heroes. In this sense, we could say that every word in narrative literature expresses a reaction to another reaction, the author's reaction to the reaction of the hero" (AA 218). Here language is not material but both the author's forming discourse that bespeaks the author's evaluative consciousness (form) and the hero's imitated discourse (content) that bespeaks the hero's. The idea of language as material has no place in this poetics, though its centrality in the formalist poetics Bakhtin is arguing with leads him repeatedly to minimize or subordinate it to the poetics of architectonic evaluative utterance he is advocating rather than to dismiss it as irrelevant.

Without language as material to complicate his poetics, though, Bakhtin can concentrate on the interrelation between content and form, between the hero's intonation and the author's forming intonation, between the rhetoric accompanying the hero's action and evaluation of the world and the aestheticizing operations through which the author shapes that rhetoric for appreciation. In a section on the "intonative structure" of the literary work added to the revised reading of a lyric poem by Pushkin that he initially turned to in *Toward a Philosophy of the Act,* he distinguishes the "realistic intonation" of the hero from the "formal intonation" of the author and shows how in drama, narrative, and lyric this distinction is variously sustained. In tragic drama, the rhythm of the verse in which the whole drama is written "expresses a reaction to a reaction—the author's unitary and uniform, purely formal-aesthetic reaction to all the contending realistic reactions of the heroes, to the whole tragic event in its entirety—and thus aestheticizes the event, i.e., extracts it out of reality (cognitive-ethical reality) and frames it artistically" (AA 216). In narrative, as we have already seen, the author's narration contains and reaccentuates the hero's discourse: "the author reacts to the reaction of the hero and consummates it aesthetically" (AA 218). This point will receive extensive elaboration in both the account of reported speech in Voloshinov's *Marxism and the Philosophy of Language* and in the typology of the prose word in *Problems of Dostoevsky's Poetics.* "In lyric," he goes on, "the author is most formalistic, i.e., he dissolves in the outward, sounding form and in the inner, pictorial-sculptural and rhythmic form, whence it seems that he is absent, that he merges with the hero or, conversely, that there is no hero and only the author is present. In reality, however, a hero and an author stand over against each other here as well, and in every word one can hear a reaction to another reaction" (AA 218). In the poem he is discussing, "the realistically sorrowing tones" of the hero are "encompassed and enveloped by the tones that sing or celebrate them—by tones that are not the tones of sorrow at all" (AA 218). Again here as in drama, the rhythm provides the aestheticizing distance that sets the suffering of the hero apart and reaccentuates it as an *appreciated* suffering, not just a directly encountered ethical suffering.[26]

But in some cases, the ones Bakhtin will later characterize as "double-voiced," the author's evaluations of heroes go beyond formally isolating them and include a cognitive-ethical evaluation of them. In these cases, "the emotional-volitional reaction of the author finds its expression not just in rhythm and intonation, but in the very choice of a hero, in the choice of theme and plot [*fabula*], in the choice of words for expressing the latter, in the choice and construction of images, etc." (AA 225). In addition, "the encompassing reaction of the author—his attitude in relation to the whole and the parts—is expressed not only through rhythm, but also through the place which a given utterance of the hero occupies in the dialogue, and through the position of the entire dialogue within the whole—through the intonational coloration of the dialogue, and sometimes through its object related meanings and images as well" (AA 226). These authorial evaluative reactions to the hero's reactions take place within the aesthetic artifact rather than within the world of the hero's or the author's ethical action, but like the hero's reactions to the objects of his or her world, the author's reactions to the hero's reactions are evaluatively charged. The author's discourse within the aesthetically set-off artifact in these cases itself has a rhetorical aspect in the broad sense that I have been using the term and in the sense that Wayne Booth often means in *The Rhetoric of Fiction* as I discussed it in Chapter 3. It is interesting that Bakhtin says, "Language in its entirety is not needed by any domain of culture save poetry" (AA 294), for he has also said, "The expression of a performed act from within and the expression of once-occurrent Being-as-event in which that act is performed require the entire fullness of the word" (TPA 31). Poetry seems to require the same fullness of the word as this latter expression, which I am calling "rhetoric," not in the sense of the specialized discipline but in the sense of evaluative discourse accompanying the act. Poetry, embodying this discourse in the verbal artifact, may itself be rhetorical in this sense. Though Aristotle's *Poetics* attempts to make language a material in which actions are imitated, I will show in Chapter 10 that he struggles unsuccessfully to suppress a poetics like Bakhtin's that makes the evaluative utterances of speaking agents, rhetoric as I have defined it here, the object of imitation.

Rhetoric thus understood is part of both the reaction that the verbal work of art embodies and the reaction to that reaction that embodies it. Even the author's cherishing reaction of the hero's reaction that is the aesthetic reaction proper might be seen as a kind of rhetorical reaction, for the author's cherishing or appreciative embodiment of a hero's reaction has a yet-to-be-accomplished aspect to it as well as a given aspect. With respect to the hero, the author's cherishing consummates and completes an action or movement of consciousness that in its own world leaves something to be accomplished. But with respect to the reader or audience of the work of art—a perspective Bakhtin does not develop in these phenomenological texts on architectonics—the aesthetic consummation of the hero's action is a call to activity, to the co-creative activity of construing and evaluating the author's reaction to the hero's reaction and the hero's reaction to the participants in his or her world. The reader, as Bakhtin will insist elsewhere, is not passive in the aesthetic transaction, and the author's discourse, while not calling for action with practical results in the world, does call up activity in the world with the aesthetic artifact itself. The author's cherishing of the hero's reaction calls for the reader's appreciation, and appreciation is an active apprehension and reaffirmation or rejection of something's value, not just a passive recognition of it. The reader's aesthetic apprehension is a kind of active participation in the world that re-creates and thereby sustains or critiques the value initially grasped by the author in the hero's activity and the value added by the author in aesthetic embodiment of that activity.

Though there is a place held for the active reader and the listener under the rubric "I-for-the other" in Bakhtin's phenomenology of the architectonic act, these figures are elaborated only in the sociological poetics he developed in conversation with or under the name of Voloshinov.[27] In the context of my present inquiry, it becomes clear that the sociological poetics set forth there translates the architectonics I have been following into a sociological register and elaborates the terms of architectonics in that new language. Far from losing in the translation, the architectonic act acquires a specificity that makes good on Bakhtin's repeated use of the epithet "historical" to characterize the act in *Toward a Philosophy of the Act*. And though sociological poetics and not sociological rhetoric is under consideration in those works, what I have been calling "rhetoric" reappears under the rubric "discourse in life" and remains essential for the account of "discourse in poetry" laid out in the Voloshinov essay whose title links those phrases.

Two premises resituate the participant consciousness and the once-occurrent act on sociological ground. *Marxism and the Philosophy of Language* declares, "The individual consciousness is a social-ideological fact. . . . Consciousness takes shape and being in the material of signs created by an organized group in the process of its social intercourse. . . . The problem of individual consciousness as the *inner word* . . . becomes one of the most vital problems in the philosophy of language" (12–14). The essay "Discourse in Life and Discourse in Art" adds, "The fact of the matter is that no conscious act of any degree of distinctness can do without inner speech, without words and intonations—without evaluations, and, consequently, every conscious act is already a social act, an act of communication." The first consequence of this socializing of consciousness as *internalized acts of communication* is to bring the listener to the fore, as the self-other emphasis of phenomenology makes the hero central. If "even the most intimate self-awareness is an attempt to translate oneself into a common code, to take stock of another's point of view," then "it entails orientation toward a possible listener . . . [a] constant *co-participant* in all our conscious acts" (DLDA 114–15). Even the inner speech accompanying unarticulated consciousness and action has an implicit interlocutor, and the relations implied between even an inner speaker and an inner listener are social relations.

Emphasis on the speaker-listener axis of social discourse calls attention to the communicative work of discourse that rhetoric is typically associated with in addition to the also rhetorical evaluative work of discourse that the speaker-hero axis foregrounds.[28] Instead of the phenomenological single participant in Being-as-event who evaluates the situation, sociologically understood discourse in life ("behavioral utterance") "always joins the participants in the situation together as *co-participants* who know, understand, and evaluate the situation in like manner." In "the given case," the discourse they participate in "*resolves the situation,* bringing it to an *evaluative conclusion,* as it were. Far more often, behavioral utterances actively continue and develop the situation, adumbrate a plan for future action, and organize that action" (DLDA 100). These "behavioral utterances" of discourse in life do the work of epideictic and deliberative rhetorical utterances.

Intonation, here as in the phenomenological account of participation in Being-as-event, remains central to the expression of evaluation, but evaluation becomes social, and intonation becomes "social par excellence" (DLDA 102). In addition to expressing evaluative responses to the hero, intonation varies as the speaker imagines listeners sharing or differing from that evaluation. Intonation doubles its orientation here: "every instance of intonation is oriented in *two directions:* with respect to the listener as ally or witness and with respect to the object of utterance as the third, living participant whom intonation scolds or caresses, denigrates or magnifies" (DLDA 104–05). And the evaluation of both listener and hero that conditions intonation depends upon social relations among the parties—hierarchical social relations obtaining among them and degrees of intimacy or proximity affecting their identification with or objectification of one another. Tone, as we know in social relations, depends on subordination or superordination or equality of the parties addressed or referred to, as it also is affected by participation in communities that mark out "we," "you," and "they" or "it." In providing social bases for evaluation of relationships, these parameters go beyond the positive and negative, interested and indifferent, poles of Bakhtin's account of phenomenological evaluation to mark out historical and institutional specificities of respect, deference, defiance, acknowledgment, and alienation of imaginable parties to concrete human relationships. The events in which agents participate gain specificity and historicity as well, as I, the other, and I-for-the-other become, for example, a father, a son, and teacher in school or an advocate, an accused, and a jury of the accused's peers in court. Intonation remains a crucial rhetorical resource in all these situations, capable of expressing the pertinent evaluations by itself, and of reinforcing or undermining arguments made to establish those evaluations (see Chapter 9).

In the sociological as well as in the phenomenological account, poetics studies the aesthetic isolation of rhetorical communication that makes utterance, evaluation, and action available for active co-creation. Artistic communication is a "special form of social communication . . . irreducible to other types of ideological communication such as the political, the juridical, the moral, and so on" (DLDA 98). Instead of defining aesthetic isolation in terms of the author's separation and consummation of the hero's action from its yet-to-be-accomplished ends, "Discourse in Life and Discourse in Art" defines it in terms of a transaction between author and contemplator: "*What characterizes aesthetic communication is the fact that it is wholly absorbed in the creation of the work of art, and in its continuous re-creations in the co-creation of contemplators, and does not require any other kind of objectification*" (DLDA 98). Whereas Bakhtin's early works posit aesthetic distance by removing the hero's desire or purpose from a world in which it could be fulfilled, Voloshinov's essay posits that distance by having the contemplator rework the work without needing to take any action beyond that reworking itself.

But introducing the contemplator or the reader of the poem into the aesthetic transaction raises additional features of the poetic work to visibility. Readers of poetry, separated from the situation of the poem's speaker's utterance, must have the features of that situation filled in or generate multiple co-creations in response to their absence.

> Discourse in art neither is nor can be so closely dependent on all the factors of the extraverbal context, on all that is seen and known,

as in life. A poetic work cannot rely on objects and events in the immediate milieu as things 'understood' without making even the slightest allusion to them in the verbal part of the utterance. In this regard more is demanded of discourse in literature: Much that could remain outside the utterance in life must find verbal representation (DLDA 106).

Verbal works of art must present necessary contexts for the utterances that they embody as well as presenting those utterances themselves. *Heart of Darkness* might be read in these terms as providing an extensive context for registering Marlowe's evaluation of Kurtz's "The horror, the horror," Marlowe's reaction to that reaction, and Conrad's aesthetic reaction to both. In addition, in the absence of the intonation of utterances in life, the implied intonation and concomitant evaluation of utterances in art must be presented through the author's choice of words, rhythm, and manner of unfolding of the poem. The work of co-creation by the contemplator/reader is largely a work of actively inferring the author's and the hero's intonations and relations from these features of the work and evaluating them within the context of his or her co-creative activity.

The sociological texts of the Bakhtin school do more than add social modifiers to the key words of Bakhtin's phenomenology of the act, though they do indeed add them: "social act," "social reality," "sociohistorical situation," "social evaluation," "the being of a given community," "social life," "social nature of intonation." "The concrete utterance . . . is born, lives, and dies in the process of social interaction between the participants of the utterance." "*Listener and hero are constant participants in the creative event.*" "Verbal discourse is a *'scenario' of an event*" (DLDA 105–09). The social modifiers re-imagine the rhetorical essence of active participation in life and the poetic contemplation of that participation, achieving a closer grasp of the concreteness of historically related agents and situations and co-participants in the events of being. They imagine active roles for the listener and contemplator without omitting the phenomenological relation of author or speaker to hero—a relation too often underestimated in audience-centered rhetorical analysis. They bring out the inseparability of act and utterance, already present in the phenomenological works but not there mediated by the idea of "inner speech." They point to a variety of social evaluations and tones correlated with specific social relations that enrich and ground the repertoire of evaluative intonations essential to the phenomenology of the architectonic act. They provide the social as a category intermediate between the individual and the universal, opening a source for making individual actions and utterances intelligible and communicable and for making agents responsive and responsible to one another in shared circumstances. Though they do not negate the uniqueness of the phenomenological truth that I experience myself "only myself, my unique self—as an I" (TPA 41), they add that "'I' can realize itself verbally only on the basis of 'we'" (DLDA 100).

The Bakhtin School's sociological texts make even clearer than the phenomenological works the close affinity of rhetoric to discourse in life, and they fruitfully elaborate a poetics that sees verbal art as an aesthetic embodiment of that discourse. The more explicit sociological accounts of social communication and specialized aesthetic social communication bring out the affinities of rhetoric and poetics that were already implied in the earlier accounts of the language accompanying the act and the aesthetic embodiment of it. Whether these extensions of earlier phenomenological concerns represent Bakhtin's colleagues' translation of his phenomenological terms into their sociological ones or his own conversion to thinking about the phenomenological issues that exercised him in what might have been their sociological categories—a conversion evident by the time he writes the speech genres essay—they represent gains in understanding that preserve even as they modify earlier terms.

The argument I have elaborated here leaves open the question of how the early phenomenological and sociological formulations of the Bakhtin School on which I have drawn here articulate with the later and more familiar dialogic ones. One crucial later figure is missing in these early texts. The dialogical account of discourse adds one further role or participant to phenomenological I, the other, and I-for-the-other relations and sociological speaker/hero/listener relations; the dialogical model of discourse adds the figure of the prior speaker(s) to whom the speaker now holding the floor is responding. In effect, the phenomenological architectonic must add a fourth term, something like "the other-for-me," and the sociological model must add a speaker who precedes its speaker or must refigure the objectified "unsaid" that precedes the utterance under analysis with a personified "already said by" that it responds to and takes for granted. The dialogical relations of speaker to speaker in Bakhtin's later work, as I anticipated earlier, include the phenomenological and sociological relations of evaluative intonation responsive to prior evaluative intonations, but they extend beyond, and reveal the artificial closure of, the paradigmatic lyric utterance of one speaker addressing one listener about one hero—the model that has held for the preceding analysis. Dramatic dialogue, narrative report of prior speech, and dialogized lyric all exemplify in different artistic ways the representation of speech responsive to prior speech.[29]

That Bakhtin in "Speech Genres" classifies all literary genres, from the proverb to the multi-volume novel, as utterances and sees complex secondary artistic utterances as internalizing the dialogic genres of everyday simple utterances suggests that a poetics of the evaluative utterance can become elaborate in its aesthetic isolation of extended rhetorical interactions among many people. The isolated discursive act, the single speech by a single speaker that is the model for the lyric poem, becomes situated as a response and prompt to other discursive acts that are taken up in aesthetic imitations of more extended discursive interactions. The novel is the most complex and to Bakhtin the most interesting of these imitations, involving as it does not just verbal interactions within the world of the novel but interactions between the narrating voice and the world whose interactions it reports, and interactions between the author's aestheticizing form and both those other interactions. As he says in his essay on speech genres,

> During the process of their formation [secondary speech genres] absorb and digest various primary (simple) genres that have taken form in unmediated speech communication. These primary genres are altered and assume a special character when they enter into complex ones. They lose their immediate relation to actual reality and to the real utterances of others. For example, rejoinders of everyday dialogue or letters found in a novel retain their form and their everyday significance only on the plane of the novel's content. They enter into actual reality only via the novel as a whole, that is, as a literary artistic event and not as everyday life. The novel as a whole is an utterance just as the rejoinders in everyday language or private letters are . . . but unlike these, the novel is a secondary (complex) utterance." (SG 62)

The same relation of discourse in life to discourse in art holds here that distinguishes the discourse accompanying the act in Being from the aesthetically set apart discourse of the lyric poem in *Toward a Philosophy of the Act*. Not just isolated rhetorical acts but extended rhetorical interactions become available for co-creation and contemplation in the novel, which sets them apart from pragmatic reality even as it introduces them into it as part of its artistic utterance. These thoughts suggest that, despite Bakhtin's later depreciation of versions of rhetoric and poetics to which he opposed his dialogic insights, a unified rhetoric and poetics grounded in the early work of the Bakhtin School may prove consistent with those insights and fruitful for understanding them.

9. Aristotle's *Rhetoric* and Bakhtin's Discourse Theory

I have shown that the work of the Bakhtin School belongs to and contributes to the rhetorical tradition, despite Bakhtin's recurrent disparaging remarks about rhetoric. The range and power of his general theory of discourse have attracted rhetorical theorists to his work, even as the place of rhetoric in his work has put them on the defensive. I have shown in Chapter 5 how Halasek attempted to downplay his placement of rhetoric on the monologic side of his fundamental distinction between dialogic and monologic discourse and imagined a Bakhtinian rhetoric more dialogic than Bakhtin allows. Articles by Walzer and Murphy, on the other hand, reaffirm the essential monologism of his account. Dentith approaches the problem by denying the distinction between dialogic and monologic discourse altogether.

This debate has addressed itself to a relatively small number of passages in which Bakhtin makes explicit pronouncements about "rhetoric" rather than to his discourse theory as a whole, where issues of concern to rhetoric arise, as I have shown, without being named as such. And it has also answered his charges against rhetoric by mobilizing some commonplace version of the art against them, without acknowledging the variety of "rhetorics" on offer in the rhetorical tradition or situating Bakhtin among their authoritative expositors. The debate has established Bakhtin's pertinence to the rhetorical tradition, but it has not established his place within it or gauged the extent to which his admission to it might transform it. One inevitable and essential expositor of rhetoric in relation to whom Bakhtin's measure must be taken is Aristotle.

I have suggested elsewhere that Bakhtin structures his work on Dostoevsky's poetics against the background of Aristotle's *Poetics* ("Dialogic Criticism"). His *Problems of Dostoevsky's Poetics* is organized as a full-scale rearrangement of Aristotle's hierarchy of parts of the tragedy—first plot, then character, thought, diction, and spectacle in that order. Bakhtin devotes chapters to developing the importance of the subordinated parts of character ("the hero"), thought ("the idea"), and diction ("discourse"). He displaces plot and plot-governed classical genres like tragedy with the multi-voiced, serio-comic, and open-ended genre of Menippean satire, in which the person-idea unites character and thought and in which dictions too are united with ideologies. His discourse theory gives primacy to the act of utterance itself, making the performative part of tragedy—spectacle—precede all others. Bakhtin does not merely deconstruct Aristotelian hierarchies by making marginal Aristotelian topics central; he articulates a world of artistic practices beyond the boundaries Aristotle established with the same thoroughness with which Aristotle settled the territory within those boundaries. Bakhtin brings into focus a "classical" tradition of anti-classical discursive practices and analyzes their principles, doubling the field covered by poetics instead of undermining its ground.

Bakhtin's thoroughgoing rewriting of Aristotle's *Poetics* at the level of its organizing distinctions raises the question of whether Bakhtin might engage Aristotle's *Rhetoric* at the same level and expand and reconfigure the "province of rhetoric" as he does the domain of poetics. I shall argue in this chapter that he does. Bakhtin turns the hierarchy of parts in Aristotelian rhetoric on its head as he does that of poetics, and he synthesizes some parts of the art with others in ways that parallel his uniting of character with thought and thought with diction in his poetics. In his theory of discourse, he rehabilitates the most abjected part of Aristotle's rhetoric—delivery—and he subordinates Aristotle's most important part—invention—to arrangement, style, and delivery. He makes the parts of poetics that Aristotle refers to the arts of rhetoric and delivery—thought and intonation—crucial to discourse in general and therefore to both rhetoric and poetics, which consequently share constitutive parts in his system instead of the secondary parts in which they overlap in Aristotle's. I will treat Aristotle's attempt to outsource thought and delivery from the *Poetics* along with his parallel effort in the *Rhetoric* and then return to the implications for his *Poetics* in Chapter 10. To think through the implications of Bakhtin's overhaul of Aristotle's rhetoric will take us beyond defending some commonplace version of "rhetoric" against his deprecations to reimagining what rhetoric might be and how its parts might relate to one another in a theory of utterance rather than a theory of argument.

Let me begin by discussing Aristotle's hypocrisy. I use this provocative word to identify a crux at which Aristotle chooses to diminish or refer elsewhere matters of *hupokrisis*—usually translated as "delivery" or "elocution"—that Bakhtin magnifies and repeatedly takes as a starting point for his accounts of discourse. The etymological matrix of this word is profoundly salient for both traditional rhetoric and for Bakhtin's dialogics, and I would like to explore it briefly before I turn to the passages in both the *Rhetoric* and *Poetics* where Aristotle sets it aside and puts it down. According to the standard lexicon (Liddell 1889), Aristotle's *Poetics* and *Rhetoric* are the only Attic sources for the two meanings translated as delivery, one that of the actor, the other that of the orator. In Ionic, however, the word and its correlative verb *hupokrinomai* have the dialogically central sense of reply or answer. Both noun and verb shade over into the meaning familiar from the English "hypocrisy" of playing a part, feigning or pretending. The *krisis* at the root of the word is the root of our "crisis," and it carries the rhetorically central senses of choice, decision, judgment, and the related senses of trial or dispute and the issue of trials and disputes. The verb *krino* can mean "to question" as *hupokrinomai* can mean "to answer," making this paradigmatic dialogic interchange available along with the paradigmatic situation of rhetorical debate and decision in the same word history.

That the act of distinguishing or separating is yet another meaning for *krino* makes it dialectically salient as well and reminds us both of the dialectical work Aristotle undertakes to distinguish the discursive practices and arts of discourse that he takes up in his several treatises and of the field of shared or overlapping meanings from which he has decided to separate those practices and arts (see Chapter 6). If he proceeds as though the domains of those practices and arts are already distinct so that he can refer topics to one rather than another, we can recall that at least some of the lines that separate those arts and practices from one another have been distinguished, separated, chosen by his own decisions. We may reasonably wonder, for example, whether the art of delivery or elocution was already *there* to be the receptacle of the matters Aristotle refers to it from the *Poetics* or whether it comes into being at his fiat to receive matters for which he needs to find a place other than poetics.

The chapter of the *Poetics* in which Aristotle refers some matters to the art of delivery or elocution is also the chapter in which he refers a whole part of poetics to rhetoric. Chapter XIX is brief and the choices it makes are critical to articulating Aristotle's views with Bakhtin's. I will quote Butcher's translation in its entirety:

> It remains to speak of Diction and Thought, the other parts of Tragedy having been already discussed. Concerning Thought, we may assume what is said in the Rhetoric, to which inquiry the subject more strictly belongs. Under Thought is included every effect which has to be produced by speech, the subdivisions being: proof and refutation; the excitation of the feelings, such as pity, fear, anger, and the like; the suggestion of importance or its opposite. Now, it is evident that the dramatic incidents must be treated from the same points of view as the dramatic speeches, when the object is to evoke the sense of pity, fear, importance, or probability. The only difference is that the incidents should speak for themselves without verbal exposition; while effects aimed at in speech should be produced by the speaker, and as a result of the speech. For what were the business of a speaker, if the Thought were revealed quite apart from what he says?
>
> Next, as regards Diction. One branch of the inquiry treats of the Modes of Utterance. But this province of knowledge belongs to the art of Delivery and to the masters of that science. It includes, for instance, what is a command, a prayer, a statement, a threat, a question, an answer, and so forth. To know or not to know these things involves no serious censure upon the poet's art. For who can admit the fault imputed to Homer by Protagoras—that in the words, 'Sing, goddess, of the wrath,' he gives a command under the idea that he utters a prayer? For to tell someone to do a thing or not to do it is, he says, a command. We may, therefore, pass this over as an inquiry that belongs to another art, not to poetry. (69–71)

The two matters touched upon here are both aspects of speech or speaking, but Aristotle refers the first to rhetoric and the other to an "art of Delivery" that belongs in neither poetics nor rhetoric.

The speech that bespeaks "Thought" here seems to encompass more than Aristotle first attributes to the category of "Thought" when he earlier distinguishes it from the speech that bespeaks "Character" in Chapter VI. There he restricts thought to the speech that "is required whenever a statement is proved, or it may be, a general truth enunciated," not the speech that "reveals moral purpose, showing what kind of thing a man chooses or avoids"—the speech that reveals character (Aristotle, 1951, p. 29). In Chapter XIX, however, speech enacting proof and refutation is supplemented with speech that shows "the excitation of feelings" and with speech that magnifies or minimizes importance. Evaluative speech, not just the relatively value neutral speech of proof and the enunciation of maxims, here falls under "Thought," even though this wider scope for thought-producing speech will make it more difficult to distinguish from character-revealing speech. Indeed, it is hard to imagine how a thought-producing speech derived from the art of rhetoric, which is defined by its orientation to advocating what to choose and what to avoid, could be separated from ethos-revealing discourse and made purely to prove or disprove or state general principles. Aristotle might have better referred "Thought" thus restricted to dialectic instead of rhetoric, and one would reasonably have expected that "Thought" encompassing proof and refutation and the excitation of feelings would also encompass the projection of ethos, completing its embodiment of the three types of proof Aristotle lists in the *Rhetoric*.

The distinction between character and thought as manifestations of speech would then be called into question by the referral of "Thought" to rhetoric, and the possibility of a theory of poetics that found thought and character united in diction or speech would emerge to challenge Aristotle's subordinated sequence of character, thought, and diction. Bakhtin, as I have already shown, develops this theory of poetics in his book on Dostoevsky. What we can now begin to see is that it is a poetics that posits rhetorical discourse, broadly understood, in its conceptual, emotional, and ethical fullness as one object of poetic imitation a view consistent with the one I derived from Bakhtin's early works in Chapter 8. Such a poetics might even be said to take rhetorical discourse thus understood as paradigmatic of the impassioned defensive discourse revelatory of person-ideas that is the dominant discourse of Dostoevsky's novels. If we take seriously Aristotle's referral of the subject of thought in poetics to the inquiry of rhetoric, Bakhtin's dialogic poetics is one of the places to which that referral may lead us. I will follow this lead to a radical revisionist reading of Aristotle's *Poetics* in Chapter 10.

The matters that Aristotle refers from poetics to the art of delivery or elocution (*hupokrisis*) will lead us to another Bakhtinian locus, but before we follow them there, let us first again set Aristotle's account of this topic in *Poetics* XIX against what he says about it elsewhere, specifically in *Rhetoric* Book III, Chapter 1. There, in the earliest extant account of delivery in the rhetorical tradition, Aristotle ambivalently acknowledges the power of this aspect of rhetoric and deprecates the influence of it. It is rare to see him take as many conflicting turns of evaluation as he does in the brief section in which he takes up this topic. In Chapter XIX of the *Poetics*, his referral of the topic elsewhere is relatively neutral, and his deprecation of its importance for poetics is accomplished in a dismissive rhetorical question, but in *Rhetoric* III.1 his tone vacillates: delivery "has the greatest force," but its power to win victories in political contests is due to "the sad state of governments." Consideration of it "seems a vulgar matter when rightly understood," but one should pay attention to delivery, not because it is right but because it is necessary, since true justice seeks nothing more in a speech than neither to offend nor to entertain; for to contend by means of the facts themselves is just, with the result that everything except demonstration is incidental; but nevertheless, [delivery] has great power, as has been said, because of the corruption of the audience. The subject of expression, however, has some small necessary place in all teaching; for to speak in one way rather than another does make some difference in regard to clarity, though not a great difference; but all these things are forms of outward show intended to affect an audience. As a result, nobody teaches geometry this way. (*On Rhetoric* 258–59)

Applying the standard first of forensic rhetoric, then of teaching, then of geometry teaching to all rhetoric, these gestures would retract not just attention to delivery but to everything beyond arguments from logos in the *Rhetoric,* and indeed the turn to geometry would retract all the probabilistic arguments that Aristotle has carefully developed for the kinds of questions rhetoric ordinarily addresses. Aristotle seems to be struggling here to name a rational discourse of sufficient power and purity to dismiss definitively the inescapable but apparently scandalous irrational force of delivery, which seems even more troubling in the province of rhetoric than in that of poetics.

His account of delivery in *Rhetoric* III.1 also reveals that the art of delivery to which he confidently referred the "Modes of Utterance" in the *Poetics* "has not yet been composed." There has been some attention to it in matters of poetics, he says, but in rhetoric it is not there yet. It is interesting that Aristotle, who rarely holds back from being the first to investigate a subject or formulate the art of a practice, dismisses this one as too vulgar to be worthy of his attention. Nevertheless, he provides a brief outline of the art in *Rhetoric* III.1:

> It is a matter of how the voice should be used in expressing each emotion, sometimes loud and sometimes soft and [sometimes] intermediate, and how the pitch accents [*tonoi*] should be entoned, whether as acute, or grave or circumflex, and what rhythms should be expressed in each case; for [those who study delivery] consider three things, and these are volume, change of pitch [*harmonia*], and rhythm. (*On Rhetoric* 258)

It is not immediately clear how this brief enumeration of the parts of the art of delivery is related to Aristotle's brief referral in *Poetics* XIX to that art of inquiry into the modes of utterance, "which includes, for instance, what is a command, a prayer, a statement, a threat, a question, an answer, and so forth."

Perhaps the difference between "Sing, goddess" as command and as prayer may be a matter of intonation: the same expression may become quite distinct types of utterance depending on its intonation. Bakhtin and Voloshinov were fascinated by such tonal variations and recurred to them as a starting point for investigating the utterance, the elemental unit of speech communication. Anecdotes regarding the adverb "Well!" (DLDA), "a certain widely used obscenity" (Voloshinov, MPL 103), and the noun "joy" (SG 87) allow Voloshinov and Bakhtin to trace the evaluative relation of the utterance to its "immediate social situation" (DLDA 104) made evident in intonation. I will show that what emerges from these discussions of the intoned utterance is an account of discourse in general that resembles nothing more than the Aristotelian rhetorical discourse to which intonation is an afterthought and a near irrelevancy. Bakhtin, starting from a topic Aristotle pushes to the margin, theorizes all discourse in ways that resemble Aristotle's theorization of rhetorical discourse, even as Bakhtin pushes rhetoric more narrowly conceived to the margins of his inquiry. But Bakhtin's starting point in delivery also foregrounds aspects of the rhetorical utterance that Aristotle's subject-matter-centered account of rhetoric minimizes or overlooks.

Much that appears in Aristotle's work as specific to rhetorical communication appears in the Bakhtin School as characteristic of all speech communication. This is not quite the same thing as "extending rhetoric's gaze to every act of speaking and writing" (Bizzell and Herzberg 926); it is rather to see many characteristics usually attributed to rhetoric as in fact properties that belong to discourse in general. Aristotle and the Bakhtin School identify the same participants in the speech situation, and both determine genre by the role of the addressee. Aristotle writes in Chapter III, "A speech [situation] consists of three things: a speaker and a subject on which he speaks and someone addressed, and the objective of the speech relates to the last (I mean the hearer)" (*On Rhetoric* I.3). In "Discourse in Life and Discourse in Art," Voloshinov writes, "*Any locution actually said aloud or written down for intelligible communication is the product of the social interaction of three participants: the speaker* (author), *the listener* (reader), and *the topic* (the who or what) *of speech* (the hero)" (DLDA 105). Elsewhere Voloshinov adds that "the dimensions and forms" of "the outwardly actualized utterance ... are determined by the particular *situation* of the utterance and its *audience*." (DLDA 96). Aristotle identifies two possible roles for the hearer, judge or spectator, and three genres of rhetoric corresponding to those roles, deliberative, epideictic, and forensic rhetoric. Bakhtin sees numerous roles for the hearer in an "inexhaustible" number of spheres of social communication that produce a "boundless" number of speech genres (SG 60): "Each speech genre in each area of speech communication has its own typical conception of the addressee, and this defines it as a genre" (SG 95). These speech genres include all types of utterance, from the military command to flirtatious drawing room banter, from the toast to the scientific treatise, from the greeting to the multi-volume novel, including the discursive genres characteristic of Aristotle's public rhetorical forums. In addition, all the "Modes of Utterance" Aristotle refers to the art of delivery in *Poetics* XIX—"a command, a prayer, a statement, a threat, a question, an answer"—are among Bakhtin's list of primary speech genres in everyday discourse.

And even the discourse of everyday and intimate settings, organizational and artistic settings—indeed all discourse, like Aristotle's rhetorical discourse—is situated and evaluative. The functions of Voloshinov's everyday discourse resemble those of Aristotle's epideictic and deliberative rhetoric. "Discourse," Voloshinov writes, sometimes "resolves the situation, bringing it to an *evaluative conclusion*. . . . [M]ore often, behavioral utterances actively continue and develop a situation, adumbrate a plan for future action, and organize that action" (DLDA 100). Bakhtin does not attribute to all utterances the ends of the forensic and scientific genres that Aristotle emphasizes, the ones that putatively require only value-free attention to the facts and arguments to determine the case, because Bakhtin takes all utterances to be evaluative and addressed. "Even the so-called neutral and objective styles of exposition that concentrate maximally on subject matter, and, it would seem, are free from any consideration of the other still involve a certain conception of their addressee" (SG 98), he writes, and Voloshinov affirms, "No utterance can be put together without value judgment" (DLDA 105).

By making rhetoric a counterpart of dialectic, Aristotle makes the social participants, audience orientation, and evaluative work of rhetoric seem peculiar to rhetoric and even aberrant from the relatively impersonal and value-neutral perspective of dialectical argument among philosophers, but by making all discourse involve social participants, audiences, and evaluations, the Bakhtin School includes both rhetorical and dialectical discourse within a common understanding of discourse in which each type of discourse defines its audience, genres, and evaluations according to its function in its sphere of communication. For the Bakhtin School, rhetorical discourse unproblematically, even paradigmatically, exemplifies the common social and evaluative features of all discourse, and it is dialectical and scientific discourse that attempt, unsuccessfully, to transcend those features.

Aristotle's linking of rhetoric to dialectic also foregrounds rhetoric's reliance upon reasoning. Aristotle's account of the enthymeme or rhetorical syllogism identifies its departure from the fully elaborated and explicit syllogism of dialectic, and Aristotle devotes a large proportion of his treatise to cataloging the propositions that might be enthymematically invoked in arguments in the three rhetorical forums he focuses on. Again, the Bakhtin School generalizes this feature of rhetoric to all discourse. Voloshinov writes,

> *The situation enters into the utterance as an essential constitutive part of the structure of its import.* Consequently, a behavioral utterance as a meaningful whole is composed of two parts: (1) the part realized or actualized in words and (2) the assumed part. On this basis, the behavioral utterance can be likened to an enthymeme." (DLDA 100)

He goes on in a note to define the enthymeme as "a form of syllogism one of whose premises is suppressed" and to conclude his discussion of the assumed part of the utterance with the claim that " every utterance in the business of life is an objective social enthymeme" (DLDA 101). Every utterance in life, then, except formal logical ones, depends upon shared unstated premises and makes its point enthymematically from those premises.

Aristotle's extensive elaboration of those premises in his long lists of the topoi upon which the three kinds of rhetoric draw, his explicit listing of what audiences for deliberative, epideictic, and forensic arguments might take for granted, reveals that his rhetoric presupposes a rhetor who does not necessarily belong to the community he is addressing and tacitly share its beliefs. The artistic rhetorician appears to be an outsider who can refer to anthropological accounts like Aristotle's of the community he is addressing to understand what his auditors might believe. He can find grounds for argument elsewhere than in his own heart and mind—the *thumos* in which unstated enthymematic premises are lodged (DLDA 100). The Bakhtin School, on the other hand, begins its inquiry into the utterance from a situation in which two interlocutors share a common space, a common view, and common values so that one can express their shared evaluation of their situation in an indignantly intoned adverb: "Well!" (DLDA). The Bakhtin School's discourse theory is in the first instance grounded in a model of native speakers' use of their first language and their unanimous unconscious assimilation of their communities' tones and values, and it moves from there to encompass sophisticated and controversial genres in which less is taken for granted.

Aristotle's perspective in the *Rhetoric* is more like that of a foreign scholar trying to codify the beliefs and language of a community alien to him, a position that may explain Voloshinov's parenthetical remark that "Aristotle is a typical philologist" (MPL 71), since philologists in his account view all language as if it were a foreign language and approach it from the outside, making explicit and formal features that for native users would remain tacit. Another way to draw this contrast, this time in terms Aristotle uses, is to recall his remark (here in the Loeb translation) that "the ignorant [are] more persuasive in the presence of crowds, . . . for the educated use commonplaces and generalities, whereas the ignorant speak of what they know and of what more nearly concerns the audience" (*"Art" of Rhetoric* 289). The ignorant know what they know as native speakers know their language, and they can speak successfully to others like themselves with ease. For Aristotle, this success of the ignorant is clearly not to their credit, but it does lead him to advise his educated rhetor to adjust to his ignorant listeners and not "argue from all possible opinions, but only from such as are definite and admitted, either by the judges or those whose judgment they approve" (*On Rhetoric* 289). Aristotle thus starts from the position of the learned and makes even the beliefs and practices of the ignorant something for the learned to study and simulate through artful effort, while the Bakhtin School's discourse theory seeks continuity between the everyday discursive practices of the speakers in ordinary life and the sophisticated practices of the learned, among which the art of rhetoric is one well developed practice.

Bakhtin proposes to consider rhetorical and literary genres "as specific types of utterances distinct from other types, but sharing with them a common *verbal* (language) nature" (SG 61). Voloshinov's "Discourse in Life and Discourse in Art" starts from the simplest of everyday utterances to discover the common verbal nature that such utterances share with poetic works. From that earliest Bakhtin School text to Bakhtin's latest notes, there is a consistent and insistent positing of "the whole utterance as speech performance" (Medvedev 132) as "the real *unit* of speech communication, for speech can exist in reality only in the form of concrete utterances of individual speaking people, speech subjects" (SG 71). This unit is bounded by the change of speaking subjects, shaped for the response of listeners or readers to whom it is addressed, and responsive to prior utterances on its topic in its sphere of communication. It takes its form as a definite speech genre, a "relatively stable typical *form . . . of construction of the whole*" (SG 78) with "relatively stable thematic, compositional, and stylistic" features and relatively stable "types of relations between the speaker and other participants in the speech communication" (SG 64). In the "utterance as speech performance" those relations among participants are always expressed through intonation, which is always "oriented . . . with respect to the listener as ally or witness and with respect to the object of the utterance as the third, living participant whom the intonation scolds or caresses, denigrates or magnifies" (DLDA 104–05), and oriented as well "toward others' utterances" regarding the object (SG 92). Intonation, "the verbal factor of greatest sensitivity, elasticity, and freedom," expresses "a living, forceful relation with the external world and with the social milieu—enemies, friends, allies" (DLDA 104–05). In particular, "it is in intonation above all that the speaker comes into contact with the listener or listeners" (DLDA 102). Intonation is a feature of all *viva voce* discourse, and it is inferred in written discourse from choices of words, the manner of unfolding, and the rhythm of the written work.

There is no "Discourse in Life and Discourse in Rhetoric" in the Bakhtin School corpus, but we may begin to construct one from this account of the utterance and from explicit remarks on rhetoric in a number of texts. Bakhtin recognizes that

> rhetorical genres have been studied since antiquity (and not much has been added in subsequent epochs to classical theory). At that time more attention was already being devoted to the verbal nature of these genres as utterances: for example, to such aspects as the relation to the listener and his influence on the utterance, the specific verbal finalization of the utterance (as distinct from its completeness of thought), and so forth. But here, too, [as in the classical study of literary genres], the specific features of rhetorical genres (judicial, political) still overshadowed their general linguistic nature. (SG 61)

This could certainly be said of Aristotle's *Rhetoric,* which defines rhetoric not primarily as an art of utterance in all spheres of communication but as an art of finding arguments for speeches addressed to judicial, political, and ceremonial occasions. For Aristotle, it is regrettably necessary, after treating these central questions, to pay some attention to verbal matters of delivery, style, and arrangement (I think this last is what Bakhtin means by "the specific verbal finalization of the utterance"). Aristotle concentrates his attention on enriching what *might be said* in cases of these kinds, whereas Bakhtin's theory of utterance focuses on the saying itself and the types of saying characteristic of various spheres of social communication.

A collection of relevant premises and lines of argument is not an utterance any more than a collection of possible grammatical forms. An utterance must present its arguments in a determinate order with or without repetition, it must present them in certain words that exclude other words, and it must present them in a definite tone that bespeaks the speaker's relation to listener, topic, and precedent utterances. An utterance is an act in the terms in which we have seen Bakhtin define acts in *Toward a Philosophy of the Act.* All of these features of the utterance have great rhetorical salience, as Aristotle acknowledges at the outset of Book III: "it is not enough to have a supply of things to say, but it is also necessary to say it in the right way, and this contributes toward the speech seeming to have a certain quality" (*On Rhetoric* 217).

The tone of delivery is not just barely relevant to "clarity," as Aristotle grudgingly allows (*On Rhetoric* 219). Any argument can be intoned to represent the topic in a way that indicates a speaker's ironic reversal of its apparent semantic force ("And Brutus is an honorable man"). An argument's tone can insult or alienate listeners or produce conviction and identification without or despite explicit argument, and it can indicate speakers' membership in the community they address or expose their foreignness. It is thus critical to the projection of the good will that is essential to an effective ethos. Tone is also essential to the arousal of emotions, for emotions depend upon impressions of the hierarchical social relations and degrees of intimacy among speaker, listener, and hero—impressions that are reflected in and projected by the tone of the utterance (DLDA 110–12). It can show respect toward precedent speakers and opponents or it can reveal contempt or distrust toward them, rhetorically modifying the "inartistic" arguments made available through the testimony of witnesses as well as affecting the audience's judgment of rhetorical antagonists. Tone, indeed, *is* an argument, a minimal enthymeme in which the intoned expression calls up the unstated premises of the situation and moves the listener to share the speaker's evaluation of the subject in question. A rhetorical theorist of philosophic disposition may be scandalized by such an argument, wanting explicit reasons to be declared and made available for critical examination, but auditors in a rhetorical situation will often identify aliens to their community precisely by their stating what should go without saying and will recognize compatriots by their taking just the right things for granted.

In "Discourse in Life and Discourse in Art," Voloshinov identifies arrangement and style—"*the manner of the unfolding*" and the "*evaluative impetus of the epithet or metaphor*"—along with the rhythm as aspects of the form of the utterance that contribute to the evaluation of content (DLDA 108). They play, in effect, the same role as tone and make it possible for written utterances to convey an analog of the tone conveyed in oral delivery. This should be clear enough in the aspect of style concerned with choice of words. The rhetor, like Voloshinov's poet, "selects words not from the dictionary but from the context of life where words have been steeped in and become permeated with value judgments. Thus he selects the value judgments associated with words and does so, moreover, from the standpoint of the incarnated bearers of those value judgments" (DLDA 107). These selections evaluate both the speaker's relation to the audience, as stylistic choices reflect the relative status and degree of familiarity in that relation, and the speaker's relation to the topic or hero. Again, clarity is not the only thing at stake in these choices.

Aristotle himself in the *Rhetoric* recognizes not only clarity but also appropriateness as virtues of style, but his initial distinction in appropriateness comes from the *Poetics*. He distinguishes between flat style and ornamented or unfamiliar style, which "makes language seem more elevated." His advice on this head is surprising: "To deviate [from prevailing usage] makes language seem more elevated; for people feel the same in regard to *lexis* as they do in regard to strangers compared with citizens. As a result, one should make the language unfamiliar, for people are admirers of what is far off, and what is marvelous is sweet" (*On Rhetoric* 221). The Loeb translation makes the point more strikingly but backs off from it in a footnote: "In this respect men feel the same in regard to style as in regard to foreigners and fellow-citizens. Wherefore we should give our language a 'foreign air': for men admire what is remote, and what excites admiration is pleasant." The note goes on, "'Foreign' does not really convey the idea, which is rather that of something opposed to the 'home-like,'—out-of-the-way, as if from 'abroad.' Jebb suggests 'distinctive'" (*"Art" of Rhetoric* 351). The uneasiness of the translator here calls attention to the oddity of the advice. It seems out of place at least for deliberative occasions, in which the speaker's credentials as fellow citizen would seem to be crucial and stylistic consanguinity most appropriate. Perhaps in epideictic occasions—those closest to the poetic—where admiration of the speaker is sometimes paramount, the advice might hold.

Aristotle's distinction between citizen's and stranger's style marks a socially constituted stylistic line of the sort the Bakhtin School draws, but it is only one among many such distinctions grounded in social distinctions that carry with them different styles. Differences of social class, gender, profession, organizational role, and family relation within a given community all affect stylistic choices in the same way as differences between members and non-members of the community. Aristotle recognizes several additional distinctions of this kind in his elaboration of the topic of appropriateness in III.7. Differences of age, gender, citizenship, or those between "a rustic and an educated person" have stylistic implications that he links to rhetorical ethos.

> The same chapter describes style in terms of tone in the expression of emotion: Emotion is expressed if the style, in the case of insolence (*hybris*), is that of the angry man; in the case of impious or shameful things, if it is that of one who is indignant and reluctant even to say the words; in the case of admirable things, [if they are spoken] respectfully; but if [the things] are pitiable, [if they are spoken] in a submissive manner; and similarly in other cases. (*On Rhetoric* 235)

Aristotle says he is distinguishing styles but seems to be describing tones, expressed evaluative relations between speaker and topic. The question of what stylistic choices would express these several tones remains open, but the close connection between style and tone is evident here.

Though it is easy to see the evaluative and therefore tonal implications of style, it is more difficult to see those implications of the "manner of unfolding" or arrangement. Traditional accounts of this topic enumerate the sequence of parts of the oration, usually based on the standardized forensic speech, sometimes subdivided and elaborated. Aristotle has little patience with the handbooks that standardize and multiply parts but fail to distinguish their function, and he sees only two essential functional parts, stating the subject and demonstrating it. Nevertheless, he goes on to show how other parts, the proem, narration, interrogation, and epilogue, function differently in each of his three rhetorical genres. His nuanced account deserves more attention than it has received from commentators on the *Rhetoric,* who, like recent rhetorical theorists, ignore arrangement altogether (see Fahnestock, "Arrangement" and "Modern Arrangement").

Bakhtin and Voloshinov do not devote extensive attention to arrangement either, but their placement of rhetoric as a type of utterance opens several new ways of thinking about the topic. First of all, it helps us recognize the "parts" of the utterance as primary speech genres incorporated into the more extended and elaborate secondary genres of rhetorical argument. Greeting, introducing, narrating, declaring, and giving reasons are elementary discursive moves familiar from everyday conversation that take a regular place in rhetorical utterances. They are the building blocks of "compositional structure" that Bakhtin identifies as the most important feature of genre recognition (SG 60).

The selection and sequence of discursive moves in an utterance, rhetorical or otherwise, will depend upon the sorts of utterances that have preceded it and the sphere of communication in which it takes place. How the given case is given or what is given in it will enable and constrain how a rhetorical utterance responds to it. Aristotle is sensitive to this principle, recognizing that the accused and the accuser will bring in different matters at different times in a forensic utterance or that everyone will already know what the issue is in a deliberative utterance so that no preliminaries may be necessary. Indeed it may not be necessary even to state the subject, Aristotle's first essential part of the oration, if all know the subject, or to state one's position on the subject if one takes the podium as the accuser, the defender, the nominator or the celebrator. What we call the question in some formal rhetorical settings is more than metaphorically a question; it is an institutional or socially constrained asking that invites certain kinds of answers and rules out others. The giving of a case, however institutionally and formally, is a move in a dialogue to which the rhetorical utterance called for is a reply.

Highly standardized and formalized situations like that of the judicial speech will be most subject to the standardization of the number and sequence of parts of an utterance addressing it. This is why the forensic speech has provided the standard account of the parts of the oration that Aristotle complicates by considering the possible function of those parts in deliberative and epideictic situations. Less formalized situations may open the way for different sequencing or elaboration of parts. The utterance that has to create its situation instead of taking it as given will be much more elaborate in its preliminaries than the one that can take its given situation for granted and address it. This difference is especially crucial to the difference between *viva voce* utterances and written ones.

In addition to the utterances that give cases, the utterances of other participants in the rhetorical situation—opponents, judges, the accused, the celebrated, those who have evaluated the hero or the situation previously—are also provocations and constraints on the types of subordinate utterances that will appear in an oration and the order in which they will appear. Aristotle, too, recognizes that the orator who comes second has a different situation to respond to than the one who comes first and may organize the "parts" of the response accordingly. And since elaborate secondary speech genres like rhetorical addresses are composed of simpler primary genres, another shaping feature of the number and sequence of parts of an utterance will be other parts of that utterance itself. Internalized questions will call ordinarily for internalized answers, unless those answers can be presupposed, making the questions rhetorical, and quotations will enable interpretations or refutations, unless they can be assumed to "speak for themselves." Claims, as Aristotle recognizes, will call for demonstrations, unless, of course, they are restating what everyone knows, and digressions will need to be followed by returns to the main point, at least if the matter at hand is a serious one.

Arrangement is thus dialogically shaped and constrained, externally and internally. It is productive of tone when, like tropes and figures, it calls attention to itself by violating established expectations or by making noticeable patterns beyond what is minimally called for. Questions or exclamations or declarations can appear out of standard sequence or interrupt familiar patterns or repeat themselves. Turns away from the subject and toward the speaker or the audience or the utterances of others or the hero—what have come to be called figures of thought—call attention to evaluations of all these parties to the discourse and stand out against the backdrop of the subject-centered decorum of serious genres (see Chapter 4). Speakers' dwelling upon themselves or worrying their relations to their listeners instead of getting to the point are matters of disposition that create tone. Expected parts of standard generic arrangements can be deferred, hurried, omitted, or expanded disproportionately. Delaying the introduction of expected considerations can give the impression of their evaluative importance or of their inconvenience to the case. Starting with things, returning to them, delaying them, repeating them are all indices of evaluation that provoke us to make inferences of tone. Even sticking to a standard pattern for standard purposes is a sign of serious and businesslike tone, just as Shandean deferral of the expected point is a sign of comic intent.

Rhetorical utterances, then, like utterances in general, deliver evaluations of their subjects and enact identifications with their listeners through *viva voce* intonation and through written signs of tone in style and arrangement. They are differentiated from other utterances by their public sphere of communication and their institutionalized occasions, which have stabilized genres of deliberation, adjudication, and celebration. Those genres call upon relatively stable lines of argument, a range of styles, and resources of arrangement suited to the several genres, some standardized, others open to expressive choice. Aristotelian rhetoric gives first and most extensive attention to the lines of argument available for those institutionalized occasions; Bakhtin's rhetoric attends to the signs of intonation in the enacted utterance that bespeak the speaker's or writer's evaluation of subject and relation to audience.

The two rhetorics are complementary, but I believe that Bakhtin's rhetoric is functionally prior to Aristotle's and ultimately governs it. There can be persuasion without argument, grounded in shared evaluation expressed through intonation, and the selection and disposition of arguments in rhetorical utterances must be ruled by their provocations and their anticipations of response, not by their availability alone. Rhetors possessed of a storehouse of available means of persuasion like the one Aristotle compiles will lack means of choosing and ordering them unless they can respond to the questions posed to them and select among those means with knowledge of what their auditors already know, believe, and hold dear. They cannot decide what to say just by knowing what might be said; they must also know what has just been said by others and what goes without saying for their audience. Their ethos and their ability to move their auditors' or readers' emotions will be as dependent on their knowing to whom and after whom they are speaking as their choice of arguments on the subject at hand. Without attention to the aspects of rhetorical utterance that Bakhtin emphasizes, Aristotelian rhetors would risk failure as pedants who bring too many arguments to bear or as outsiders who bring the wrong ones. Their audiences would distrust them as the proverbial pointy-headed intellectuals or not laugh at their jokes or be moved by their sentiments. Entechnic argument is no substitute for enthymematic utterance that shares the unspoken beliefs and evaluations of those it aims to persuade and delivers that unspoken understanding through persuasive intonation.

10. Rereading the Place of Rhetoric in Aristotle's *Poetics* in Light of Bakhtin's Discourse Theory: Rhetoric as *Dianoia*, Poetics as an Imitation of Rhetoric

I anticipated in the last chapter that a reading of Aristotle's *Poetics* that focuses on its referral of thought or *dianoia* to his *Rhetoric* may lead us to a position close to Bakhtin's dialogic poetics as I have elaborated it in Chapter 8, and I began that reading by looking at Aristotle's passages on *dianoia* and *hypocrisis* in the *Poetics*. This chapter will pursue that anticipation further and return to those passages for a closer and more critical reading. It is a reading that goes against the grain of the argument Aristotle is trying to make and consequently against the many subsequent interpretations of the *Poetics* that consider him to have successfully made it. I will take seriously his discrepant accounts of *dianoia*, discrepancies that I am not the first to notice,[30] and read them from the point of view of his *Rhetoric*, as previous commentators have not done. In addition, in the present Bakhtin School context I will read the relationships I uncover not as incoherences but as signs of a pre-disciplinary view of discourse in which something like the Bakhtinian relationship between a primary "rhetorical" discourse and a poetic discourse that imitates it shines forth. Along lines close to those P. Christopher Smith follows in his "destructive" Heideggerian readings of these Aristotelian texts, I read Aristotle, in his attempt to limit utterance to the category of *dianoia* or thought, as actively resisting and repressing but not entirely obscuring earlier sophistic and even Platonic accounts of poetry as utterance and imitation of utterance. I read him as engaged in what Bakhtin would call "hidden dialogue" or "hidden polemic" with a precedent poetics of utterance as he tries to establish a poetics of imitated action that treats language as the material in which the imitation is made.

I will pose two questions: What part does Aristotle's *Rhetoric* play in his *Poetics?* Second, what part of his *Rhetoric* is *in play* in his *Poetics?* If the first question were a test question for students of the *Poetics,* the answer would be: Of the six parts of tragedy Aristotle derives in Chapter VI of the *Poetics*—plot, character, thought, diction, melody, and spectacle—*Rhetoric* is assigned the tertiary role of thought, or *dianoia*. He himself assigns it this role in Chapter XIX where he writes, in Halliwell's Loeb translation, "The discussion of thought can be left to my discourses on rhetoric, for it is more integral to that enquiry" (1456a 33–35). This cross reference allows for a very brief elaboration of what *dianoia* entails within the *Poetics* itself and a quick turn to the next part—diction, or *lexis*. This would be a good answer, though it would not yet have explained how Aristotle characterizes *dianoia* in the *Poetics* or how his several characterizations of it fit with one another or with his *Rhetoric*—topics to which I shall return in a moment.

The second question would not have an immediately obvious answer. Indeed, the cross-reference to the *Rhetoric* points to no obvious part of the work we know. *Dianoia,* or thought, is neither a major nor a minor heading in Aristotle's *Rhetoric*. Neither the Greek term nor its English translation merits an index entry in Kennedy's translation. Is Aristotle referring us, then, to the whole of the *Rhetoric* and inviting us to re-conceive it under the rubric of "thought" rather than "persuasion," or has he simply cryptically neglected to indicate which part of the text he is referring to? We will see below that he gives us at least one clue.

If it is not clear where to go from the *Poetics* to the *Rhetoric,* it is disorienting to come from the *Rhetoric* to the *Poetics* and read the several versions of the part that Aristotle assigns there to rhetoric as the locus of *dianoia*. As I showed in Chapter 9, we first encounter *dianoia* in his Chapter VI as one of the "factors which allow us to ascribe qualities to [a character's] actions"(1450a). It is immediately distinguished from character, *ethos,* however, in the following terms: "I use . . . 'character' to mean that in virtue of which we ascribe certain qualities to the agents, and 'thought' to cover the parts in which, through speech, they demonstrate something or declare their views." Coming from the *Rhetoric,* one may wonder at least two things about this distinction: First, is speech, which is explicitly linked here to thought but not to character, something in virtue of which we ascribe certain qualities to agents? In rhetoric, it is all we have to go on—artistically—in ascribing character to a speaker, though we may have inartistic supplements from the testimony of witnesses or from what torture might reveal. Second, if character too is revealed in speech, do "the parts in which, through speech, they demonstrate something or declare their views" stand apart from the parts in speech in which they reveal their qualities as agents? If so (and we will have reason in a moment to think Aristotle thinks so), then thought would seem to be closer to vernacular rhetoric's vernacular dialectical counterpart than to vernacular rhetoric itself, as Aristotle first distinguishes them in the opening chapter of the *Rhetoric*—this is the distinction from which my second chapter begins. It is through vernacular dialectic in the *Rhetoric*'s opening paragraph that all people try, impersonally, it would seem, to "test and maintain an argument," while it is in vernacular rhetoric that they try, with their characters at stake, "to defend themselves and attack others" (*On Rhetoric* 29). Janko's translation of *dianoia* as "reasoning" instead of "thought" emphasizes this affinity with Aristotle's dialectic and reminds us that *dianoia* is also associated with the third level of Plato's divided line in the *Republic*, not quite Plato's highest level of dialectic that aspires toward *nous*, but above the lower half of the line concerned with opinion, where rhetoric belongs (8).

The only part of the *Rhetoric* this account of *dianoia* would comport with is the part that draws upon the reduced dialectical proofs, consisting of enthymemes and examples, that fall under the head of *logos*. Though Aristotle gives special emphasis to this class of proofs and seems sometimes to wish that it were the only kind, he recognizes sometimes that in rhetoric such proofs are always associated with the proofs of *ethos* that come from the character of the speaker and the proofs of *pathos* that come from the audience's responses to representations of the situation and the speaker. It is only philosophers who aspire to produce formally complete proofs that "demonstrate or declare their views" without revealing their characters or appealing to one another's feelings.

When we next find Aristotle distinguishing character from thought later in Chapter VI at 1450b, readers coming from his *Rhetoric* will again not quite recognize the rhetoric they have just left. It will sound familiar to hear "thought" understood as rhetoric defined as "the capacity to say what is pertinent and apt, which in formal speeches is the task of politics and rhetoric," for thought here is a power or *dunamis* as it is in the *Rhetoric*, and it manifests itself in speeches, often political ones. But a power of finding means of "persuasion" in a particular case that is specified in the *Rhetoric* as one of three kinds of cases is here replaced by a power of saying what is pertinent and apt in indeterminate cases with indeterminate ends. Suasion may or may not be what speeches revealing thought may aim at, and the occasions that prompt those speeches and in relation to which they will be found pertinent and apt are no longer given deliberative, epideictic, or forensic cases but, one imagines, whatever words or action that have already been said or done in whatever situation by whomever is involved in that situation. Rhetoric or speech here expands to include all kinds of utterances as I have shown Bakhtin's analysis in "Speech Genres" does.

Chapter VI at 1450b goes on to clarify two points that we questioned at 1450a. Aristotle says,

> Character is that which reveals moral choice—that is, when otherwise unclear, what kinds of things an agent chooses or rejects (which is why speeches in which there is nothing at all the speaker chooses or rejects contain no character); while thought covers the parts in which they demonstrate that something is or is not so, or declare a general view.

So some speeches *do* reveal character when they express choices and preferences, while other speeches reveal no character but only show that something is or isn't the case or declare impersonal truths that say nothing about the character of the one who declares them. Though the character-revealing speech is much closer to the sort of speech Aristotle's art of rhetoric considers, while the truth-declaring and proving speech would seem to belong in his dialectical domain, Aristotle nonetheless refers *dianoia* to his *Rhetoric*, not to his *Topics* or his *Analytics*. Those of us coming from his *Rhetoric* should be wondering why he would refer *dianoia* there, and those starting from the *Poetics* should be thinking that the only relevant parts of the *Rhetoric* for their purposes might be the chapters on logos—rhetorical syllogisms and inductions in Books I and II—which they might want to supplement with Aristotle's consideration elsewhere of real syllogisms and inductions.

But the concluding words of Book II of the *Rhetoric* seem to say that *dianoia* has been the subject not just of a few chapters of the first two books but of the whole treatise so far. Though Kennedy does not index *dianoia* or thought, he calls attention to both terms in his translation of this concluding passage. His translation reads:

> Since there are in fact three things that should be systematically worked out in discussion of speech, let us regard what has been said as enough about the paradigms and maxims and enthymemes and in general about thought [*dianoia*] and the sources of arguments and how we shall refute them. It remains to go through the subject of style [*lexis*] and arrangement [*taxis*].

I am surprised here to find that the three things necessary to a speech are *dianoia, lexis, and taxis,* instead of *logos, ethos, and pathos* and to find the previous two books summarized as if *logos* were their sole subject and *ethos* and *pathos,* had not been treated in them at all. Either *ethos* and *pathos* have been forgotten in this summary despite their taking up the first seventeen chapters of Book II, or they are to be understood somehow as among the "sources of argument" and to be *part* of *dianoia.*

The efforts we have seen Aristotle make in Chapter VI to separate *dianoia* from *ethos* argue against his including *ethos* as part of *dianoia,* but the account he gives of *dianoia* in Chapter XIX of the *Poetics* raises this question in a new form. Chapter XIX seems to incorporate the whole of the *Rhetoric* into the *Poetics* or at least almost all of it:

> The discussion of thought can be left to my discourses on rhetoric, for it is more integral to that inquiry. "Thought" covers all effects, which need to be created by speech: their elements are proof, refutation, and the conveying of emotions (pity, fear, anger, etc.), as well as enhancement and belittlement. It is clear that the same principles should also be used in handling of events, when one needs to create impressions of what is pitiable, terrible, important, or probable—with this difference, that the latter effects must be evident without direct statement, while the former must be conveyed by the speaker in and through speech. For what would be the point of the speaker, if the required effects were evident even without speech?

Here "all effects which need to be created by speech" are covered by "thought," and the enumeration of their elements includes not just the principal aspects of proofs from *logos* (proof, refutation, and amplification) but also the appeals to *pathos* (pity, fear, anger, etc.). What is strikingly absent from this enumeration is that one of the principal "effects to be created by speech" is *ethos,* which we learned in Chapter VI was an aspect of *character as opposed to thought.* Here in Chapter XIX it appears that character, at least as it is revealed by speech rather than "events," is not opposed to thought but should be one more of the effects created by speech that belong to thought. Characters are not just agents but speaking agents, and thought as here defined includes the effects of speeches that bespeak their reasoning, their passions, and, though it is not mentioned, their characters. The distinction in the last part of this passage between events—what is visibly done—and speeches—what is said—includes explicitly the passions on both sides and should include the presentation of character on both sides as well. We can recognize the melodramatic villain from his sneer, his leer, his laugh and his twirling of his moustache as well as from his spoken threats. Reasoning alone would seem to belong only on the side of speaking, though a good mime can at least mime getting an idea. Speech/*dianoia*/ thought gives enormously greater latitude to the imitation of reasoning, but *dianoia* is not confined to reasoning utterance alone. It also includes impassioned and characterizing utterance.

It would appear, then, that though Aristotle in the earlier passages tried to maintain a distinction between character and thought, thought *includes* character as it manifests through speech. The more fundamental distinction is between what is communicated by bodily action alone and what is communicated by speech or *dianoia*. Tragic drama would be distinguished from mime by its imitation of *speaking and acting* agents, dianoetic agents—embodied rhetorical agents communicating their reasoning, passions, and characters through "pertinent and apt" words and bodily movements. Epic would be distinguished by its communication of the speaking of its agents through the speaking (but not the bodily acting) of its narrator—a part of narration we now recognize but that Aristotle did not.[31] In epic both the narrator and the speaking agents reveal their reasoning, passions, and characters, the one directly through speaking, the others only through the narrator's reporting of their speech and actions. It could be thought of as a rhetoric that reports other rhetoric and action, as Bakhtin's double-voiced discourse that makes the novel so interesting to him. Lyric poetry, which Aristotle does not discuss, would be an imitation of speech alone that does not report other speaking and acting or imitate acting, an imitation of rhetorical utterance alone without bodily movement.

But these revised distinctions of poetic kinds still depend upon a problematic separation of speech from bodily movement. Speaking, after all, is a kind of bodily movement, a kind of physical action. It issues from the muscles, the breath, the mouth and tongue in motion. To call the speech in poetry "thought" or *dianoia* is to occlude its bodily manifestation, its utterance, to mentalize or disembody it.[32] Aristotle's naming of speech as thought is part of his more extensive effort that Jeffrey Walker and P. Christopher Smith have documented in both the *Poetics* and the *Rhetoric* to disembody speech and make it rational. I have already considered the relevant passages on delivery in Chapter XIX of the *Poetics* and the first chapter of Book III of the *Rhetoric* in Chapter 9 above, but I return to them here to emphasize a crucial point.

Immediately after the section we just reviewed in Aristotle's Chapter XIX, he turns from thought to diction and writes, "As for matters of diction, one type of study concerns the forms (*schemata*) of utterance (knowledge of which belongs to the art of delivery and the person with this mastery— namely what is a command, prayer, narrative, threat, question, reply, and all the like. Knowledge or ignorance of these things can support no serious criticism of poetry.)" Delivery, the embodied utterance of words that distinguishes a question from an assertion or a command from a prayer by how the words are intoned, has no relevance, he tells us, to poetics or tragedy, even though, as we have just seen, tragic drama is distinguished by its imitation of speaking agents acting and speaking. The words, it appears, should reveal their meaning to the reader of the play without attention to how they might be spoken. Aristotle, as his remark later about reading tragedy confirms, is focused on the text rather than the performance, on the thought it contains abstracted from the utterance that delivers it.

Aristotle's ambivalent treatment (and his interesting analysis) of delivery in the opening of Book III of the *Rhetoric* is too long to quote in full, but his preference for the rational and conceptual over the embodied utterance and his grudging attention to the latter are evident there, as we have seen in Chapter 9. Aristotle deprecates outward show in favor of what must be inward thought, the *dianoia* that he has just said was the subject of the previous two books. He gives precedence to the monotonous teaching of geometry, where concept trumps expression of character and emotion, over delivered rhetorical or poetic utterance, where as he had said earlier, "the voice should be used in expressing each emotion" through tone, pitch, and rhythm (218). As in *Poetics* XIX, so at the beginning of *Rhetoric* III, the thought should be clear apart from its delivery, and embodied speaking introduces distracting irrelevancies into what ought to be rational communication. Embodied delivery is inescapable in spoken discourse, however, as even Aristotle grudgingly concedes of rhetoric, and we have seen that recovery of intonation from written text is crucial for poetry, where the reader (and also the actor of drama) must co-create the tones in the scripted utterance. Speech, Bakhtinian utterance scripted for delivery or imaginative co-creation, is that through which poems are realized, and even Aristotelian dramatic plots must come into being through it.

In both the *Poetics* and the *Rhetoric,* we have seen Aristotle attempting unsuccessfully to reduce speech to thought, even as he must sometimes acknowledge thought's inescapable participation in embodied speech that expresses emotion and reveals character even as it reasons. What answers does this recognition offer to my opening questions: First, what part does Aristotle's *Rhetoric* play in his *Poetics?* Second, what part of his *Rhetoric* is *in play* in his *Poetics?* In answer to the first, I would say that speakers engaged in rhetorical utterance, broadly understood as saying "what is pertinent and apt" on all sorts of occasions, are the object of all poetic imitation, sometimes organized into plots and presented as acting and speaking like those Aristotle analyzes in tragic drama, sometimes narrating what others have said and done and felt and thought, sometimes speaking and arguing in response to an unlimited number of interesting exigencies and provocations. The *Rhetoric* plays a bigger part in the *Poetics* than Aristotle explicitly grants it, though we find him on the edge, in Chapter XIX, of recognizing that character, like reasoning and passion, is not a separate part of tragedy but a function of the rhetoric or speech in poetry and that tragedy imitates not just men in action but men acting *and speaking*. If speech replaced thought or *dianoia* among the parts of tragedy Aristotle enumerates as an object of imitation, character, *ethos,* would be manifested through it as well as through imitated actions, and the *Rhetoric*'s part in the *Poetics* would begin to emerge. I think, however, that its part is larger still, as my answer to the second question will suggest.

What part of the *Rhetoric* is in play in the *Poetics?* All of it, though some parts will be more directly relevant than others. The *pisteis,* or kinds of proof, we have seen, are central. The Aristotelian genres of rhetorical occasion are unnecessarily limiting, although they can provide a model for analyzing less definitely delimited kinds of utterances that say what is "pertinent and apt" on a number of less institutionalized occasions, a model Bakhtin follows in his analysis of the unlimited number of speech genres by content, style, and compositional structure addressing the numerous exigencies of multiple spheres of communication. The epideictic, least central of the genres in the *Rhetoric,* takes on greater importance in a rhetorical poetics, as Jeffrey Walker has shown, and exemplifies the evaluative function that Bakhtin finds in all discourse. The *Rhetoric*'s account of logos—the enthymeme and example, and rhetorical topoi—have profound relevance to poetic discourse, which depends upon, appeals to, and calls attention to the taken-for-granted and the taken-to-heart, as Voloshinov shows in "Discourse in Life and Discourse in Art." The analysis of the passions provides a powerful analytic for poetic as well as rhetorical interactions of persons and articulates important determinations of the tones that various hierarchical and intimate social relations produce. Aristotle's analysis shares the independent variables of hierarchy and intimacy/distance with the Bakhtin School. The underdeveloped account of *ethos* might be elaborated with examples of poetic characters, just as the genres of discourse might be expanded in more open contexts of poetic utterance. The treatment of style in Book III of the *Rhetoric* is in many ways more appropriate to the *Poetics* than the peculiar account of it that Aristotle gives in the *Poetics* itself. Style in the *Rhetoric* considers the appropriateness of diction to the speaker's character, while the treatment of language as material in the *Poetics* underwrites the formalist materialist poetics Bakhtin opposes because it reveals the poet's manipulations of language but not the speaker's evaluation of his topic or hero. The account of arrangement in the

Rhetoric supplements the exclusive treatment of plot in the *Poetics* with attention to the various unfoldings of utterance and argument Bakhtin points to in "Speech Genres." The deprecation of delivery in both treatises—the main point of difference between Aristotle and Bakhtin as I have shown in Chapter 9—needs to be reversed, and a good starting place is Aristotle's brief analysis of it in the first chapter of Book III. I believe that the whole of the *Rhetoric* is not a footnote to the *Poetics* or an optional cross-reference but rather its most important part, without which poetry cannot be properly understood.

Recalling that for Bakhtin action is a fundamental category but that speech is not only a kind of action but also an essential accompaniment to action that makes it intelligible as action, we can now expand Aristotle's poetics of imitated action to a poetics of acting implied by scripted speech and scripted speech that becomes action when it is uttered. We could say that poetry imitates *logos* not in the restricted Aristotelian sense of reasoning but in Gorgias's sophistic sense of the word or speaking, and that plots are one, but not the only, shape that a sequence of *logoi* can take. Arguments, dialogues, all the genres of speaking that lyric poems imitate and elaborate—toasts and boasts, aubades and lullabies, curses and blessings, commands and prayers—and an unlimited number of kinds of utterances and combinations of them into more elaborate utterances would all be among objects it imitates. The structuralist narratological privileging of stories over discourse is reversed in this Bakhtinian and revised Aristotelian poetics, as is the formalist privileging of verbal material over verbalized utterance.[33]

I will be the first to admit that even bringing this version of Aristotle's *Poetics* to the aid of Bakhtin's poetics of utterance will not easily displace the well-established Aristotle's *Poetics* in which narratologists, my mentor Wayne Booth, and a pervasive and enduring tradition have long invested. And I will also readily concede that Aristotle's *Poetics* as it is usually read has proved itself fruitful in analysis of its paradigmatic topic, tragic dramatic poetry. There plots do take special importance, and the signs of the author's evaluative stance are all indirectly inferable from the shape and style (and sometimes stage directions) the author made, mediated by the interpretations of actors, directors, and a battery of costumers, lighting specialists, and set designers who, from Aristotle's perspective, make it more difficult to make out what the playwright made. But studies of narrative have not benefited by starting from a poetics that has no conception of the narrator and privileges dramatic showing over telling, and studies of lyric poetry have been blinded by formalist appropriations of Aristotle's account of diction as material. As Voloshinov puts it, "However far we go in analyzing all the properties of the material and all the possible combinations of those properties, we shall never be able to find their aesthetic significance unless we slip in the contraband of another point of view that does not belong within the framework of analysis of the material" (DLDA 97). The Bakhtin School, on the other hand, has little to say about drama (Caryl Emerson has recently explored this lack at an International Bakhtin Conference in Stockholm), and the most familiar Bakhtin School texts have advanced our understanding of reported speech and novelistic narrative discourse while reinforcing an unproductive monologic account of lyric poetry.

The poetics of utterance I have drawn out of Aristotle's *Poetics* and explicated from translations of Bakhtin's earliest manuscripts, Voloshinov's "Discourse in Life and Discourse in Art," and Bakhtin's late essay on speech genres has ample room for lyric poems, understood as scripts imitating simple and complex utterances of all kinds by single speakers, available for imaginative co-creation of the evaluative acts those speakers perform.[34] As I have shown both from Bakhtin School texts and from this chapter's reading of Aristotle, this poetics of utterance is intimately connected with an expansive understanding of rhetoric as the domain of evaluative utterances or discursive acts. Those utterances or discursive acts may be systematically studied for various disciplinary purposes—to make those acts more persuasive in certain institutional contexts (what we commonly call "rhetoric"), to delimit the style and shape of those acts for certain special kinds of inquiry like philosophy and science ("dialectic") or certain kinds of institutions like business or the military, or to make aesthetic imitations of those acts interesting to co-create and to learn to co-create those imitations enjoyably and instructively ("poetics"). There are other lines of inquiry that aim simply to describe such acts accurately or to account for their differences across time and societies. I believe that the most important contribution of the Bakhtin School to these inquiries was not the first one I imagined, to add a discipline or art of dialogics to the already extant disciplines of rhetoric, dialectic, and poetics. More important was Bakhtin's architectonic effort to make all of these disciplines along with linguistics, stylistics, and philology responsive to the predisciplinary scene of action informed and articulated by evaluative discourse and Voloshinov's and Bakhtin's location of that evaluative discourse in concrete historical social situations.

Bender and Wellbery grasped this contribution, even before the early manuscripts were translated, when they saw Bakhtin's works as "virtual treatises on the nature and functioning of rhetoricality" (p. 37), a "generalized rhetoric that penetrates to the deepest levels of human experience, . . . bound to no specific set of institutions, . . . no longer the title of a doctrine and a practice . . . [but] something like the condition of our existence" (p. 25). Aristotle recognized in the first paragraph of the *Rhetoric* that the practices from which he planned to derive an art of rhetoric (and implicitly an art of dialectic too) were already being practiced with varying degrees of success by "all men" before he tried to systematize them (*On Rhetoric* 4). We cannot dwell, however, in this predisciplinary world as if, Wordsworth writes, we "were [Earth's] first-born birth / And none had lived before" us (*Lyrical Ballads* 104). Aristotle and the organizations of knowledge and art that have followed in his footsteps have made that world inaccessible except through radical inquiries of the sort Bakhtin and Heidegger undertook in the 1920s.[35] But we can refer our sometimes calcified institutionalized disciplines at least to an imagined, reconstructed common world that preceded them and still underwrites them, to a discourse of evaluative concerns against which they must still justify themselves and from which they can still refresh and renovate themselves. Rhetoric in the sense to which I have expanded its range is that discourse, and poetry is the discourse that isolates and heightens rhetoric thus understood in forms we can co-create, contemplate, and critique.

11. Liberal Education, Writing, and the Dialogic Self

In academic writing it is conventional to revise oral presentations for publication by suppressing those figures of thought through which speakers register the presence of their auditors and the remarks of participating colleagues. Such revision deletes the signs of what Mikhail Bakhtin calls the dialogizing background of the utterance to generalize the contexts of its reception and universalize the appearance of its claims. It is also conventional to cover up the signs of such revision, presenting the argument as unified and the self that underwrites it as of one mind about it. Such silent revision enhances the appearance of authoritativeness and hides the possibility that the author did or could think otherwise. These conventions of published authority are part of what we teach in teaching academic writing, and my failure to abide by them in this chapter anticipates my questioning of that pedagogy. I foreground the occasions and the revisions of this piece, then, as part of my attempt to redialogize the practice and teaching of academic writing.

I begin accordingly by talking (as if I were still talking) about how I have revised this chapter and revised myself for two occasions with similar audiences but diverse co-participants. My auditors on both occasions were interested in how to think about teaching writing in a college or university, and I, on both occasions, was bringing them word of how Bakhtin's dialogic theories might clarify their purposes and inform their practices. If, as rhetoricians say, my relation to my audience governs my discourse, it might not have been necessary to revise my talk and myself from one occasion to the next, for the genre of my presentation was the same and the speaker-audience relation that determines it was the same. If the community of discourse, its conventional genres, and its commonplaces remain constant, why should I have had to rewrite my talk for a new gathering of essentially the same community? After all, the visiting pastor does not write a new sermon for each new congregation of the same faith.

Two changes between the first and second presentations of the paper nevertheless compelled me to change it, and both, I think, raise theoretically interesting questions about the notions of discourse communities, genre conventions, and commonplaces I have invoked. First, between the 1984 special session on authentic voice of the Conference on College Composition and Communication and the 1987 Chicago Conference on Interpretive Communities and the Undergraduate Writer, many members of my audience had heard about Bakhtin's dialogics. A lot of us had been saying a lot about Bakhtin in the forums many of us attend and in the publications we read, and no one needed any longer to explain who he was and how we had come to possess his work. By 1987 his name was appearing in almost every issue of *College English,* and even undergraduates were using his dialogic terms in their senior theses. So my second audience knew more about Bakhtin and his work's implications for the teaching of writing than my first audience did, and even if I abided by all the appropriate conventions of our community of discourse, my telling them what they already knew would have bored them. If, indeed, the community of discourse I was addressing and the genre conventions and commonplaces of my talk remained the same, my talk could not stay the same because the history of the discussion had changed. Academic discourse is not a ritual discourse that rehearses the same commonplaces every Sunday; academic discourse moves, and we must, as we say, keep up with it.

The second change between presentations of my paper was itself doubleedged: first, the voice that provoked and shaped much of my earlier paper was scarcely in evidence among the voices that addressed the participants in the Chicago conference, and, second, many of the voices that did address that conference were much closer to Bakhtin and me than was my original friendly adversary. My former colleague Peter Elbow first invited me to participate in the CCCC session he organized, and he encouraged me to reformulate his "self-centered" idea of "authentic voice" in the social and contentious terms of dialogics. Although Elbow's work was not unknown to my Chicago audience and some of its members even declared their allegiance to his position from the floor, his psychological and individualistic stance, which dominated the first occasion of my talk, was clearly marginalized on the second one. The psychologists who spoke in Chicago were more interested in problem solving and stages of development than in authentic voice, and the social constructionists who dominated the meeting already shared Bakhtin's view that our individual voices should be defined as relations to others, not as relations to ourselves. A Bakhtinian who shared the podium with Joe Williams, Tori Haring-Smith, Elaine Maimon, Kenneth Bruffee, Gregory Colomb, Linda Peterson, Richard Lanham, and David Bartholomae, among others, did not need to argue for a social understanding of discourse as I did when I shared the stage with Elbow. My earlier provocation to speech was placed in the background by the gathering of another group of speakers, and I needed to search for new provocations from other people whose positions were closer to my own. Though again the discourse community and the generic conventions and commonplaces of my paper remained constant, a change in the field of speakers involved and in the range of positions they represented compelled me to change my talk.

In my first talk I appropriated Elbow's terms for a social notion of authentic voice that I did not need to emphasize at the Chicago conference. Here is a part of the earlier paper that reveals its dialogic ties with Elbow:

> Voice, as I am defining it, is not so much a matter of how my language relates to me as it is a matter of how my language relates to your language and to the language of others you and I have heard address our topic. Voice is never something speakers have before they speak but something they create by defining a relation to the other voices that have already opened the discussion and to those that wait to enter into it. "I" am—and "my self" is—created in the course of my assimilating, responding to, and anticipating the voices of others. Language, from the time I first begin to hear it from my parents and siblings and friends and teachers, is always somebody else's first and becomes mine without entirely losing its otherness. Does this other-directed notion of voice deprive my voice of authenticity, as Peter Elbow understands it, as a resonant and effortless expression in an utterance of the person uttering it? Does my notion of voice so alienate my own voice that nothing distinctive to me remains? I think not, but I do think I must redefine what I mean when I talk about speaking in an authentic voice. If voice as I have defined it is to be heard in the speaker's responsiveness to the voices of others who have spoken on the topic as well as to the voices of those who now listen but may yet speak, then an authentic voice in my terms would be one that vitally and productively engaged those voices. It would be authentically situated, if you will, evidently aware of its place in the ongoing conversation about its topic, relevant to preceding utterances, alert to those about to follow, and clear about its own

contribution. In these terms, an inauthentic voice would be "out of it"—unresponsive to what had been said or what might be said on its topic, dead to possibilities that others who share the language and the world could hear and expect responses to.

Ah, there's the rub. A paper perfectly responsive to what has been said by *some* others is suddenly "out of it" in a field of *other* others. An introduction will not do where the parties are already acquainted, and a point worth making in response to a strong opponent leaves us out of it when we make it among allies who take the point for granted. And of course a chapter written still later and re-published many years later risks being even further from pertinent to those who read it. Plato was right about the written word saying the same thing again and again.

Furthermore, we can commit faux pas that expose us as "out of it" without leaving a single discourse community or leaving its system of commonplaces or breaching its decorum of genres. It is not enough, it seems, to learn to mind our academic manners, for we can still make fools of ourselves by not knowing to whom or after whom we are speaking. A student who writes a critical essay on "My Last Duchess" without mentioning a book the teacher has written on it may not impress that teacher no matter how well the essay otherwise reflects the decorum of the opening review of the literature, and the professional critic who submits a book or article for publication always takes the same risk of having ignored the major work of some anonymous referee. Knowing the conventions is indispensable, but it also helps to know who is out there.

It may appear, however, that in undergraduate instruction the conventions will suffice without the specific knowledge of prior voices. After all, one way the discourse of undergraduate instruction differs from the discourses of more advanced study and of professional academic writing is that we do not require undergraduate writers to situate their writing in the history or current published discussion of their topic. (Indeed, we sometimes do not expect our graduate students or ourselves to do so.) What this distinction means in practice, however, is not that the undergraduate student adopts conventions and exploits commonplaces without regard to specific prior uses of them but that we or our class discussions or our sets of readings establish such specific prior uses for the working purposes of the class. We define a field of the "already said" and the "might be said" in our classes, and we trust our students to recognize the conventions of our discourse and to discover the opportunities and limitations set by the specific voices we take on or admit into those classrooms. Our students' writing depends not just on their learning the ropes but on their coming into contact with some representative voices from the field whose examples suggest projects to pursue and whose differences reveal problems to address. Their writing relies, in short, on whom they have heard of and whom they have heard out.

A dialogic orientation to teaching writing differs from other social theories of discourse in its vision of ideologically situated persons involved in struggles over the meanings of things and the ownership of words. It de-emphasizes rhetorical commonplaces, calling attention instead to the appropriated, if not always proper, places of persons who have identified themselves with certain words, ideas, ways of talking, and social positions. And it envisions what Bakhtin calls "an individual's ideological becoming," not just as the learning of "information, directions, rules, models" or conventions, as my social constructionist colleagues argued in Chicago, but as the individual's struggle to make other people's language his or her own and to resist being owned completely by alien languages. As Bakhtin puts it, "the struggle and dialogic interrelationship of [authoritative and internally persuasive discourse] are what usually determine the history of an individual ideological consciousness" (DI 342).

In that struggle, the voice that speaks the authoritative word is set apart in what Bakhtin describes as a distanced zone; the authoritative word can be received and repeated but is not to be responded to, modified, or questioned. It is the voice of the textbook or the lecturer that students learn to parrot back on tests, the voice of the instructor's summary judgment, the voice of given rules and conventions that must be observed but that do not have to account for themselves. The internally persuasive word is not, however, a word belonging solely to the inner world of the student, a dialectical counterpart to a wholly external authoritative word. Bakhtin writes that

> the internally persuasive word is half-ours, half-someone else's. Its creativity and productivity consist precisely in the fact that such a word awakens new and independent words, that it organizes masses of our words from within, and does not remain in an isolated and static condition. It is not so much interpreted by us as it is further, that is, freely, developed, applied to new material, new conditions; it enters into interanimating relationships with new contexts. (DI 345–46)

Just as the authoritative word is set apart in the distanced zone, the internally persuasive word is in the "zone of contact" in which its receiver is also its user (DI 345). This word differs from the authoritative word not so much as inner to outer, though Bakhtin uses these misleading terms, but as proximate to distanced, touchable to untouchable, answerable to unanswerable language. It is not inert and indigestible, nor does it dominate from within as the authoritative word appears to dominate from without. Rather, Bakhtin writes, "it enters into an intense interaction, a *struggle* with other internally persuasive discourses" (DI 346). The internally persuasive word does not settle things and take over the voice but engages actively with other such words in vital dialogue that marks the authentically situated voice. The authoritative word remains aloof from that dialogue, co-opts it, or even silences it. The voice under the influence of the authoritative word might repeat it thoughtlessly, imitate it confusedly, cite it passively, comply with it formally, or defer to it silently.

Although the participants in the Chicago conference who emphasized teaching students the conventions of scholarly writing may also have intended to demystify the norms of authoritative discourse, I feared and still fear that their primary emphasis risks teaching no more than formal compliance with those norms. Many disciplinary courses already aim no higher than enforcing such conformity, and I would be sorry to see the writing course, whether in English or across the disciplines, confine itself to explaining the conventions that the disciplinary courses mutely impose.

As I see it, the writing class opens up a space in which individual ideological development can become not just the accidental outcome of encounters with the disciplinary languages but also the deliberate goal of a reflective practice. Such a class can modify the terms of disciplinary education in the students' favor by letting them in on the secrets of genre and convention that the disciplines silently observe, by sharing with students the power produced by switching genres and defying conventions, and by suspending for the sake of students' development some of the conditions of disciplinary discourse itself. Though we would not want to train students to transfer inappropriate genres to their courses in history or biology or even in other English classes, we are free to engage them in intellectual struggles from which they learn to hold their own and choose their own genres, not just to behave themselves according to whatever conventions may hold in any given situation.

The special conditions we set up in our writing classrooms depend on how we understand new college writers and the specific problems of developing their individual ideological consciousnesses. Such students are beginning to encounter a number of disciplinary languages that claim, in their domains of expertise, to be more precise and comprehensive than the languages students bring with them. To master these disciplines, students are expected to assimilate disciplinary languages and to write them in preference to the languages they ordinarily speak. There is a powerful pressure to adopt these authoritative languages, even though students do not find them internally persuasive and feel alienated when they use them in written discourse. The vocabulary and tone of these disciplines seem remote to students and their form of presentation seems complicated. Developed arguments, articulated parts, and elaborate tropes replace the face-to-face exchange of words or opinions or tones or the tweets that have mimed such exchange in writing. Finally, the classical texts or textbooks of some of these disciplines are set apart in time, in language, and in authority. Students are often invited to defer to the language of such texts instead of engaging it.

As part of a college education designed to initiate students into reflective use of these authoritative languages, the study of college writing should not permit students to conform without struggle to the new academic languages or to retreat from the challenges they present by falling back on languages they already know. If they simply abandon or compartmentalize the language they already have and adopt the disciplinary languages the university offers each in its own department, they will pass their courses but pass through school uneducated. If, however, they are encouraged to imagine the language they already have as their own authentic language, which the new alien languages threaten from without, they will be deterred from engaging in the struggle of making their own the new resources those languages offer for seeing and saying. The college writing course can cultivate students' understanding of their ambivalent situations and validate their struggles to remake themselves and the languages imposed on them.

Recognizing languages as languages and exploring the worldviews inherent in them allows us to engage languages in a new way: responsibly, self-consciously, and openly, or—for it amounts to the same thing—authentically. To know our minds as the site of dialogue among languages is to discover both the relevance of other people's words to our predicaments and the relevance of our contributions to others with whom we share the world and the ongoing dialogue about it. It is to take up membership not just in the community defined by the authority of a given discipline or religion or class and its language, but in the whole community where those languages are in contention within and among the voices of writers and speakers for whom they are internally persuasive.

Two practices to cultivate authentically situated voice follow from the goals I have described—objectifying students' words and having them retell others' words in their own. Students need to examine the words they arrive with and take for granted, whether those words are the prose of *Reader's Digest* and *Time* (What dated sources! Perhaps these days Facebook and Twitter) or the unexamined languages of class, party, religion, age group, gender group, or region. We need to encourage students to characterize these languages and to respond to what they have characterized. Paul Cardacci of Georgetown University reported at the Chicago conference that he uses George Lakoff and Mark Johnson's *Metaphors We Live By* to help basic-writing students recognize the metaphors that orient their thought and to help them make those metaphors available for criticism. Bakhtin suggests that inventing characters who speak a particular social-ideological idiom is a good way to objectify those idioms and liberate ourselves from their authority. Here the genre in question is ultimately that of the novelist, not the professional academic, but the function of such portraiture in individual ideological development is important enough to give it a place in the writing classroom.

The professional and high-cultural languages that intimidate students from without need to be demystified and rewritten in terms available to students. Assignments in which students retell or even parody these authoritative voices and styles can bring these languages into the zone of contact. While a disciplinary course encourages students to appropriate its languages and conventions accurately and completely, a writing course can put students in a position to minimize their authority and finality. We should authorize our students to reaccent, not just reproduce, the disciplinary languages we and our colleagues impose on them.

For Bakhtin, retelling in one's own words is not a sterile exercise in paraphrasing but a working-out of evaluative relations between the reporting and the reported discourse—a necessarily double-voiced practice that "includes within it the entire series of forms for the appropriation while transmitting of another's words" (DI 342). This range of forms includes the journal that copies out a quotation on the left page and responds to it on the right, the marginal annotation, the admiring or parodic imitation, the quoted passage preceded by the writer's point in quoting and followed by the writer's interpretation, and many others. These forms are of interest not just as conventions to be learned but as sites where productive verbal-ideological work goes on. Most handbooks on argumentation treat the quotation as a technical citation in support of the author's claims in genres like the research paper, but I suggest that quotation is the very act in which one voice creatively absorbs another and defines itself in relation to that second voice. When we interrupt the quoted text, interrogate it, clarify its point, or expose its ambiguities, we make an opening for our own utterances and give shape to our own roles in the conversation. The point of this exercise is to practice aligning what we are saying with other voices, whether we affirm, redefine, differ with, or develop them. The exercise should avoid confronting students with too many voices or with overelaborated voices, concentrating instead on making significant contact between the student writer's words and the words he or she reproduces.

I have been urging that we engage our writing students not just with disciplinary conventions, genres, and commonplaces but with specific other voices in relation to which they may define their own voices, but I should note here that we may imagine those other voices in several ways. David Bartholomae—my colleague now, as Elbow was at the beginning of my career—and whose groundbreaking essay "Inventing the University" accords with my position in many respects, uses the striking image of "'off-stage voices,' the oversound of all that has been said." He continues:

> These voices, the presence of the "already written," stand in defiance of a writer's desire for originality and determine what might be said. A writer does not write (and this is Barthes's famous paradox) but is, himself, written by the languages available to him. (143)

In this passage, previous voices merge first into the "already written" and then into overwhelming available "languages," losing their individual profiles and characteristic limitations as they acquire the power to defy efforts of origination and to write the writer who would write in them. As this passage transforms them, they are no longer individual voices but Foucauldian discourses that contain within themselves all the possibilities of utterance. They do not situate and provoke our own utterances as specific other voices do but anticipate and contain them. Our only choice, if we wish to participate in the writing these off-stage voices authorize, is to move inside them and assume the position of privilege they grant us. Their authority, in this formulation, is absolute and does not allow for our taking them as "half-ours and half-someone else's," as Bakhtin says we take the internally persuasive word (DI 345).

But Bartholomae's essay suggests elsewhere a position closer to Bakhtin's, for Bartholomae admires the student essay that Bakhtin would call double-voiced, the essay that Bartholomae says displays "two gestures . . . one imitative and one critical" (157). Furthermore, Bartholomae repeatedly opens the alternative between a single code or discourse and competing codes or discourses that might question and debate any single claim to authority. But the drama he points to "in a student's essay, as he or she struggles with and against the languages of our contemporary life" (162) or "against competing discourses" (158) would be even more dramatic if the characters in it were permitted to assume their identities as specific dramatis personae, other persons whose use of the languages of our contemporary life provokes the students to respond. The languages or discourses imagined as disembodied systems of inescapable terms and commonplaces have too much power to make the struggle with them dramatic, unless the drama is the tragic one of our own and our students' futile struggles against the gods of a Foucauldian universe.

Elaine P. Maimon's essay "Maps and Genres" also offers an image of other voices as the student writer encounters them:

> The lonely beginner condemned to the linearity of ink on the blank page hears all the wrong voices. As he tries to imagine those absent strangers to whom he must write, he hears the voices of doubt and despair: "You don't belong here. This paper will show your smart English teacher how stupid you are. You never could write anyway." We want students to drown out these voices with other voices—voices that impersonate the missing readers. Nancy Sommers's research in revision makes clear that experienced writers know how to imagine a reader who is "partially a reflection of themselves and functions as a critical and productive collaborator—a collaborator who has yet to love their work. " (124)

The voices in this drama are all voices from the pedagogical situation itself—the discouraging voice of the teacher, who will unmask the student writer's masquerade as an academic writer, and the encouraging voices of the student's collaborative colleagues, whose criticism does not threaten ostracism from their community. But in this image neither the teacher's voice nor the voices of other students shape the lonely beginner's utterance or provoke it; they only judge it, either harshly or kindly. Acknowledgment of others' help remains a ritual in this community because no one in it has discovered the other voices whose prior writing provides the language and the provocation for the beginner's utterance. Its members are innocent of the kind of debt with which Bartholomae's writers are all too burdened.

Bakhtin's prose writers enjoy no such innocence, but neither do they meet other voices as embodiments of all-powerful intimidating discourses. For them other voices are writers like themselves who are already on the scene and already having their say about the world:

> Any concrete discourse . . . finds the object at which it was directed already as it were overlain with qualifications, open to dispute, charged with value, already enveloped in an obscuring mist—or, on the contrary, by the "light" of alien words that have already been spoken about it. It is entangled, shot through with shared thoughts, points of view, alien value judgments and accents. The word, directed toward its object, enters a dialogically agitated and tension-filled environment of alien words, value judgments and accents, weaves in and out of complex interrelationships, merges with some, recoils from others, intersects with yet a third group: all this may crucially shape the discourse, may leave a trace in all its semantic layers, may complicate its expression and influence its entire stylistic profile. . . . For the prose writer, the object is a focal point for heteroglot voices among which his own voice must also sound; these voices create the

> background necessary for his own voice, outside which his artistic prose nuances cannot be perceived, and without which they "do not sound." (DI 276–78)

Other voices for Bakhtin give our voices their occasions and provocations, their reasons for saying one thing rather than another, their differences that make them distinguishable and audible among the many voices in the forum.

Bakhtin's open forum that excludes no prior or contemporary voices is the ultimate forum in which the voices we learn in our disciplinary and pedagogical communities get their hearings and find their meanings. Its manners are rough-and-tumble, its genres are mixed, its commonplaces are always getting appropriated, and its only convention is the taking of turns by all the voices it has convened, though there is no guarantee they will not interrupt one another. Specialized discourses branch off from the forum but cannot entirely separate themselves from it into purified universes of discourse invulnerable to parodic revoicing from some other language's point of view.

Classrooms protect the young from its full cacophony to cultivate students' capacities to speak up and be heard in it, but they offer no permanent refuge from it; indeed, they cannot even do without some sample of its voices, selected to provoke students without overwhelming them. Even the communities of our national languages and our cultural groups give us only partial shelter from translated voices from outside and their barbarous neologisms (like Bakhtin's *heteroglossia* and my *dialogics*).

Bakhtin suggests that novelists make this entire heteroglot forum the object of their discourse, while scholars and teachers confine themselves to their specialized objects and their more decorous genres. But if we aim for individual ideological development, we cannot leave this forum to the novelists. In the final analysis, what Bakhtin calls the "linguistic consciousness of the educated person" resembles the novelist's language:

> Within it, intentional diversity of speech . . . is transformed into diversity of language . . . ; what results is not a single language but a dialogue of languages, . . . a highly specific unity of several "languages" that have established mutual contact and mutual recognition with each other. (DI 294–95)

To clarify the character of this consciousness, I offer one last long quotation from Bakhtin:

> Concrete socio-ideological consciousness, as it becomes creative . . . discovers itself already surrounded by heteroglossia and not at all a single, unitary language, inviolable and indisputable. The

> actively literary linguistic consciousness at all times and everywhere . . . comes upon "languages," and not language. Consciousness finds itself inevitably facing the necessity of *having to choose a language.* . . . Only by remaining in a closed environment, one without writing or thought, completely off the maps of socio-ideological becoming, could a man fail to sense this activity of selecting a language and rest assured in the inviolability of his own language, the conviction that his language is predetermined.
>
> Even such a man, however, deals not in fact with a single language but with languages—except that the place occupied by each of these languages is fixed and indisputable, the movement from one to the other is predetermined and not a thought process; it is as if these languages were in different chambers. They do not collide with each other in his consciousness, there is no attempt to coordinate them, to look at one of these languages through the eyes of another language. (DI 295)

Those different chambers are not unlike different knowledge communities, each insulated from the others in its own department and each enterable by those who adopt its taken-for-granted conventions and learn its language. The students' movement from one such community to another is, as Bakhtin says, often predetermined and not decided by a thought process—a fact of requirements and schedules. Students can learn the conventions and language of each community without undergoing any "socio-ideological becoming" at all as long as they learn the manners appropriate in each department and never see one from the point of view of any other. Bakhtin illustrates such insulation of verbal domains in the life of a peasant who moves from the language of church to the language of family to the language of official transactions without giving the differences among them a second thought.

But in the forums and in the consciousness where all these languages meet and compete to be chosen, no such blithe passage from one to another is possible, and the participation in diverse knowledge communities opens a struggle among them that knowledge of conventions and mannerly behavior cannot resolve. For Bakhtin, self-conscious participation in that struggle marks the free and educated consciousness—the dialogic self. The writing course, like the novel and the public square, may be one of the forums in which that consciousness comes into being.

Notes

1. The place of poetry and poetics among the arts of discourse complicates the division Aristotle posits at the opening of his *Rhetoric*. For him, poetry is not an art of discourse at all but a nondiscursive product made out of, among other things, language. He regards poetics as a science of such products and their functioning, not, like both rhetoric and dialectic, as an art of improving discursive practice. But despite his efforts to separate poetry and poetics from the arts of discourse, his distinction between rhetoric and dialectic has shaped much of the subsequent discussion and practice of poetry (and of science, for that matter) in the West.

2. For a rich articulation of these arts in ancient thought, see Trimpi's account of philosophical discourse and rhetorical discourse. In late twentieth-century literary criticism allegiances to rhetoric and dialectic were quite explicit. Paul de Man's and J. Hillis Miller's deconstructionist projects were brought forward under the banner of "rhetoric" as were the Marxist proposals of Frank Lentricchia and Terry Eagleton *(Walter Benjamin* 101–13; *Literary Theory),* though "rhetoric" does not mean the same thing to both pairs of critics, or even to both members of each pair. Wayne Booth, of course, viewed critical discourse in rhetorical terms. See also the essays by Bashford, Mailloux, and Wess. "Dialectic," too, had its adherents—Fredric Jameson, for example, in the camp of Marxist criticism and Hans-Georg Gadamer in the arena of argument about discourse in the humanities. For versions of dialectical criticism, see also Watkins's book and McGann's article.

3. In one of his earliest works, "Author and Hero in Aesthetic Activity," Bakhtin distinguishes between a purely theoretical unity of a character's worldview and the modifications of that theoretical unity in the context of the whole character taken as a human being. See also Clark and Holquist 63–94, the chapter entitled "The Architectonics of Answerability"). In an essay of the mid-1930s, "Discourse in the Novel," Bakhtin focuses again on the speaking person in the novel as "an *ideologue*" and treats style from the point of view of the "concrete socio-ideological language consciousness" (*Dialogic Imagination* 295, 332–34).

In the Bakhtin-School works of Voloshinov and Medvedev, the emphasis shifts somewhat from the unity of person and idea to the context of persons ideologically invested in social and historical worlds occupied by other such persons. Both *The Formal Method* and *Marxism and the Philosophy of Language*, for example, reject the ideas of transcendent meaning and of the isolated subjective consciousness in favor of a materially embodied world of interacting, ideologically involved persons engaged in socially specific verbal practices. The verbal practices Bakhtin treats, however, are not the arts I have stressed but genres like the novel and forms of utterance like reported speech.

4. Three books demonstrate that we may practice dialogics, as well as rhetoric and dialectic, without identifying our practice with an art of that name. In a "critical articulation" of Marxism and deconstruction, Michael Ryan brings together voices that have not listened to one another and draws out their mutual implications from his own committed standpoint, placing his own voice on the same plane as the voices of his subjects instead of objectifying them as subjects of a "comparative study" (xiii). Jane Roland Martin thematizes her book's dialogic practice in its title, *Reclaiming a Conversation*, and produces a critical symposium by recalling a forgotten dialogue among earlier writers, creating a conversation where it had not yet taken place, and responding critically to the voices she reclaims. Martha Nussbaum provocatively continues the conversation in her review, which called my attention to Martin's book. Wallace Martin's survey of narrative theories refuses to reduce the ideas of various theorists to a common vocabulary and imagines within each theory he treats "the opposing voice of another theoretical perspective" to which it is a dialogic reply (10). He represents the field of narrative theory as "a discussion, or a series of arguments" (30) rather than as a systematic discipline, and he organizes diverse theories to "have them address each other" (10).

5. The term *chaos* gained currency from its appearance in the title of the first chapter of I. A. Richards's *Principles of Literary Criticism*, "The Chaos of Critical Theories." Wayne Booth uses *scandal* to describe "the criti-

cal disagreement revealed to anyone who compares two or three critics on any one story" (*Rhetoric* 315).

6. Todorov's French essay is the last chapter of his *Critique de la critique,* which refers explicitly to Bakhtin and includes a chapter on his implications for critical practice. Thomas Whitaker points out Brown's debt to Gentile in his introduction to *The Double Lyric.*

7. Todorov's practice in his book on Bakhtin confirms Bakhtin's judgment, for Todorov in fact interprets Bakhtin using the terms of other critics, such as Kristeva and Jakobson, and does not in the end refrain himself from "engaging Bakhtin in dialogue." The dialogue is more overt in the essay on Bakhtin in *Critique de la critique,* but a subsequent reading of *Mikhail Bakhtin: The Dialogical Principle* makes clear how, even there, Todorov's concerns shape his ostensibly objective exposition of Bakhtin's views. I am grateful to Todorov for personal correspondence that clarified the issues between our views of dialogic criticism.

8. The quoted phrase is from Wordsworth's 1805 *Prelude* (10.814). For the use of the name "rhetoric" to cover what I am calling "dialogics," see Booth, *Modern Dogma,* and Bashford.

9. Warnke offers an extended critique of Rorty's appropriation of Gadamer, 139–66.

10. Georgia Warnke says that Gadamer "often" describes "the text that is handed down as a fusion of previous opinions about it, a harmony of voices" (90), but she cites only the passage I have quoted. I do not find this a common emphasis in *Truth and Method,* and I believe that the emphasis is primarily Warnke's own, her supplement to Gadamer's argument that gives greater emphasis than he does to the possibility of differing with tradition and to what she calls "the dialogic structure of understanding" (100). That structure, as Warnke acknowledges, is still dialectical in the sense I have been using.

11. See Warnke's sections on "The Dialogic Structure of Understanding" and "The Dialogic Character of Understanding" in Gadamer for a careful separation of these conservative tendencies from other directions in Gadamer's thought she takes to be more characteristic and consistent with his basic premises.

12. Todorov identifies him as "a linguist and marginal Formalist destined to become the official guiding light of Soviet Stylistics" (9), and Shukman calls him "the doyen of the Soviet school of stylistics" (v). See also Busch for an extended discussion of Vinogradov.

13. See Bakhtin's remark that in dealing with the stylistic dilemma posed by the novel, "the re-establishment of rhetoric, with all its rights,

greatly strengthens the Formalist position. Formalist rhetoric is a necessary addition to Formalist poetics" (DI 267).

14. I discovered Billig's work through the use made of it in Leith and Myerson, who also draw extensively upon Bakhtin's work in their construction of their introductory textbook on language—a self-conscious revival of rhetoric. Their book is a sign of the *pedagogical* revival of the trivium today.

15. Bakhtin's critique of theoretical cognition or epistemology runs pp. 3–13 in the English translation, his critique of aesthetics from pp. 13–18, his critique of ethics from pp. 21–27.

16. Liapunov's footnotes suggest that this whole passage may not have been available to Morson and Emerson; the reduced comment they may have seen in an earlier Soviet edition lacked the critical qualifications restored to the English edition.

17. They also express, and here the Voloshinov essay enters territory unexplored by *Toward a Philosophy of the Act,* an evaluation of the listener.

18. This point is developed in Voloshinov and was first elaborated for composition studies by Schuster.

19. Other aspects of *Toward a Philosophy of the Act* open the way to later developments but do not yet elaborate the notions that the later works will present. The central notion of intonation, as I have already suggested, is close to half of the account of intonation in "Discourse in Life and Discourse in Art," the half that registers the speaker's relation to the hero of the utterance, and it enriches our understanding of why all topics are really value-charged heroes. But it completely ignores the other half of the account of intonation that registers the speaker's relation to the listener and indeed ignores the listener of the utterance completely. It never asks *to whom* the answerable act and utterance are answerable, though its emphasis on acting and speaking in concrete historically unique situations would seem to make this a reasonable question. In this respect, as in several others, we might say that the utterance as act has not yet been fully socialized or rhetoricized or historicized.

The same can be said of Bakhtin's account in this text of the relation of the utterance as act to prior utterances. We might find a latent version of this central feature of Bakhtin's dialogics in the idea that "everything I have to do with is given to me in an emotional-volitional tone" (33), for all we would have to do is recognize that the emotional-volitional tones in which everything is given to me are the tones of those who have already spoken about everything and colored everything for better or worse with their own intonated words. Again it is illuminating to see that this later notion derives from an earlier recognition of the world of anyone's experience as always already charged with value and shot through, as he will later put it, with intonation. But the populated world of Bakhtin's later thought is here still focused on the singular relations of I and the other. The later work goes a long way toward specifying what participative consciousness participates *in* and *with whom* it participates. The value that permeates the world of the participant in ongoing being is not yet parsed as primarily *social* value, to which I respond at least in part as one who does or does not share the social positions of the ones who have previously expressed them and the ones being addressed.

20. "Writing with Teachers" (64). The debate between these figures has attracted large audiences and informed a series of publications, beginning with Elbow (1973) and Bartholomae (1985), both paradigmatic works in composition studies. Their differences took the formal shape of debate at the 1989 CCCC Convention. Their talks from the 1991 convention and further responses from them and others, including my "Romantic Resonances," appear in *CCC* 49 (February 1995). Much of the debate is reproduced as part of the disciplinary heritage for graduate students in composition studies in Villanueva.

21. Eskin cites the commonplace views of poetics drawn from these sources, generally concerned with their devaluation of poetry (379). He counters that commonplace by drawing on the same sources and a few untranslated works, gesturing in the direction of *Toward a Philosophy of the Act* in his conclusion but not elaborating a poetics drawn from it. Wesling goes back to Voloshinov's sociological work and points toward Bakhtin's earlier phenomenological work as well (98). With rhetoric as with poetics, arguments drawn from these texts mainly counter or come to terms with Bakhtin's devaluation of the art.

22. Aristotle introduces both the art of rhetoric and the science of poetics as deriving from the discursive practices and natural dispositions of "all men," but the art and science that he goes on to codify eventually come to be enshrined in a cultural curriculum that purports to define and regulate those practices and dispositions. He points to the argumentative discursive practices that precede the art of rhetoric in order to justify making rhetoric into an art, and he points to the evaluative and imitative discursive practices that precede poetics in order to show the emergence of truly dramatic imitative poesis from its evaluative and narrative predecessors, but once he arrives at definitions of the task of the art and the object of the science, all of his effort goes into elaborating their definitions and systematizing them. Both his treatises establish disciplines derived from pre-disciplinary discursive practices, but neither treatise looks back at those practices for long or returns to them later to ask what might be the consequence of disciplining them.

23. P. Christopher Smith arrives at a parallel argument for rhetoric similarly understood as the primordial discursive mode—"original argument," he calls it—through a Heideggerian "destructive" reading of Aristotle's *Rhetoric*.

24. See my Bakhtinian reading of this poem in *KB Journal*.

25. There is a crucial ambiguity in the use of the term "hero" in Bakhtin School texts that needs to be made explicit here. In "Author and Hero in Aesthetic Activity" the hero of the lyric poem is the speaker, but in Voloshinov's "Discourse in Life and Discourse in Art" the hero is the personified topic or person whom the speaker of the poem evaluates. In the one it is the author's relation to the figure he or she represents that makes that figure the hero; in the other it is the represented speaker's relation to the character or personified topic he or she speaks about that makes that character or topic the hero. Both relations are essential to a fully developed Bakhtin School poetics. I prefer Voloshinov's usage but follow Bakhtin's here where I am following his argument.

26. A sentence from Wordsworth's Preface to *Lyrical Ballads* makes this point forcefully: "Now the music of harmonious metrical language, the sense of difficulty overcome, and the blind association of pleasure which has previously been received from works of rhyme or metre of the same or similar construction, all these imperceptibly make of a complex feeling of delight, which is of the most important use in tempering the painful feeling which will always be found intermingled with powerful descriptions of the deeper passions" (266–267). The surrounding context deepens this insight.

27. The question of the authorship of the disputed texts is not one I can decide. I prefer to retreat to speaking of the "Bakhtin School" when it arises and to treating the names of the published authors as the authors of the texts. The texts have important ideas in common though they differ sometimes in their use of terms and their argumentative framing. Bakhtin, for example, makes a critical remark about sociological method in "Content, Material, and Form in Verbal Art," noting that it "not only transcribes the ethical event in its social aspect—the event experienced and co-evaluated in aesthetic contemplation—but it also passes beyond the bounds of the object and draws the event into broader social and historical interconnections. Such studies can have great scientific significance, and for the literary historian they are indispensable, but they do go beyond the bounds of aesthetic analysis proper" (AA 290). The sociological method offered in "Discourse in Life and Discourse in Art" counters this tendency of the sociology of art and tries to provide a distinctive immanent mode of aesthetic sociological analysis of artistic form. Bakhtin himself seems to elaborate the terms of this essay many years later but without explicit reference to it in "The Problem of Speech Genres."

28. Here I am using "hero" in Voloshinov's sense. See note 25.

29. For an extensive account of dialogized lyric, see chapters 3, 4, and 5 of my *Wordsworth, Dialogics, and the Practice of Criticism*.

30. Blundell reads the distinction in the *Poetics* from the perspective of the *Ethics* as well as the *Rhetoric*. She notes that the treatment of *dianoia* in the *Rhetoric* "suggests that dramatic *dianoia* is coextensive with rhetorical argument in general. But the *Poetics* omits any mention of the third rhetorical 'proof,' the proof from the *ethos* of the speaker." She speculates on several reasons for this omission and concludes: "The absence of *ethos* is therefore best regarded as an oversight, and should not be taken to imply that *dianoia* excludes the kind of rhetorical argument which represents the speaker or others as being 'of a certain kind.' Dramatic *dianoia* is thus broadly the production of rhetorical effects through the techniques discussed in *Rhetoric* I and II but focuses more particularly on the kinds of argument summarized at the end of Book II" (167–68). Dale notes that "so long as we leave these in a vague translation 'Character' and 'Thought' may seem ordinary and relevant enough in a discussion of drama, but the more we pursue them, the more elusive and lacking in self-consistency they seem to become" (147). He also notes that *ethos* is "deliberately omitted" in Chapter XIX of the *Poetics* from the trio of *pisteis* Aristotle lists in the *Rhetoric* (152).

31. He does not carry over this distinction from Book III of Plato's *Republic* from which his distinctions of manner otherwise derive. See my "Narrative Diction in Wordsworth's Poetics of Speech."

32. This is how Derrida reads *dianoia* in the *Poetics*: "the area of what is allotted to language or to be thought in language, a cause, effect or content of language, but not the linguistic act itself (enunciation, diction, elocution, *lexis*) in "White Mythology" (32). I find it interesting that he conflates diction/*lexis* with enunciation/elocution/delivery here.

33. See my "Bakhtin versus Chatman on Narrative" and "Dialogics, Narratology, and the Virtual Space of Discourse."

34. I have completed another book manuscript that works out the implications of this poetics for reading lyric and narrative poetry. See my *How to Play a Poem: A Bakhtin School Pedagogy for Poetry*.

35. P. Christopher Smith draws upon Heidegger's 1924 lectures on Aristotle's *Rhetoric* to arrive at this "original mode of speech" that precedes philosophical divisions of the disciplines, unites *ethos, pathos,* and *logos,* derives its arguments from prior "tonal voicings," and constitutes a more broadly interpreted evaluative rhetoric that precedes any art of rhetoric. See especially his second chapter. Nancy Struever in work in progress is finding a similar turn in the same period in the work of R. G. Collingwood.

Works Cited

Arac, Jonathan. *Critical Genealogies: Historical Situations for Postmodern Literary Studies*. New York: Columbia UP, 1987.
Aristotle. *Aristotle's Poetics*. Trans. Stephen Halliwell. Chicago: U of Chicago P, 1986.
—. *Aristotle's Theory of Poetry and Fine Art with a Critical Text and Translation of the Poetics*. Trans. S. H. Butcher. New York: Dover, 1951.
—. *On Rhetoric*. Trans. George Kennedy. New York: Oxford UP, 1991.
—. *Poetics*. Ed. and trans. Stephen Halliwell. Loeb Classical Library. Cambridge, MA: Harvard UP, 1995.
—. *Poetics*. Trans. Richard Janko. Indianapolis and Cambridge: Hackett, 1987.
—. *Rhetoric*. Trans. Lane Cooper. New York: Appleton-Century-Croft, 1932.
—. *The "Art" of Rhetoric*. Trans. J. H. Freese. Cambridge, MA: Harvard UP, 1926.
Armstrong, Edward. *A Ciceronian Sunburn: A Tudor Dialogue on Humanistic Rhetoric and Civic Poetics*. Columbia: U of South Carolina P, 2003.
Atwill, Janet. *Rhetoric Reclaimed: Aristotle and the Liberal Arts Tradition*. Ithaca: Cornell UP, 1998.
Auerbach, Erich. *Mimesis: The Representation of Reality in Western Literature*. 50th Anniversary Edition. Princeton: Princeton UP, 2003.
Austin, J. L. *How To Do Things with Words*. Cambridge, MA: Harvard UP, 1962.
Bacon. Francis. *The Advancement of Learning*. Ed. G. W. Kitchin. London: J. M. Dent, 1962.

Bakhtin, M. M. *Art and Answerability: Early Philosophical Essays of M. M. Bakhtin*. Ed. Michael Holquist and Vadim Liapunov. Trans. Vadim Liapunov. Austin: U of Texas P, 1990.

—. *The Dialogic Imagination: Four Essays by M. M. Bakhtin*. Ed. Michael Holquist. Trans. Caryl Emerson and Michael Holquist. Austin: U of Texas P, 1981.

—. "Extracts from 'Notes' (1970–1971)." *Bakhtin: Essays and Dialogues on His Work*. Ed. Gary Saul Morson. Chicago: U of Chicago P, 1986.

—. *Problems of Dostoevsky's Poetics*. Trans. R. W. Rotsel. Ann Arbor, MI: Ardis, 1973.

—. "The Problem of Speech Genres." *Speech Genres and Other Late Essays*. Ed. Michael Holquist and Caryl Emerson. Trans. Vern W. McGee. Austin: U of Texas P, 1986.

—. *Problems of Dostoevsky's Poetics*. Ed. and trans. Caryl Emerson. Minneapolis: U of Minnesota P, 1984.

—. *Rabelais and His World*. Trans. Helene Iswolsky. Cambridge, MA: MIT P, 1968.

—. *Toward a Philosophy of the Act*. Ed. Vadim Liapunov and Michael Holquist. Trans. Vadim Liapunov. Austin: U of Texas P, 1993.

Bartholomae, David. "Inventing the University." *When a Writer Can't Write: Studies in Writer's Block and Other Composing Problems*. Ed. Mike Rose. New York: Guilford, 1985. 134–65.

—. "Writing With Teachers: A Conversation with Peter Elbow." *College Composition and Communication* 46 (1995): 62–71.

Bashford, Bruce. "The Rhetorical Method in Literary Criticism." *Philosophy and Rhetoric* 9 (1976): 133–46.

Bender, John, and David E. Wellbery. *The Ends of Rhetoric: History, Theory, Practice*. Palo Alto: Stanford UP, 1990.

Bernard-Donals, Michael. *Mikhail Bakhtin: Between Phenomenology and Marxism*. Cambridge: Cambridge UP, 1995.

—. "Mikhail Bakhtin, Classical Rhetoric, and Praxis." *Rhetoric Society Quarterly* 22:4 (1992): 10–15.

Bialostosky, Don H. "Bakhtin versus Chatman on Narrative: The Habilitation of the Hero." *University of Ottawa Quarterly* 53 (1983): 109–116.

—. "Dialogic Criticism." *Contemporary Literary Theory*. Ed. G. Douglas Atkins and Laurie Morrow. Amherst: U of Massachusetts P, 1989. 214–28.

—. "Dialogics, Literary Theory, and the Liberal Arts." *Cross Currents: Recent Trends in Humanities Research*. Ed. E. Ann Kaplan and Michael Sprinker. London: Verso, 1990. 1–13.

—. "Dialogics, Narratology, and the Virtual Space of Discourse." *Journal of Narrative Technique* 19 (Winter 1989): 167–73.

—. *How to Play a Poem: A Bakhtin School Pedagogy for Poetry.* Pittsburgh: U of Pittsburgh Press, 2016.
—. "Liberal Education, Writing, and the Dialogic Self." *Contending with Words.* Ed. Patricia Harkin and John Schilb. New York: MLA, 1991. 11–22.
—. *Making Tales: The Poetics of Wordsworth's Narrative Experiments.* Chicago: U of Chicago P, 1984.
—. "Narrative Diction in Wordsworth's Poetics of Speech." *Comparative Literature* 34 (1982): 305–29.
—. "Romantic Resonances." *College Composition and Communication* 46 (1995): 92–96.
—. "Symbolic Action and Dialogic Social Interaction in Burke's and the Bakhtin's School's Sociological Approaches to Poetry." *KB Journal* 11 (2015).
—. *Wordsworth, Dialogics, and the Practice of Criticism.* Cambridge: Cambridge UP, 1992.
Billig, Michael. *Arguing and Thinking: a Rhetorical Approach to Social Psychology.* Cambridge: Cambridge UP, 1987.
Bizzell, Patricia and Bruce Herzberg. *The Rhetorical Tradition: Readings from Classical Times to the Present.* Boston: St. Martin's, 1990.
Blundell, Mary Whitlock. "*Éthos* and *Dianoia* Reconsidered." *Essays on Aristotle's Poetics* Ed. Amélie Oksenberg Rorty. Princeton: Princeton UP, 1992. Pp. 155–75.
Booth, Wayne C. *The Company We Keep: An Ethics of Fiction.* Berkeley: U of California P, 1988.
—. *Critical Understanding: The Powers and Limits of Pluralism.* Chicago: U of Chicago P, 1979.
—. Introduction. *Problems of Dostoevsky's Poetics.* By M. M. Bakhtin. Ed. and trans. Caryl Emerson. Minneapolis: U of Minnesota P, 1984.
—. *Modern Dogma and the Rhetoric of Assent.* Chicago: U of Chicago P, 1974.
—. *The Rhetoric of Fiction.* Chicago: U of Chicago P, 1961.
—. *The Rhetoric of Fiction.* 2nd ed. Chicago: U of Chicago P, 1983.
—. "The Rhetoric of Fiction and the Poetics of Fictions." *Novel: A Forum on Fiction* 1 (1968): 105–17. Rpt. in *Towards a Poetics of Fiction.* Ed. Mark Spilka. Bloomington: Indiana UP, 1977. 77–89.
—. *A Rhetoric of Irony.* Chicago: U of Chicago P, 1974.
Brown, Merle. "The Idea of Communal Creativity in F. R. Leavis's Recent Criticism." *The Double Lyric: Divisiveness and Communal Creativity in Recent English Poetry.* New York: Columbia UP, 1980. 201–22.
Bruffee, Kenneth. Letter to "Forum." *PMLA* 102 (1987): 216–17.

Busch, Robert. "Bakhtin's 'Problemy tvorchestva Dostoevskogo' and V. V. Vinogradov's 'O khudozhestvennoi proze'—A Dialogic Relationship." *Social Discourse* 3 (1990): 311–32.
Carroll, David. "The Alterity of Discourse: Form, History, and the Question of the Political in M. M. Bakhtin." *Diacritics* 13.2 (1983): 65–83.
Chatman, Seymour. *Story and Discourse.* Ithaca: Cornell UP, 1978.
Clark, Katerina, and Michael Holquist. *Mikhail Bakhtin.* Cambridge, MA: Harvard UP, 1984.
Cole, Thomas. *The Origins of Rhetoric in Ancient Greece.* Baltimore: Johns Hopkins UP, 1991.
Crane, R. S. *Critics and Criticism, Ancient and Modern.* Chicago: U of Chicago P, 1952.
Curtius, Ernst Robert, and Willard R. Trask. *European Literature and the Latin Middle Ages.* Princeton: Princeton UP, 1990.
Dale, A. M. "Ethos and Dianoia: 'Character' and 'Thought' in Aristotle's Poetics." *Oxford Readings in Ancient Literary Criticism.* Ed. Andrew Laird. Oxford: Oxford UP, 2006. 142–57.
De Man, Paul. "Dialogue and Dialogism." *Poetics Today* 4 (1983): 99–107.
—. *The Resistance to Theory.* Minneapolis: U of Minnesota P, 1986.
—. "Rhetoric." *Allegories of Reading.* New Haven: Yale UP, 1979. 1–131.
Dentith, Simon. "Bakhtin Versus Rhetoric?" *Face to Face: Bakhtin in Russia.* Ed. C. Adlam, V. Makhlin, and A. Renfrew. Sheffield: Sheffield Academic P, 1997. 311–25.
Derrida, Jacques. "White Mythology." *New Literary History* 6 (1974): 5–74.
Eagleton, Terry. *Literary Theory: An Introduction.* Minneapolis: U of Minnesota P, 1983.
—. *Walter Benjamin: Or, Toward a Revolutionary Criticism.* London: Verso, 1981.
Elbow, Peter. "Being a Writer vs. Being an Academic: A Conflict in Goals." *College Composition and Communication* 46 (1995): 72–83.
—. *Writing Without Teachers.* New York: Oxford UP, 1973.
Eliot, T. S. *The Waste Land and Other Poems.* New York: Harcourt, 1934.
Emerson, Caryl. "The Tolstoy Connection in Bakhtin." *PMLA* 100 (1985): 68–80.
Eskin, Michael. "Bakhtin on Poetry." *Poetics Today.* 21 (2000): 379–391.
Ewald, Helen Rothschild. "Waiting for Answerability: Bakhtin and Composition Studies. *College Composition and Communication* 44 (1993): 331–48.
Fahnestock, Jeanne. "Arrangement." In *Encyclopedia of Rhetoric and Composition.* Ed. T. Enos. New York: Garland, 1996.

—. "Modern Arrangement." In *Encyclopedia of Rhetoric*. Ed. T. Sloane. New York: Oxford UP, 2001.
—. *Rhetorical Figures in Science*. New York: Oxford UP, 1999.
Farmer, Frank. *Landmark Essays on Bakhtin, Rhetoric, and Writing*. Mahwah, NJ: Hermagoras, 1998.
—. *Saying and Silence: Listening to Composition with Bakhtin*. Logan: Utah State UP, 2001.
Fish, Stanley. *Doing What Comes Naturally*. Durham and London: Duke University P, 1989.
Gadamer, Hans-Georg. *Truth and Method*. New York: Seabury, 1975.
Genette, Gérard. *Figures of Literary Discourse*. New York: Columbia UP, 1982
Gentile, Giovanni. *Genesis and Structure of Society*. Trans. H. S. Harris. Urbana: U of Illinois P, 1966.
Goodson, A. C. "Structuralism and Critical History in the Moment of Bakhtin." *Tracing Literary Theory*. Ed. Joseph Natoli. Urbana: U of Illinois P, 1987.
Halasek, Kay. *A Pedagogy of Possibility: Bakhtinian Perspectives on Composition Studies*. Carbondale: Southern Illinois UP, 1999.
—. "Starting the Dialogue: What Can We Do About Bakhtin's Ambivalence Toward Rhetoric?" *Rhetoric Society Quarterly* 22:4 (1992): 1–9.
Hartman, Geoffrey H. "The Culture of Criticism." *PMLA* 99 (1984): 371–97.
Haskins, Ekaterina V. *Logos and Power in Isocrates and Aristotle*. Columbia: U of South Carolina P, 2004.
Hirschkop, Ken. *Mikhail Bakhtin: An Aesthetic for Democracy*. New York: Oxford UP, 1999.
Holquist, Michael. "Answering as Authoring: Mikhail Bakhtin's Trans-Linguistics." *Critical Inquiry* 10 (1983): 307–19.
Howell, Wilbur Samuel. *Eighteenth-Century British Logic and Rhetoric*. Princeton: Princeton UP, 1971.
Jameson, Fredric. *Marxism and Form: Twentieth-Century Dialectical Theories of Literature*. Princeton: Princeton UP, 1971.
—. *The Political Unconscious: Narrative as a Socially Symbolic Act*. Ithaca: Cornell UP, 1981.
Jarratt, Susan C. *Rereading the Sophists: Classical Rhetoric Refigured*. Carbondale: Southern Illinois UP, 1991.
Joseph, Miriam. *Rhetoric in Shakespeare's Time: Literary Theory of Renaissance Europe*. New York: Harcourt, 1962.
—. *Shakespeare's Use of the Arts of Language*. New York: Columbia UP, 1947.
Kant, Immanuel. *Critique of Pure Reason*. Trans. Norman Kemp Smith. New York: Bedford Books: 1969.

Klancher, Jon. "Bakhtin's Rhetoric." *Reclaiming Pedagogy: The Rhetoric of the Classroom.* Ed. Ellen Quandahl. Carbondale: Southern Illinois UP, 1989. 83–96.

Kristeva, Julia. "Bakhtine, le mot, le dialogue, et le roman." *Critique* 23 (1967): 438–65.

Kuhn, Thomas. *The Structure of Scientific Revolutions.* Chicago: U of Chicago P, 1962.

LaCapra, Dominick. "Bakhtin, Marxism, and the Carnivalesque." *Rethinking Intellectual History: Texts, Contexts, Language.* Ithaca: Cornell UP, 1983. 291–324.

Lanham, Richard. *A Handlist of Rhetorical Terms.* Berkeley: U of California P, 1968.

Leith, Dick, and George Myerson. *The Power of Address: Explorations in Rhetoric* London and New York: Routledge, 1989.

Lentricchia, Frank. *Criticism and Social Change.* Chicago: U of Chicago P, 1983.

Liddell, H. G. *An Intermediate Greek-English Lexicon.* Oxford: Clarendon P, 1889.

MacCabe, Colin. "Towards a Modern Trivium for English Studies." *Critical Quarterly* 26 (1984): 69–83.

Mailloux, Steven. "Rhetorical Hermeneutics." *Critical Inquiry* 11 (1985): 620–41.

Maimon, Elaine. "Maps and Genres: Exploring Connections in the Arts and Sciences." *Composition and Literature: Bridging the Gap.* Ed. Winifred Bryan Horner. Chicago: U of Chicago P, 1983. 110–25.

McCloskey, Donald N. "The Rhetoric of Economics." *Journal of Economic Literature* 21 (1983): 481–517.

McGann, Jerome J. "Some Forms of Critical Discourse." *Critical Inquiry* 11 (1985): 399–417.

Martin, Jane Roland. *Reclaiming a Conversation: The Ideal of the Educated Woman.* New Haven: Yale UP, 1985.

Martin, Wallace. *Recent Theories of Narrative.* Ithaca: Cornell UP, 1986.

Matejka, Ladislav, and Krystyna Pomorska. *Readings in Russian Poetics.* Ann Arbor: Michigan Slavic Publications, 1978.

Medvedev, P. N., and M. M. Bakhtin. *The Formal Method in Literary Scholarship.* Trans. Albert Wehrle. Baltimore: Johns Hopkins UP, 1978.

Miller, J. Hillis. "On Edge: The Crossways of Contemporary Criticism." *Romanticism and Contemporary Criticism.* Ed. Morris Eaves and Michael Fischer. Ithaca: Cornell UP, 1986. 96–111.

—. *Speech Acts in Literature.* Stanford: Stanford UP, 2001.

Morson, Gary Saul, ed. *Bakhtin: Essays and Dialogues on His Work*. Chicago: U of Chicago P, 1986.
Morson, Gary Saul, and Caryl Emerson. *Mikhail Bakhtin: Creation of a Prosaics*. Palo Alto: Stanford UP, 1990.
—. *Rethinking Bakhtin: Extensions and Challenges*. Evanston: Northwestern UP, 1989.
Murphy, John M. "Mikhail Bakhtin and the Rhetorical Tradition." *Quarterly Journal of Speech* 87 (2001): 259–77.
Needham, Lawrence D., and Don H. Bialostosky, eds. *Rhetorical Traditions and British Romantic Literature*. Bloomington: Indiana UP, 1995.
Neel, Jasper. *Plato, Derrida, and Writing*. Carbondale: Southern Illinois UP, 1988.
Nussbaum, Martha. "Women's Lot." *New York Review of Books* 30 (Jan. 1986): 7–12.
Olson, Elder. "The Dialectical Foundations of Pluralism." *On Value Judgments in the Arts and Other Essays*. Chicago: U of Chicago P, 1976. 327–59.
Payne, Robert O. *The Key of Remembrance: A Study of Chaucer's Poetics*. New Haven: Yale UP, 1963.
Perlina, Nina. "Mikhail Bakhtin in Dialogue with Victor Vinogradov." Unpublished conference paper. University of Cagliari Conference, "Bakhtin: Theorist of Dialogue," June 16–18, 1985. Expanded and revised as "A Dialogue on the Dialogue: The Baxtin-Vinogradov Exchange (1924–65)." *Slavic and East European Journal* 32 (1988): 526–41.
Phelan, James. *Living to Tell About It: A Rhetoric and Ethics of Character Narration*. Ithaca: Cornell UP, 2005.
—. *Narrative as Rhetoric: Technique, Audiences, Ethics, Ideology*. Columbus: Ohio State UP, 1996.
—. *Worlds from Words: A Theory of Language in Fiction*. Chicago: U of Chicago P, 1981.
Phelan, James, and Peter J. Rabinowitz. *A Companion to Narrative Theory*. Malden, MA: Blackwell, 2005.
—. *Understanding Narrative*. Columbus, OH: Ohio State UP, 1994.
Pirsig, Robert. *Zen and the Art of Motorcycle Maintenance*. New York: Morrow, 1974.
Poirier, Richard. "Hum 6, or Reading before Theory." *Raritan* 9 (1990): 14–31.
Rabinowitz, Peter J. *Before Reading: Narrative Conventions and the Politics of Interpretation*. Ithaca: Cornell UP, 1987.
Richards, I. A. "Introduction." *Interpretation in Teaching*. New York: Harcourt, Brace, and Company, 1938
—. *Principles of Literary Criticism*. 1925. New York: Harvest, 1961.

Richter, David H. "Bakhtin in Life and in Art." *Style* 20 (1986): 411–19.
—. "Dialogism and Poetry." *Studies in the Literary Imagination* 23 (1990): 9–27.
Rorty, Richard. *Philosophy and the Mirror of Nature*. Princeton: Princeton UP, 1979.
Ryan, Michael. *Marxism and Deconstruction: A Critical Articulation*. Baltimore: Johns Hopkins UP, 1982.
Schiappa, Edward. "Did Plato Coin *Rhêtorikê?*" *American Journal of Philology* 11 (1990): 457–70.
Scholes, Robert. "A Flock of Cultures—A Trivial Proposal." *College English* 53 (1991): 759–72.
Schuster, Charles. "Mikhail Bakhtin as Rhetorical Theorist." *College English* 47 (Oct. 1985): 594- 607.
Shelley, Percy B. *Shelley's Poetry and Prose*. Ed. Donald H. Reiman and Sharon B. Powers. New York: Norton, 1977.
Shukman, Ann, and L. M. O'Toole, eds. *Russian Poetics in Translation*. No. 5 (1978).
Smith, John H. *The Spirit and Its Letter: Traces of Rhetoric in Hegel's Rhetorical Bildung*. Ithaca: Cornell UP, 1988.
Smith, P. Christopher. T*he Hermeneutics of Original Argument: Demonstration, Dialectic, Rhetoric*. Evanston: Northwestern UP, 1998.
Struever, Nancy. "Humanities and Humanists." *Humanities and Society* 1 (1978): 25–34.
—. "Topics in History." *History and Theory* 19 (1980): 66–79.
Todorov, Tzvetan. *Critique de la critique*. Paris: Seuil, 1984.
—. "A Dialogic Criticism?" Trans. Richard Howard. *Raritan* 4 (1984): 64–76.
—. *Mikhail Bakhtin: The Dialogical Principle*. Trans Wlad Godzich. Minneapolis: U of Minnesota P, 1984.
Trimpi, Wesley. *Muses of One Mind: The Literary Analysis of Experience and Its Continuity*. Princeton: Princeton UP, 1983.
Tuve, Rosemond. *Elizabethan and Metaphysical Imagery: Renaissance Poetic and Twentieth-Century Critics*. Chicago: U of Chicago P, 1947.
Vickers, Brian. *In Defence of Rhetoric*. Oxford: Clarendon P, 1988.
Villanueva, Victor, Jr. *Cross-Talk in Comp Theory: A Reader*. Urbana, IL: NCTE, 1997.
Voloshinov, V. N. "Discourse in Life and Discourse in Art." In *Freudianism: A Critical Sketch*. Ed. Neil H. Bruss. Trans. I. R. Titunik. Bloomington: Indiana UP, 1987.
—. *Marxism and the Philosophy of Language*. Trans. L. Matejka and I. R. Titunik. New York: Seminar, 1973.

Walker, Jeffrey. *Rhetoric and Poetics in Antiquity.* New York, Oxford UP, 2000.
Walzer, A. "Aristotle's Rhetoric, Dialogism, and Contemporary Research in Composition." *Rhetoric Review* 16 (1997): 45–57.
Warnke, Georgia. *Gadamer: Hermeneutics, Tradition and Reason.* Stanford: Stanford UP, 1987.
Watkins, Evan. *The Critical Act.* New Haven: Yale UP, 1978.
Wells, Susan. "Bakhtin and Rhetoric." Unpublished paper presented at the International Bakhtin Society Conference, Urbino, 1990.
Wesling, Donald. *Bakhtin and the Social Moorings of Poetry.* Lewisburg: Bucknell UP, 2003.
Wess, Robert. "Notes toward a Marxist Rhetoric." *Bucknell Review* 28 (1983): 126–48.
Williams, Raymond. *Culture and Society 1780–1950.* New York: Columbia UP, 1958.
Wordsworth, William. *The Prelude: 1799, 1805, 1850.* Norton Critical Editions. Ed. M. H. Abrams, Stephen Gill, and Jonathan Wordsworth. New York: Norton, 1979.
—. *Wordsworth and Coleridge: Lyrical Ballads.* Ed R. L. Brett and F. R. Jones. London and New York: Methuen, 1963.
Zima, Peter V. "Bakhtin's Young Hegelian Aesthetics. *Critical Studies* 1 (1989): 77–94.

About the Author

An early adopter of Bakhtin School ideas, Don Bialostosky first mobilized them to rehabilitate Wordsworth's narrative experiments in *Making Tales* (Chicago 1984) and extended them to rethink his lyric poetry and the critics who wrote about them in *Wordsworth, Dialogics, and the Practice of Criticism* (Cambridge 1992). Participant in the first international Bakhtin conferences in the early 1980s and contributor to the first bibliographies of the *Bakhtin Newsletter*, he introduced Bakhtin to a CCCC convention in 1984 and published the first article on Bakhtin in *PMLA* in 1986. His forthcoming book *How to Play a Poem* from the University of Pittsburgh Press brings Bakhtin School poetics to a pedagogy for poetry. Rhetoric has been on his radar since his undergraduate studies in the Analysis of Ideas and the Study of Methods at Chicago, where his engagement with the art was reinforced by graduate work with Wayne Booth, to whose memory this volume is dedicated. He has taught at the Universities of Utah and Washington, at Stony Brook and Toledo and Penn State. Currently he is Professor in the Composition, Literacy, Pedagogy, and Rhetoric track and Chair of the English Department at the University of Pittsburgh.

Photograph of the author by Sue Bialostosky.
Used by permission.

Index

Aarsleff, Hans, 40
Abrams, M. H., 51
act, the, 38, 86–89, 91–96, 98, 105–112, 114–115, 118–120, 122-123; answerable, 95, 96, 110, 164;
actor: dramatic, 123, 143, 145
addressee, 127–128
aemulatio, 72
aesthetic: activity, 106; communication, 117; consummation, 115; contemplation, 166; distance, 117; experience, 103; imitations, 120, 146; isolation, 112, 117, 120; object, 111, 114, 115; seeing, 94, 103, 104, 110, 112; transactions, 115, 117; values, 104
aesthetics, 24, 88, 94, 97, 103–106, 110–112, 114–115, 117–120, 146, 164, 166
agents, 27, 88, 115, 117–118, 138, 140–143
agonism, 69, 110
allegory, 55
answerability, 24, 32, 85, 86, 89, 91, 93, 95–96, 99, 106, 108–110, 152, 164
Antczak, Fred J., x, 5

anti-logoi, 77, 79–81
antithesis, 21–22
architectonici concrete, 94, 103–104, 106
architectonics, 14, 15, 88, 95, 102–107, 110–113, 115, 118–119, 146
argument: entechnic, 136; enthymematic, 129, 136
Aristotelian, 5, 7–8, 12, 15, 33, 43–44, 49, 51, 53–54, 70–71, 76, 77, 80–81, 108, 122, 127, 136, 137, 143–145
Aristotle, xi, 4–8, 13–14, 19–22, 26, 32–33, 46, 51, 55, 71, 76, 80, 104, 106, 109, 112, 114, 121–129, 131–146, 161, 165–167; hierarchy of parts, 122
Armstrong, Edward, 57
arrangement, 10, 21, 58–59, 73, 122, 131–132, 134-136, 140, 144
arts, verbal, 6, 8–9, 13–14, 19–20, 22, 24-27, 30, 31–34, 38, 41–42, 51, 57, 59, 64, 75–76, 81–82, 87, 91, 99, 102, 105, 110, 122–126, 128, 130-132, 140, 142, 146-147, 161-162
Atwill Janet, 7
audience, 10, 13, 20–22, 44, 60,

62-63, 65, 73, 77, 80, 82, 106–107, 115, 126–130, 132, 135–136, 139, 148–149, 165
Auerbach, Erich, 57
Austin, J. L., 60–61
author, 10, 25, 27–28, 43–47, 52-56, 61, 89, 95–96, 106, 111-118, 120, 127, 145, 148, 155, 166

Bacon, Francis, 25, 66
Bakhtin School, x, 3–6, 8–12, 14, 60–62, 66–67, 69, 102, 119–121, 127–131, 133, 137, 144, 146, 162, 166–167
Bakhtin, Mikhail: *Dialogic Imagination, The*, x, 4, 11, 162; *Problems of Dostoevsky's Poetics*, 4, 11, 32, 43, 45, 77, 102, 113, 122; *Toward a Philosophy of the Act*, xi, 14, 86–92, 94, 96, 99–106, 110, 113, 115, 120, 131, 164–165
Bakhtinians, 6, 14, 77, 100
Bartholomae, David, 101, 150, 156–157, 165
Bashford, Bruce, 161, 163
Bateson, F. W., 27
being: human, 34, 88, 94, 103, 111, 162
Being-as-event, 108, 110, 114, 116
Bender, John, 14, 58, 74, 82, 146
Benjamin, Walter, 161
Berlin, Isaiah, 27
Bernard-Donals, Michael, x, 11, 14, 67–71, 74
Bialostosky, Don, 57, 60
Billig, Michael, xi, 14, 76–82, 164
Bizzell, Patricia, 3, 11, 14, 72, 127
Blakesley, David, xi
Blundell, Mary Whitlock, 167
Booth, Wayne, ix–x, 3–5, 13, 40, 43–55, 66, 114, 145, 161–163; chaos of critical theories, 25–26, 32, 47, 162; *Critical Understanding; The Powers and Limits of Pluralism*, 45, 47, 49–52; *Rhetoric of Fiction*, 3, 5, 43–47, 51, 55–56, 114

Brown, Merle, 13, 26–29, 163
Bruffee, Kenneth, 31, 150
Brutus, 132
Bulgaria, 26
Burke, Kenneth, 51; Burkeans, 66; parlor, 67
Busch, Robert, 163

Cardacci, Paul, 154
carnival, 43–44, 86
character, 33, 44, 46–47, 82, 94–95, 105, 108–109, 120, 122, 124–125, 138–144, 158, 162, 166
characters, 21, 43–44, 46–47, 53–55, 139, 141–142, 144, 155–156; *See also* hero
Chatman, Seymour, 4, 9, 167
Chicago School, 5, 50, 53–54, 56
clarity, 42, 44, 126, 131–132
Clark, Katerina, 91, 162
classical rhetoric, 4–7, 9, 14, 20, 30, 32, 42, 55, 57, 61, 64–66, 77, 80, 82, 100, 106, 109, 122, 131, 154
co-creation, 115, 117–118, 120, 143, 146–147
Coleridge, Samuel Taylor, 7, 50
College Composition and Communication (journal), 165
Collingwood, R. G., 167
Colomb, Gregory, 150
comic, 43, 136
commonplaces, 22, 25, 50, 59, 121–122, 129, 149–152, 155, 156–158, 165
communication, x, 3, 6, 57, 61–62, 73, 97, 116–117, 119, 127–128, 130, 134, 136, 142–143; social, 73, 117, 119, 127, 131; speech, 62, 120, 127, 130; spheres of, 62, 131, 144
community, ix–x, 15, 21, 26, 32, 41, 51–52, 68, 70–71, 77–78, 117–118, 129, 132–133, 149–151, 154, 157–159
composition, ix, 3, 6, 11, 14, 54, 57, 67, 85–87, 91, 95, 99, 101, 148-159, 164–165

compositionists, 97, 100–101
Conference on College Composition and Communication, ix–x, 15, 149, 165
consciousness, 36, 46, 48, 69, 88–89, 93, 97–99, 104, 106–107, 109–112, 115–116, 152–153, 158–159, 162; act-performing, 104; historical, 36, 37; individual, 72, 97, 116; participative, 87–89, 100, 103, 105–107, 112, 115, 165
consummation, 111–113, 115, 117
conversation: dialogic, 26, 34, 37; disciplined, 30; hermeneutical, 33–34, 36, 37; of mankind, 30; ordinary, 30, 38–39
conversations, 13, 21, 25–26, 30, 33–34, 36–39, 49–50, 52, 64, 67, 115, 134, 150, 155, 162
conversion, 26–27, 119
co-participants, 116, 118, 148
Crane, R. S., 49–50, 66
creativity, 13, 27, 29, 31, 152
crisis, 97, 99, 105, 123
criticism, 3, 4, 7, 9, 14, 24–28, 39, 40–41, 47, 50, 53–57, 59, 65–69, 71, 73, 143, 155, 157; Chicago School, 5, 55–56; collaborative, 26; culture of, 40, 43, 47, 51; deconstructive, 54; dialectical, 29, 161; dialogic, 13, 25–27, 40, 45, 48, 163; literary, 5, 20, 24–25, 32, 47–48, 53, 57–59, 65, 86, 161; Marxist, 161; New, 7, 50, 56, 65; post-structuralist, 8; rhetorical, 3, 13, 26, 43, 53–55, 57, 59–61, 64–69, 71, 73, 75; scientific, 69; structuralist, 26
critics, 6–9, 13, 15, 24–28, 40, 47–51, 57, 59, 64–68, 73, 151, 161, 163; Anglo-American, 24, 41, 43; British, 27, 40
Curtius, Ernst Robert, 57

deconstruction, 6, 11, 33, 53–56, 65, 67, 122, 162
deconstructionists, 53, 56, 161

deliberation, 70, 72, 80, 96, 136
deliberative rhetoric, 30, 58, 71, 79–80, 104, 116, 127–129, 133–135, 140
delivery, 8, 13, 59, 122–123, 125–128, 131–132, 142–143, 145, 167; *See also* elocution
democracy, 41, 50
Derrida, Jacques, 71, 76, 167
development: ideological, 34, 72, 152–153, 155, 158
dialectic, 6, 8–9, 13, 19–26, 29–41, 44, 50–52, 68, 71–72, 75–77, 82, 106, 123, 125, 128, 139–140, 146–147, 152, 161–163
dialogic, 3, 8–9, 11, 13–15, 20–29, 31, 33–38, 40–48, 50–52, 54, 61, 63, 67, 69, 71–73, 76–79, 82, 86, 91, 94–95, 102, 109–110, 119–123, 125, 135, 137, 148–150, 152, 157, 159, 162–163, 167
dialogics, 8, 13–15, 20–22, 24, 28, 30–32, 34, 38–41, 46–49, 51, 72, 75–78, 81–82, 123, 146, 149, 158, 162–164
dialogism, 42, 44–45, 86
dialogue, 21–24, 26–29, 34, 42–43, 45–46, 51,–52, 71, 73, 77–79, 86, 87, 114, 119–120, 134, 138, 145, 153–154, 158, 162–163
dianoia (thought in Aristotle's *Poetics*), 15, 137–144, 167
Dickens, Charles, 81
diction, 4, 7, 33, 51, 122, 125, 138, 142, 144–145, 167; *See also* style
Diderot, Denis, 28
disciplines, 4, 5, 6, 11, 14, 15, 21, 26, 30–32, 38–39, 63, 76, 81–82, 87–90, 99, 100, 103–105, 110, 114, 146–147, 153–154, 162, 165, 167; ancient, 5, 43, 82, 161
discourse: abnormal, 31; arts of, 9, 19–20, 22, 32, 123, 161; authoritative, 79, 97, 153; critical, 25, 27, 48, 49, 161; dialectical, 19, 24, 30, 128; dialogic, 3, 20–21, 24, 36; double-

voiced, 38, 73, 142; internally persuasive, 98, 100, 109, 152–153; monologic, 79, 121; normal, 31; novelistic, 8, 43, 110; objectified, 35–38; ordinary, 30; poetic, 8, 137, 144; person-centered, 20-21 rhetorical, 19, 45, 73, 105, 109–110, 125, 127–128, 161; scientific, 30, 128; single-voiced, 37; thesis-centered 20
Dostoevsky, Fyodor, 8, 10, 13, 20–22, 25, 43, 45, 122, 125
double-voiced, 34, 38, 42, 73, 77, 114, 142, 155, 156
drafts, 96–97
drama, 7, 8, 73, 113, 124, 142-146, 156, 157, 165, 167
dunamis, 139

Eagleton, Terry, 161
edification, 30, 32–33, 38
education, 5, 56–57, 65–66, 100, 129, 133, 153–154, 158–159
Elbow, Peter, ix, 101, 149–150, 156, 165
Eliot, T. S., 99
elocution, 123, 125, 167; *See also* delivery
embarrassment, 25
embodiment, 58, 88, 94, 97, 111–112, 115, 119, 125, 142–143, 157, 162
Emerson, Caryl, 11, 14, 24, 45, 76, 85, 86, 88–89, 91–93, 95, 98–99, 102, 146, 164
emotion, 94, 110, 126, 132–133, 136, 141, 143
emotional-volitional, 93, 98, 104–106, 108-109, 111, 113–114, 164
empathy, 111
enthymeme, 59, 128–129, 132, 139–140, 144
enunciation, 124, 167
epic, 43, 142
epideictic rhetoric, 6, 30, 54, 58, 71, 80, 104, 116, 127–129, 133, 135, 140, 144
epistemology, 30–31, 88, 164

epithet, 89, 90, 115, 132
ethics, 11, 14, 47, 85–86, 88–89, 91, 94, 100, 102, 105, 164
ethos, 108, 125, 132–133, 136, 138–139, 141, 144, 167
event: artistic, 120; creative, 118; ongoing, 98, 104, 107, 109; tragic, 113
events, 13, 62, 92–93, 98, 104–105, 107–109, 111, 113, 117–118, 141, 166
Ewald, Helen Rothschild, 11, 14, 85–86, 88
exercitatio, 72
exotopy, 52
expectations, 6, 8, 13, 24, 57, 59, 88–89, 135
experiences, 14, 29, 34–38, 59, 89, 94, 99, 104, 105, 107, 109, 111, 119, 146, 164

fabula, 114
Facebook, 154
Fahnestock, Jeanne, 14, 55, 59, 60–62, 64, 134
familiarization, 44
Farmer, Frank, 3, 85
fear, 124, 141, 153
feeling, 44, 87, 91, 109, 124, 139, 166
feminism, 6, 50, 66, 76
fiction, 9, 43–47, 51, 66
figurality, 56
figures, 5–6, 11, 14, 20, 26, 39, 41–42, 51, 55–56, 58, 59–64, 66, 73, 115, 119, 135, 148, 165–166; of speech, 56, 73; of thought, 14, 55, 59–64, 66, 73, 135, 148
Fontanier, Pierre, 54
foreignness, 129, 132–133
forensic rhetoric, 30, 71, 80, 126–129, 134, 140; *See also* judicial rhetoric
formalism, 6, 7, 8, 43, 69, 73, 112–113, 144–145
Foucault, Michel, 156
foundationalism, 34
freedom, 27, 47, 130

Gadamer, Hans-Georg, x, 13, 33–39, 161, 163
Garver, Eugene, 5
Genette, Gérard, 54
genre, 5, 11, 13, 22–23, 33, 42–44, 47, 48, 60, 62–64, 66, 68, 71, 73, 77, 79–82, 94–96, 120, 122, 127,–129, 131, 134–136, 144, 145, 148–149, 151, 153, 155, 158, 162
genres: literary, 63, 119, 130–131
Gentile, Giovanni, 26
gestures, 11, 50, 60, 62, 73, 94, 106, 156
Goodson, A. C., 75
Gorgias, 20, 78, 145
grammar, 5, 8–9, 54, 61, 75, 76, 82, 98, 100, 111, 131

habit, 30, 51, 57, 89
Halasek, Kay, x, 3, 9, 14, 67–70, 73, 121
Halliwell, Stephen, 7, 8, 138
Harkin, Patricia, ix–x
harmonia (change of pitch), 126
Hartman, Geoffrey, 40–41, 47
Haskins, Ekaterina, 7
Hegel, Georg Wilhelm Friedrich, 35, 72
Hegelian, 9, 35, 75, 77
Heidegger, Martin, 147, 167
Heideggerian, 5, 137, 166
hermeneutics, 13, 30–38, 66
hero, 25, 27, 33, 44–46, 61–63, 73, 92–93, 96, 103, 106–107, 111–119, 122, 127, 132, 135, 144, 164, 166–167
Herzberg, Bruce, 72, 127
heteroglossia, 32, 48, 61, 71, 86, 157, 158; authentic, 42, 48
hierarchy, 6, 9, 26, 32, 44, 117, 122, 132, 144
Hirschkop, Ken, 10
historians, 7, 58
historicism, 40, 65, 78
historicity, 35, 89, 117

history, 5–6, 8, 20, 22, 27, 36, 39, 51–53, 56–59, 65, 66, 68, 70, 72, 78, 81, 88–90, 93, 100, 108, 118, 123, 149, 151–153, 164; literary, 66
Holquist, Michael, x, 11, 75, 91, 162
Homer, 124
Howell, Wilbur Samuel, 65
humanism, 6
hybris, 133
hypocrisis, 137

ideas, 5, 7, 12, 20–22, 25–28, 31, 41–42, 52, 62, 88, 91, 101, 152, 162, 166; person-ideas, 15, 21, 22, 29, 50, 67, 125; voice-ideas, 21, 24
identity, 25–26, 32, 38–39, 41, 77–78, 81, 156
ideological, 21–23, 26–27, 34, 45, 72, 94, 117, 152–153, 155, 158, 162
ideology, 45–46, 94
imagination, 38, 50
imitatio, 72
imitation, 8, 38, 115, 120, 125, 138, 142–143, 146, 155
individual, 26–27, 34-38, 42, 49–50, 52, 71-72, 77, 82, 86, 88–89, 92, 95, 97–98, 107, 116, 118, 130, 150, 152–153, 155–156, 158
individualism, 86, 149
individuality, 38, 52
induction, 140
interlocutors, x, 22, 28, 31, 33–34, 76, 78, 116, 129
International Bakhtin Conference, x, 12, 71, 146
interpretatio, 72
intonation, 92–93, 96, 104, 108, 112–114, 116, 118–119, 122, 127, 130, 136, 143, 164–165; *See also* tone
intrusion: narratorial, 55, 73
invention, 59, 73, 122
irony, 55, 85
Isocrates, 7
istoricheskoi (historical), 89

Jakobson, Roman, 163
Jameson, Fredric, 9, 11, 75, 161
Janko, Richard, 139
jargon, 31
Jarratt, Susan, 76
Jarrell, Randall, 56
Jost, Walter, xi, 5
Joyce, James, 56
judicial rhetoric, 131, 134; *See also* forensic rhetoric

Kant, Immanuel, 88, 103; *Critique of Pure Reason*, 103
Kastely, James, 5
Kazakhstan, 10
Kennedy, George, 6, 138, 140
Kneupper, Charles, 67
knowledge, 11, 32, 40, 56, 64, 70, 76, 87, 92, 97–100, 103–104, 106, 108, 124, 136, 142, 147, 151, 159
Koestler, Arthur, 27
krino (to question), 123
krisis, 123
Kristeva, Julia, 11, 163
Kuhn, Thomas, 31

Laertius, Diogenes, 77
Lakoff, George, 154
language, 7–10, 11, 13–14, 21–23, 27, 31, 34, 36, 42, 45–46, 48, 49–50, 53–55, 60, 64, 67–69, 74–75, 78–79, 82, 86–87, 91,–94, 99, 102, 106, 108, 112–116, 119–120, 129–130, 132, 138, 144, 150, 152–159, 161–162, 164, 166, 167; alien, 24, 52, 152, 154, 157
language-consciousness, 112
Lanham, Richard, 72, 150
laughter, 44
laws, 88, 97, 105
learning, 57–58, 63, 66, 151, 152
Leavis, F. R., 13, 26–29
Leith, Dick, 164
Lentricchia, Frank, 161
lexis, 133, 138, 140–141, 167; *See also* diction

Liapunov, Vadim, 164
liberal arts, 75, 81
liberal education, 15, 148-159
limitations, 13, 34, 36, 76, 151, 156
linearity, 157
linguistics, 11, 34, 59, 73, 81, 87, 92, 98, 112, 131, 146, 158–159, 167
linguists, 163
listener, 42, 61–62, 68, 80, 106, 115–116, 118–119, 127, 130–132, 135–136, 164
literary, 5–7, 14, 20, 23–29, 32, 44, 47–49, 53–54, 57–59, 61–63, 65–66, 75, 86–87, 113, 119–120, 130–131, 159, 161, 166
literary studies, 14, 27, 29, 57, 75
literature, 6, 9–10, 27, 43, 57–59, 65–67, 75, 86, 91, 113, 118, 151
Loeb Classical Editions, 129, 133, 138
logic, 8, 19, 25, 33, 42, 61, 75, 81, 92, 104, 108, 129
logos, 33, 76–77, 79–80, 108, 126, 139–141, 144–145, 167
Longinus, 47
Lunsford, Andrea, xi
Lycidas, 63
lyric, 43, 103–104, 110, 112–113, 119, 120, 145–146, 166–167

Mailloux, Steven, xi, 161
Maimon, Elaine, 150, 156
Martin, Jane Roland, 162
Marxism, 4, 6, 11, 70, 89, 113, 115, 162
Marxists, 69, 75, 90, 161
materialism, 8, 69, 89, 144; historical, 89, 93
maxims, 77, 124, 140
McCloskey, Deirdre (Donald), 30
McGann, Jerome, 161
McKeon, Richard, 5, 51
medieval, 57, 75
Medvedev, P. N., 3–4, 10, 69, 130, 162
Menippean satire, 9, 33, 79, 122
mentors, ix, 26, 49, 145

metalinguistics, 82
metaphor, 8, 72, 95, 132–134, 155
Miller, J. Hillis, 61, 161
mime, 142
models, 13, 20, 23, 27–28, 32–34, 36–38, 43, 49, 52, 61–62, 68, 72, 91, 101, 119–120, 129, 144, 152
modernism, 7, 99
monologism, 9, 23, 27, 32, 37, 42–46, 48, 68–69, 71, 77,–79, 96, 110, 121, 146
Morson, Gary Saul, 14, 76, 85–86, 88–89, 91, 93, 95, 98–99, 102, 164
movements, 6, 26, 69, 81–82, 109, 115, 142, 159
multivoicedness, 33, 42, 77, 122
Murphy, John M., 121
Myerson, George, 164

narration, 4, 8, 27, 43, 46, 54–55, 61, 101, 113, 120, 134, 142–145
narrative, 4, 8, 23, 26, 54–55, 99, 100, 113, 119, 142, 145, 162, 165, 167
narratology, 7, 9, 54, 75, 145
nature, 14, 35, 37, 62, 74, 82, 118, 130–131, 146
Needham, Lawrence D., 57
Nietzsche, Friedrich, 55, 74
novel, 3, 5, 8, 11, 13–14, 40, 42–47, 56, 68, 71, 73, 76, 79, 94, 95, 102, 110, 119–120, 125, 128, 142, 146, 155, 158–159, 162–163
Nussbaum, Martha, 162

objectification, 15, 35–39, 47, 97, 112, 117, 119, 154, 162
objectivity, 26–27, 33–34, 45, 98, 100, 106–107, 127–129, 163
objects, 6, 8, 28, 35, 39, 63, 65, 88, 92, 93, 104, 106, 107, 109, 111, 114, 118, 145, 158
occasions, 15, 19, 47, 66, 73, 131, 133, 136, 139, 143–144, 148–149, 158
Olmsted, Wendy, xi, 5
Olson, Elder, 50

Ong, Walter, 4
open-ended, 33, 42, 45, 65, 71–72, 78–79, 122
openness, 23, 37–38, 79
orators, 59, 123, 135
oratory, 42, 69, 80, 134–135
orientations, 8, 75
originality, 9, 12, 156
origins, 12, 64–65, 93
Orpheus, 63
otherness, 29, 37, 150

paradigms, 32–33, 41, 76, 81-82, 86, 98, 140, 165
Paris (Gorgias's "Helen"), 78
parody, 36, 38, 68, 70, 81, 155, 158
participants, 12, 20, 22, 26, 29, 45, 48, 50, 59–63, 79, 88, 92, 98, 106–112, 115–116, 118–119, 127–128, 130, 135, 149, 153, 165
participation, 26, 44, 52, 79–80, 87–90, 96, 98–101, 103–108, 110–112, 115–116, 118, 143, 159, 165
pastoral, 63
pathos, 108, 139, 141, 167
patterns, 59, 64, 135
Pausanias (Plato's *Symposium*), 23
Payne, Robert O., 57
pedagogy, ix, 4, 11, 55, 61, 66, 68, 72, 148, 157–158, 164
performance, 15, 44, 61, 89, 91–92, 108–109, 112, 130, 143
performative, 61, 109, 122
Perlina, Nina, 42, 69, 77
person-idea, 15, 21–22, 29, 41, 50, 67, 122, 125
personification, 62, 119, 166
persuasion, 12, 19, 21, 25, 41, 47, 54–55, 66, 69–71, 79, 80, 109–110, 129, 136, 138–139, 146, 152–154, 156
Peterson, Linda, 150
Phelan, James, 5
phenomenology, 11, 88, 90, 96, 105–106, 110, 115–119, 165
philology, 12, 56, 129, 146

philosophers, 13, 32, 128, 139
philosophy, 3, 6, 8, 11, 14, 20, 25–26, 30, 32, 38, 50, 69, 71–72, 88–89, 100–103, 105–107, 116, 132, 146, 161, 167; moral, 88, 103, 106
Pirsig, Robert, 76
pisteis, 144, 167
pity, 124, 141
Plato, 4, 20, 23, 33, 41, 69, 71, 76, 106, 138–139, 151, 167; *Phaedrus*, 20, 23, 69
plot, 7, 8, 33, 54–55, 114, 122, 138, 143, 145
pluralism, 5, 14, 45, 47, 48, 51, 53, 56
poesis, 165
poetics, 4–8, 13–14, 32, 42–43, 45, 50–51, 53–54, 58, 69, 94, 102, 104–105, 111–115, 117–120, 122, 123–126, 130, 133, 137, 142–146, 161, 164–167; sociological, 115
poetry, 7–8, 25, 28–30, 47–48, 53–54, 58, 63, 73, 102–105, 110–115, 117–118, 120, 124, 138, 142–147, 161, 165–167
poets, 32, 50, 63, 112, 124, 132, 144
Poirier, Richard, 12
polemic, 14, 38, 42–43, 57, 68, 70–71, 73, 138
politics, 15, 27, 30, 41, 50, 57, 62, 68–70, 81, 90, 94, 97, 104, 110, 117, 125, 131, 139
polyphonic, 9, 42
postmodernism, 74
post-structuralist, 8, 68
power, 9, 20, 22–23, 25, 38, 40–41, 51–52, 54, 61, 69, 72, 77, 79–81, 97, 99, 108, 121, 125–126, 139, 144, 153, 156, 166
practices, 7, 9, 13–14, 19–22, 24, 26, 29–33, 38–39, 41, 44, 47–48, 50–51, 54–56, 64–66, 70–72, 76–77, 81–82, 85, 105–106, 122–123, 126, 130, 146, 148, 151, 153–155, 161–163, 165
pragmatics, 60
pragmatism, 76

pravda (truth), 98, 107–108
praxis, 58, 70
prayer, 124, 126–128, 142
priznanie (acknowledgment), 98
proofs, 61, 124, 139, 141, 144, 167
Protagoras, xi, 14, 77, 124
psychology, 69, 76, 81
Pushkin, Alexander, 113

Quintilian, 55, 60–61, 64, 73

Rabelais, Francois, 4, 10
rationality, 43
reader, 13, 23–24, 27–29, 34, 43–45, 48, 52, 54–59, 61–62, 73, 111–112, 115, 117–118, 127, 130, 136, 143, 157
reading, 5, 20, 23, 28–29, 52–53, 55, 58–59, 69, 95, 125, 137, 166; deconstructive, 53, 55; dialogic, 23, 52; Heideggerian, 5, 36, 137, 166; rhetorical, 23, 52
reason, 34, 76, 103, 105
reasoning, 8, 128, 139, 141–142, 144–145
reduction, 36, 38, 45, 51, 89
relations: human, 40, 50, 117
relativism, 68
relativity: joyful, 43–44, 68
Renaissance, 56
resistance, 29, 33, 38–39, 44, 51–52, 88, 93, 101, 138, 152
rhetor, 15, 47, 49, 52, 71, 79, 80, 106, 129, 130, 132, 136
rhetoric, ix, 3–6, 8–9, 11–14, 19–26, 29–34, 38–39, 41–47, 49, 50–62, 64–73, 75–78, 80–82, 85, 87, 92, 94, 100–102, 104–110, 112–144, 146, 152, 161–167
rhetoricality, 14, 74, 82, 146
rhetoricians, 4, 6, 9, 13, 15, 42, 48, 58–60, 64–65, 68–69, 78, 129, 148
rhetorics, 57, 66, 68, 121, 136
rhythm, 113–114, 118, 126, 131–132, 143
Richards, I. A., 48, 75, 162

Richter, David, 5
romanticism, 99
Rorty, Richard, x, 13, 30–34, 38, 39, 68, 76, 163
Russia, 4, 8, 10–11, 43, 68, 92

satire, 33, 79, 122
Saussure, Ferdinand de, 8, 75
schemata, 142
Schiappa, Edward, 76
Schilb, John, ix–xi
Scholes, Robert, 75
Schuster, Charles, 3, 164
science, 6, 25, 30–31, 59, 62, 68–71, 81–82, 90, 97, 99–101, 103–104, 106–107, 124, 128, 146, 161, 165–166
seeing, 24, 111, 154
selectio, 72
self-consciousness, 13, 19, 24, 30, 46, 51, 154, 159, 164
semantics, 35, 37–38, 73, 132, 157
seriocomic, 42–44, 46, 77, 122
Shelley, Percy Bysshe, 99
Shukman, Ann, 163
signature, 87
situatedness, 112; concrete, 89–90, 92, 108
situations, 13, 14, 44, 47–48, 50, 59–61, 68, 71–73, 81, 82, 90–92, 97–99, 106–110, 112, 116–118, 123, 127–129, 132, 134–135, 139–140, 146, 153–154, 157, 164
Slavic, 11, 14, 75, 85
Smith, P. Christopher, 5, 137, 142, 166–167
social constructionism, 85
social relations: hierarchical, 117, 132
sociolinguistics, 69
sociology, 6, 11, 14, 115–119, 165–166
Socrates, 31, 33
sophists, 14, 33, 76–78, 81–82, 138, 145
Soviet Union, 9, 10, 12, 42, 69, 163–164
speaker-hero axis, 116

speaker-listener axis, 116, 148
spectacle, 25, 122, 138
spectator, 44, 127
speech, 4, 6, 27, 37, 42–44, 59–64, 69, 72–73, 78, 87, 108, 113, 116, 119–120, 124–127, 130–131, 134–135, 138–146, 150, 158, 162, 167; character-revealing, 125, 140; inner, 80, 116, 118; prior, 4, 119
speech act theory, 59–61
speech genres, 61–64, 72, 119–120, 127, 130, 134–135, 144, 146
Stendhal (Marie-Henri Beyle), 28
strategies: rhetorical, 41, 69–70, 76
strength, 11, 33, 90
structuralism, 7, 9, 26, 54, 145
structure: compositional, 73, 134, 144
Struever, Nancy, 75, 111, 167
students, 4–6, 10, 13, 15, 54, 59, 72, 76, 78, 99, 100–101, 138, 151–159, 165
style, 8, 26, 42–45, 59, 73, 122, 128, 130–133, 136, 140, 144–146, 155, 157, 162–163; *See also* diction
stylistics, 42, 81, 146, 163
subjects, 6, 21, 24–25, 29, 34, 45, 62–63, 68-70, 70–72, 74, 78–79, 81, 97, 100, 124–128, 130, 132, 134–136, 140–141, 143, 162
syllogisms, 128–129, 140
systems, 42, 66, 69, 103, 122, 151

teachers, ix, 3, 5, 6, 96, 101, 117, 150–151, 157–158
teaching, 5, 8, 10, 15, 41, 56, 78, 85, 126, 143, 148–149, 152–153
techniques: fictional, 41, 43, 45, 47, 69, 167
texts: sociological, 11, 118–119
theorists, x, 3–4, 6, 7, 9, 25, 39, 45, 57, 61, 68–69, 75, 121, 132, 134, 162
theory, 3, 4, 7, 9–10, 14, 15, 24, 26, 28, 39, 43, 51, 53–54, 61, 64, 66–68, 70, 74–75, 86–89, 97–98, 102, 121–122, 125, 131, 148, 152,

162; composition, 3; critical, 24, 27, 44; discourse, 121–122, 129, 130; literary, 6, 54, 75; narrative, 54, 162; rhetorical, ix, 7, 14, 54–55, 58, 65, 68
theses, ix, 4–5, 19–20, 22
Thomson, Clive, x
thought; *See dianoia*
Todorov, Tzvetan, 11, 13, 26–29, 36, 52, 163
tone, 46, 79, 86–87, 92–93, 95, 96, 98, 104, 108–110, 112–114, 116, 118–119, 122, 125, 127, 129, 130–133, 135–136, 143–144, 153, 164; emotional-volitional, 93, 98, 104, 105, 108–109, 111, 164; *See also* intonation
tonoi, 126
topics, 15, 22–23, 33, 50, 55, 59, 61–63, 73, 93, 96, 106–107, 122, 127, 130-133 138, 140, 144, 150–151, 164, 166
topoi, 13, 22, 50, 129, 144
torture, 139
totalitarianism, 27
Tower of Babel, 48
tradition, 4, 7, 9, 24, 30, 32, 34–35, 36–38, 41, 44, 47, 50, 54–55, 57–60, 66, 68–69, 72–74, 76, 82, 106, 108, 121–123, 125, 145, 163
tragedy, 33, 43–44, 122, 138, 143–144
transactions, 13, 54, 61, 117
translation, x, 3–4, 6–7, 10–14, 24, 31, 45, 47, 52, 67, 72, 76, 86, 89, 105, 115, 119, 123, 129, 133, 138–140, 146, 158, 164, 167
treatises, 7, 14, 19, 23, 56, 59, 74, 82, 87–88, 90, 95, 100–101, 123, 128, 140, 145–146, 165
tribes: critical, 49
Tristram Shandy (Sterne), 136
trivium, 5–6, 8–9, 13, 39, 75–76, 81–82, 164
tropes, 8, 54–56, 58–59, 73, 135, 154
truth, 21, 25–26, 28–30, 32–34, 37,
39, 49, 73, 92, 97–98, 107-108, 119, 124, 140
tweets, 154
twentieth-century, 4–6, 26, 60, 76, 161
two-sidedness, 77–79

utterance, 5, 15, 22–23, 42, 48, 58, 60–64, 69–70, 73, 77–80, 86–87, 90–91, 92, 94–96, 98, 104, 108, 111, 113–114, 116–120, 122, 126–132, 134–137, 140, 142–146, 148, 150, 155–157, 162, 164; behavioral, 116, 128–129; concrete, 112, 118, 130

validity, 25, 37–38, 97, 105, 107, 111
value, 14, 23, 30, 32, 38, 44–45, 50–51, 58, 71, 78, 90, 92–94, 97–98, 103-108, 111-112, 115, 124, 128–129, 132, 157, 164
value judgments, 32, 132, 157
vernacular, 64, 139
Vickers, Brian: *Defence of Rhetoric*, 56–57, 70, 72
Villanueva, Victor, 165
Vinogradov, Victor, 9, 42–44, 69, 77, 163
voice, ix, 20–28, 34, 36–39, 41–44, 46, 48–49, 51, 61-64, 69, 71, 79, 81, 99, 106, 120, 126, 143, 149–158, 162–163
voice-ideas, 21, 24
volition, 91, 96, 109
Voloshinov, V. N., 3–4, 10–11, 69, 92, 102, 113, 115, 117, 127–130, 132, 134, 144–146, 162, 164, 165–167

Walker, Jeffrey, 6, 58, 142, 144
Walzer, Art, 121
Warnke, Georgia, 34, 163
Watkins, Evan, 161
Wegener, Charles, ix, 5
Wellbery, David, 14, 58, 74, 82, 146
Wells, Susan, 71, 80

Wesling, Donald, 165
Wess, Robert, 161
Whitaker, Thomas, 163
Williams, Joe, 150
Williams, Raymond, 11, 27
Wordsworth, William, 50, 54, 60, 147, 163, 166–167
writing, 3, 15, 20, 27, 32, 56, 58, 68, 73, 79, 85, 87, 95, 98–99, 101, 127, 148–149, 151–157, 159; college, 154

Zebroski, James, xi, 67
Zima, Peter, 75
znanie (knowledge), 98
Zumthor, Paul, 40